Circular Reflections

The International Library of Group Analysis

Edited by Malcolm Pines, Institute of Group Analysis, London

The aim of this series is to represent innovative work in group psychotherapy, particularly but not exclusively group analysis. Group analysis, taught and practised widely in Europe, derives from the work of SH Foulkes.

other titles in the series

Active Analytic Group Therapy for Adolescents
John Evans
International Library of Group Analysis 6
ISBN 1 85302 617 4 hardback
ISBN 1 85302 616 6 paperback

Attachment and Interaction
Mario Marrone and Nicola Diamond
International Library of Group Analysis 3
ISBN 1 85302 587 9 hardback
ISBN 1 85302 586 0 paperback

Self Experiences in Group
Intersubjective and Self Psychological Pathways to Human Understanding
Edited by Irene Harwood and Malcolm Pines
International Library of Group Analysis 4
ISBN 1 85302 596 8 hardback
ISBN 1 85302 597 6 paperback

Dialogue in the Analytic Setting
Selected Papers of Louis Zinkin on Jung and Group Analysis
Edited by Hindle Zinkin, Rosemary Gordon and Jane Haynes
International Library of Group Analysis 5
ISBN 1 85302 610 7

INTERNATIONAL LIBRARY OF GROUP ANALYSIS 1

Circular Reflections

Selected Papers on Group Analysis and Psychoanalysis

Malcolm Pines

Foreword by Saul Scheidlinger

Introduction by Earl Hopper

Jessica Kingsley Publishers
London and Philadelphia

First published in the United Kingdom in 1998 by
Jessica Kingsley Publishers Ltd
116 Pentonville Road
London N1 9JB, England
and
1900 Frost Road, Suite 101
Bristol, PA 19007, U S A

Library of Congress Cataloging in Publication Data
A CIP catalogue record for this book is available from the Library of Congress

British Library Cataloguing in Publication Data
A CIP catalogue record for this book is available from the British Library

ISBN 1 85302 492 9 pb
ISBN 1 85302 493 7 hb

Printed and Bound in Great Britain by
Athenaeum Press, Gateshead, Tyne and Wear

Contents

List of tables

Acknowledgements

This book owes its life to my dear friend and colleague, Meg Sharpe, without whose enthusiasm, gentle pressure, patience and hard work, it would have been stillborn. When Meg entered group analytic training many years ago I could not have imagined this partnership. We have travelled and worked together over many years and my admiration and respect continue to grow. She shares my sense that our work is a privilege.

My career has been in psychiatry, therapeutic community, psychoanalysis and group analysis. On these many pathways to myself I have had good fortune and good companionship. I began my psychiatric training at the Maudsley Hospital, the postgraduate centre for psychiatry in London, which was then under the stern rule of Sir Aubrey Lewis. We juniors argued for hours over the biological and psychodynamic approaches to mental illness and I have never lost the Maudsley imprint for discussion and integration. After the Maudsley I spent several years at the Cassel Hospital, a marvellous place to concentrate on individual and group psychotherapy and community psychiatry. Tom Main, the Director, was a stimulating mentor to me, as he was to many young analysts. After the Cassel I took up the challenge extended by Professor Arthur Crisp to help in the conversion of the traditional inpatient facility at St George's Hospital to one using psychodynamic principles. I greatly appreciated this opportunity and have great admiration for the department that Professor Crisp built up. I both contributed and learnt from the very high standard of psychiatry practised there. I returned to the Maudsley as a Consultant in the Psychotherapy Unit for some memorable years, where I inherited the tradition set down by my own analyst and teacher, Michael Foulkes, encouraging novice psychiatrists to practise group psychotherapy and supervising individual work. My final stage was in the Adult Department of the Tavistock Clinic, where my brief was to encourage group psychotherapy, as that had ceased to be a major part of the Department's work. This was an uphill struggle in a department largely devoted to individual psychotherapy, staffed by persons intent on psychoanalytic training which made it difficult to extend their vision to the group analytic frame of reference.

Throughout these years I maintained a private practice in both psychoanalysis and group analysis, taught at the Institute of Psychoanalysis, helped to found its Applied Section and to found the Institute of Group Analysis in London. I also began to teach in other countries which led to much pleasure in working with my group analytic and psychoanalytic colleagues in Denmark, Norway, Italy, Russia, the former Yugoslavia and the USA, to my companions on these journeys – Meg Sharpe, Liesel Hearst, Harold Behr, Colin James, Jonathan Pedder, Murray Cox –

heartfelt thanks for your good spirits, for what you have taught me and for the good times that we have had together.

In the background of a busy life has been my wife, Iris, from whom I learned what cannot be learned in training: loving care for children and family; to see how a natural brave and cheerful spirit can transform the humdrum of daily life; the security of home, midst the welter and turmoil of the strange life of a psychotherapist.

I have lived so many lives with my patients and am very grateful for what they have given to me.

Finally, for rendering my tapes and papers into coherent and readable form, thank you Barbara, June and Peter.

Malcolm Pines
Group Analytic Practice

Foreword

This book's modest title fails to convey the uniquely erudite, creative and wide-ranging nature of its contents. In this collection of lectures and essays by Malcolm Pines, a distinguished British psychiatrist, psychoanalyst and group therapist, all mental health professionals will find an amalgam of cogent philosophical, sociological, historical and psychological insights over a period of four decades.

While loyal to the cardinal precepts of the late S.H. Foulkes, his erstwhile analyst and mentor and the acknowledged Moses of *Group Analysis*, Pines, in his emerging role of Joshua, broadens the movement's perspectives. His new territories encompass highly sophisticated intrusions into the fields of systems theory, of modern child development and of Heinz Kohut's self-psychology.

The American reader is bound to be especially interested in the volume's historical material which unfolds the origins of psychoanalysis in Europe. He will learn about the intriguing interplay among the psychoanalytic centres of Vienna, Zurich, Budapest and London. Intertwined are the august figures of Freud, of Adler, of Jung, of Ferenczi and of Jones, among others – none devoid of our human foibles. (I, for one, was distressed by the account of Melanie Klein having chastised her mentor Jones for hurting British psychoanalysis by offering asylum to the Freuds). Equally revealing are the histories of such often-cited institutions as London's Tavistock Clinic, as well as the Maudsley and Cassel Hospitals. Last, but not least, is the uniquely *British way* in which the bitter conflict between the Anna Freud and Melanie Klein camps was contained. Pines' Heidelberg lecture, which deals with Germany's relation to the Jews, is especially timely in the face of the recent reopening of the issue of the Holocaust by the expositions of Havard's Professor Goldhagen.

Having been privileged to follow Dr Pines' outstanding work over many years, I was happily surprised to find in this book a gift of his, hitherto unknown to me – profound clinical wisdom. Here are a mere two samples drawn from among many such gems contained in this volume: 'The process of communication is identical to the process of therapy'; and, 'Theory should not be a procrustean bed for us to be tied to and to which we should not attempt to bind our patients'.

Saul Scheidlinger, PhD
Emeritus Professor of Psychiatry (Psychology)
and Adjunct Professor of Clinical Psychology in Psychiatry
Cornell University College of Medicine, New York

Introduction

The work of Malcolm Pines hardly needs an 'Introduction', especially in the United Kingdom and Europe. Although S.H. Foulkes, his training analyst and mentor and the founder of group analysis, had more than one child, it is widely acknowledged that Malcolm Pines is the eldest son. It is virtually impossible for the eldest son of a founding father to be acknowledged as a 'father' in his own right, but Malcolm *personifies* the institutionalisation of group analysis.

The Group Analytic Society developed from the interests and activities of a small circle of multilingual refugees from Nazi atrocities, a few English colleagues, mostly younger than themselves, and their new students and patients. Inevitably, as their numbers grew, lineages were established, marked by specialisations – if not tribalisations – in the study and treatment of families, median and large groups, therapeutic communities, group analysis proper, and so on. The elders have not always danced at one another's family weddings, and have not even known when they occurred.

Malcolm has led the process of bringing together these many and diverse social, cultural and intellectual interests, often within an inhospitable climate of opinion. His work on committees and his teaching, lecturing and writing have been prodigious. He helped to found the Group Analytic Society and the Institute of Group Analysis, and he now edits *Group Analysis*. He is Past-President of the International Association for Psychotherapy, and is an 'Honorary Ambassador' for group analysis.

It can be readily understood how and why Malcolm has taken these roles. He was the youngest son of a Russian Jewish immigrant who was a well-known ophthalmic physician, whose mirrors and ophthalmoscope were among Malcolm's strongest memories from his childhood in the East End of London. Having become a psychiatrist and then a psychoanalyst at a very young age, he continued his search for a form of sociology that would help him understand the sociality of human nature, eventually finding his own version of the hermeneutic developmental sociology of Norbert Elias, tempered by an interest in socio-linguistics. His very involvement with group analysis was part of this intellectual and emotional journey from the brain to the mind, the organism to the person, and the family to the society. Malcolm has searched for a school of psychoanalysis that he felt was compatible with group analysis. As an alternative to classical Freudian psychoanalysis and British object relations thinking, he eventually found self-psychology, again tempered by his own interpretations of it. His search for Englishness is manifest in his breadth of knowledge of novels, poetry and philosophy in several languages and cultural traditions, rather than in his depth of mastery of the theories and facts of formal social science. It is also seen in his intellectual style, which is evocative, free-associational and eclectic, more in the tradition of the self-taught patrician amateur than of the trained professional sociologist or social psychologist. Readers in North America will recognise this in the distinction that used to be drawn between Harvard and Columbia, perhaps similar to the distinction in England between Cambridge University and the University of London. Following his retirement as a Consultant at the Cassel Hospital, St George's Hospital, the Maudsley Hospital and the Tavistock Clinic, London's leading centres for training in psychiatry and psychotherapy, he has shown an increasing interest in the social and cultural origins of our disciplines and their distinguishing ideas, and in the forces that tend to institutional schism, as well as their integration and growth.

Such antimonies are not without their tensions, and this volume of selected essays, compiled by Mrs Meg Sharpe, a Jungian analyst, a close colleague and one of the first graduates of the Institute of Group Analysis, reflects Malcolm's attempts to make creative use of them. The essays are distinguished by several common themes: the relationship between individuals and their groups and institutions, as seen especially in processes of mirroring and echoing; the coherency of mind and society as seen in groups of all kinds, but especially in training institutions within the mental health field; the unconscious constraints of social and cultural factors on personality and group process; and the social, cultural and historical contexts of psychoanalysis, group analysis and psychodynamic psychotherapy. However, the breadth of knowledge and the depth of clinical insight are not conveyed by the titles of the specific papers, most of which originated in presentations at various conferences throughout the world during the last 15 years, but have been reworked for publication.

The eye and the ear and their personal and social vicissitudes are the hallmark of the collection, and healthy narcissism is its driving force. I would argue that the most creative, original contributions are found in the shift from his own 'father' theme of benign and malignant mirroring, with which the book begins, to what may be his own 'maternal' theme of aural dialogue. For many of us this shift involves the unconscious step from the maternal eye to the paternal ear; language involves a marriage of 'mother tongue' with the 'father grammar, syntax and vocabulary of language'. Malcolm has made creative use of this difficult developmental phase in his focus on his understanding of the coherency of persons and their groups on the basis of the development of the capacity for self-reflection through internal dialogue based on the introjection of language, its speakers and their cultures. In North America, these issues are reminiscent of the development from Cooley's ideas about mirroring and the 'looking glass self' to G.H. Mead's ideas about 'mind, self and society' in connection with the transformation of Mother to the Generalised Other on the basis of language and 'symbolic interaction' in general. However, no other psychoanalyst and group analyst has made these ideas the basis of his own theoretical and clinical work. If Foulkes was the first to focus on the social and cultural dimensions of seeing and hearing as group-specific phenomena, Pines has developed these insights into contributions of substance which have influenced the way we see and hear our patients within their total situation.

As a whole, these essays reflect a personal quality that has always informed Malcolm's clinical and intellectual style. It is not generally known that Malcolm is especially sensitive to the barely formed, the fragile and the vulnerable. It is not accidental that his major theoretical and clinical orientations have found their most mature expression in his treatment of borderline patients, and in his essay about this. His motto might be: To protect the particular from the Universal, the person from the theory, and the group from the institution. I would suggest that, like many others who have found intellectual nourishment in self-psychology, Malcolm's work is marred by his apparent neglect of the forces of destruction and perversion, but he is always sensitive to the needs of the down-trodden. He is markedly sensitive to how necessary it is to keep hope alive, and when and where it seems not to exist, to instil it.

I have known Malcolm Pines since 1967. He was my first supervisor for a training case in psychoanalytical psychotherapy, and one of my first teachers. I have worked with him in a mental hospital and therapeutic community, and I have been his associate in private practice. We have served together on many committees. Yet, on reading these fascinating essays, I have learned for the first time how similar are our intellectual interests. I do not always agree with Malcolm's views, nor he with mine, but I am grateful to him for having modelled the importance of making one's own integration from diverse interests and personal characteristics. The work of Dr Malcolm Pines should be seen and heard within the circular mirrors of our international community of group psychotherapists of all kinds, and of the wider community of scholars and people interested in the study of persons and their groups.

Earl Hopper, PhD
Psychoanalyst and Group Analyst
President International Association for Group Psychotherapy

PART I

Group Analysis

CHAPTER I

Reflections on Mirroring[1]

My lecture is dedicated to the memory and work of Dr S.H. Foulkes, *fons et origo* of group analytic theory technique and my own analyst and mentor. In my dedication I couple with his the name of my father, Dr Noe Pines, whose ophthalmic mirror and ophthalmoscope are amongst my strongest childhood memories. With these mirrors he made deep and original studies of the retina of the eye and its blood vessels (Pines 1950), and when I was a medical student he shared with me the wonder of seeing the living brain.

My study has been of the mind through the instruments of psychoanalysis and in the network of group analysis; when, in the course of preparing this lecture, I realised that the word retina means a network, then a hitherto obscured transgenerational link was revealed to me.

I begin with a quotation:

> A woman has two images. There is a magical person seen or remembered by those who love her, her finest qualities are flesh and spirit illuminated. She herself knows this ideal self; she projects it, if she is confident; or she day-dreams her ideal self; or she recognises it with gratitude in the admiring eyes of others. There is at the same time a second image: the woman as seen by those who dislike or fear her. This cruel picture has an all too powerful mirror in her own negative idea of herself. She sees with fear her own ravaging impulses and most painful of all, a graceless, freakish, and unlovable physical self, this was the mirror her parents held before Edith. Her brothers saw her with love. She herself knew both images. Her life, and her poetry, constituted a flight from the second one.

This evocative passage (Glendinning 1981, p.35) introduces my theme of imagery: the self, as seen in self-reflection, and how the mind's mirror is cast in the matrix of human relationships. That the same word, reflection, is used for the mirror image and the process of reflective thought, sets the scene.

1   Sixth Annual Foulkes Lecture of the Group-Analytic Society, 10 May 1982. Published in: (1) *Group Analysis* (1982) 15, Supplement. (2) *International Review of Psychoanalysis* (1984) *11*, 1, 27–42.

The starting point for my lecture, these reflections and some speculations about mirroring, this journey into mirror land, is what S.H. Foulkes wrote about mirroring as a therapeutic factor in group analysis. His clear and thoughtful capacity to observe the happenings of the small group of patients with whom he met in 1939, in the newly discovered role of group conductor, led to his recognition of 'group-specific phenomena', events that appear for the first time in the new psychotherapeutic situation. Amongst these he included mirror phenomena:

> Mirror reactions are characteristically brought-out when a number of persons meet and interact. The person sees himself, or part of himself – often a re-pressed part of himself – reflected in the interactions of other group members. He sees them reacting in the way he does himself, or in contrast to his own be-haviour. He also gets to know himself – and this is a fundamental process in ego development – by the effect he has on others and the picture they form of him. (Foulkes 1964, p.110)

> ('Oh would some power the giftie give us to see ourselves as others see us: it would from many a blunder free us'. (Robert Burns: *Ode to a Louse*)).

Elsewhere Foulkes writes of the child's emergence from narcissism through the greater awareness of the self evoked by reflection coming from outside, which helps him to differentiate between what he is and what he is not (Foulkes 1965). Note therefore that the mirror reactions refer both to therapeutic processes and to early developmental processes. As to the mechanism of the mirror reactions, he says that it, 'can be dissected into a number of psychoanalytic concepts, e.g. projection, identification, etc. but there are good grounds for putting these together and giving them a collective name emphasising the "mirror" aspect' (Foulkes 1964, p.81). Thus it is not a concept derived from psychoanalysis, it is derived from the field of observation of the small group, the new therapeutic context that he had established. 'Mirror reactions are characteristically brought out when a number of persons meet and interact' (p.110). Each person is in the position of an observer: 'he can observe from the outside another member reacting in the way he himself reacts, can for instance see how the conflicts and problems are translated into neurotic behaviour' (p.81). The mirror reaction is a concept based upon a self-and-other psychology, of persons becoming aware that their selves are incomplete and who can recognise aspects of themselves, 'in particular a repressed part', in other persons. Foulkes noted that by observing fellow group members, patients could often more easily recognise how conflicts and problems are translated into neurotic behaviour. However, Foulkes said relatively little about mirroring phenomena, though recently Leal (1982), Zinkin (1981) and Wooster (1983) have each made important contributions to the group analytic literature.

Yet in the 40 years that have passed since he began his first work with groups, the term 'mirroring' has appeared with increasing frequency in the psychoanalytic literature, both as a therapeutic and developmental factor of high significance. Probably Kohut's (1971) description of mirror transference in the analysis of narcissistic personalities and his emphasis on the need for phase-appropriate mirroring (from 18 months to 3 years) in the development of a healthy narcissistic economy – the child that is the gleam in the mother's eye – has received most attention. Kohut's baby is born strong, not weak, and he is born into the psychological matrix of responsive self-objects. He is simultaneously inside and outside of self-objects as oxygen is simultaneously inside and outside of him physically: 'Being reflected by the self-objects (mirroring), being able to merge with their calmness and power (idealisation), sensing a silent presence of their essential alikeness (twinship), the baby is strong, healthy and vigorous' (Meyers 1981, p.157). Earlier there is Lacan's (1977) 'mirror stage' of development when the child of six months and upwards becomes enchanted and enraptured seeing himself in a mirror and begins to live 'out there' in his specular image, abandoning his lived-in body-self which is so poor a vehicle by comparison with the beautiful magical child in the mirror. Earlier still are Mahler (1967) and Winnicott's (1971) observations (Table 1.1). Greater clinical experience of those elusive persons whom we cluster under the rubric of borderline personalities has focused our attention on the psychodynamics of very early childhood and on the earliest interactions of the child.

Bandler and Grindler (1979) emphasise what they call 'mirroring' in neuro-linguistic programming. The psychodramatic technique of 'doubling' (Elefthery 1982) is a 'mirroring' technique. In all this literature the term 'mirroring' appears, though used in many different ways. I shall try to bring together, and also to differentiate, the phenomena that are all condensed in the one concept of mirroring and try to see if we can grasp the underlying truth which makes different people use the same word, though in differing ways, developmentally and therapeutically. I shall use the term as a kind of 'ideo-gram', that is, as a pictorial symbol, 'a word in visual, not its auditory form, the mere tracing of which evokes the whole group of ideas or notions that it connotes' (Lichtenstein 1977, p.208). If we go to the root of our word we find that mirror derives from the French *miroir*, which in turn derives from the Latin *mirare*, to look at, and is related to *mirari*, to wonder. Thus the visual and the wonderful overlap in the word as they do in myths, dreams and fairy tales and as they also do in our own magic years of childhood. The word *mirage* has the same root as mirror, and the mirage image may be sought for in the mirror by the ailing and the ageing, the narcissistically vulnerable, searching for the mirror that can be made to say 'you are the fairest of them all'. A recent article from New York in *The Times* (1981) had the title: 'Mirror mirror on the wall – lie to me' and began, 'Plastic surgeons seem

Table 1.1 Separation–Individuation and Mirroring

Months	Phase	Reference
0 – 4	Symbiotic	Winnicott (1971): *Mother's Face* Mahler (1967): *'Mirroring Frame of Reference'*
10	Differentiation	Lacan (1977): *Physical Mirror and Specular Image* Merleau-Ponty (1964): *Alienation from Self, Externality*
18	Practising	Abelin (1980): *Early Triangulation* Amsterdam (1980): *Painful Self- Consciousness* Kohut (1971): *Grandiose Self*
36	Rapprochement	Kohut (1971): *Grandiose Self* Zazzo (1975)/Bach (1980) *Perspective on Self as Subject/Object*

poised to take over from psychiatrists as merchants of the American dream'. The official emblem of the American Society of Plastic Surgeons is a scalpel-clutching hand rampant before the Venus de Milo, a Venus reconstructed according to the ideal image of the time. The mirror has been a symbol for truth and purity (Cirlot 1962); Jesus, Mary, the Bible, the sky of heaven, have all been called mirrors for man's contemplation. The pure virgin mirror will only reflect truth (Goldin 1967). Yet Plato abhorred the mirror, for it can only reflect reality and be a two-dimensional representation of three-dimensional reality, and for Plato mankind runs the continual danger of being seduced from the ideal truth and the ideal form by the arts and by the mirror. Later the neo-Platonist Plotinus (AD 204–270) wrote that we see the world only through the mirror of the mind (Whyte 1979, p.23): 'But when this, the mirror in us, is broken, on account of the disturbed harmony of the organism, then the mind and soul think without the mirror image, and then thought is present without an inner image of itself'. What a powerful image that is! It brings to mind Roy Schafer's (1968) work on reflective self-representation and W.R. Bion's work on thinking (Bion 1970; Hamilton 1982). The reflective self-representation is that of oneself as thinker of the thought, and when the function is suspended the thinker vanishes but the thought remains. In the parliament of mind there is no self-representation without self-reflection and without self-representation there is only reaction. The philosopher, Richard Rorty, in his recent book *Philosophy and the Mirror of Nature* (1980) writes:

It is pictures rather than propositions, metaphors rather than statement, which determine most of our philosophical convictions. The picture which holds traditional philosophy captive is that of the mind as a great mirror, containing various representations – some accurate, some not and capable of being studied by pure non-empirical methods. Without the notion of the mind as mirror, the notion of knowledge as accuracy of representation would not have suggested itself. (p.12)

Cartesian and Kantian philosophy try getting more accurate representation by inspecting, repairing and polishing the mirror. According to Rorty, Wittgenstein, Heidegger and Dewey have tried to create a new philosophy out of the vision of a new kind of society in which culture is no longer dominated by the idea of objective cognition but now by that of aesthetic enhancement.

This metaphor (Rorty 1980) of the mind as a mirror has been dominant in Western literature, philosophy and epistemology. Abrams (1953) in his book *The Mirror and the Lamp* has shown that until the eighteenth century the mirror was the predominant poetic metaphor for the mind, reflecting reality that is outside the self, and how with the rise of the romantic movement this altered, so that now the mind of the poet and of the novelist became likened to lamps that illuminate small areas of the great darkness of the human mind. Insight replaced outsight; the poet Gerard Manley Hopkins (Caws 1981, p.87) created the word 'inscape', a word which telescopes two terms, 'inner' and 'landscape', the eye turned inwards. And as night follows day, the mirror turning inwards leads to the insights of psychoanalysis.

The metaphor of the mirror image condenses multiple images so that we can then grasp the picture as a whole. In the seventeenth century suddenly the mirror in Dutch paintings intensified the depth of field of the picture and filled it out with new angles and perspectives. In the nineteenth century Stendhal wrote that the novel is, 'a mirror strolling down a broad highway. Sometimes it reflects the azure blue of the skies and while sometimes the mire stagnating made muddy ditches'. The poet Bonnefoy wrote, 'words like the sky, infinite. But in the brief puddle suddenly entire'. A man's life, his character and achievements may be said to represent the mirror of his age, that he is a prism through which multiple rays will centre. The vision actively grasps an image that reduces diversity to unity. The physical mirror extends the range of perceptions, for with a mobile mirror we can reach all sides of an object and thus obtain multiple perspectives and, though remaining in one position, we can visually circle the object. Thus with hand and eye working together we extend our visual grasp to achieve greater mastery of our environment, as hand and eye have done together throughout human physical and cultural evolution. Circling round an object and viewing from all sides involves the sharing of space with the other viewers, the shared neutral space of the forum.

As the historian of ancient Greek art, Denys Haines (1981) has written:

> Shared space is a necessary condition for the differentiation of the individual; it
> is only when we see people together that we can compare them and recognise
> what is unusual or unique in each. With shared space we develop the capacity
> for taking a perspective on a common object of perception. In a shared world
> the individual discovers his identity, his difference from others; at the same time
> it subjects that world to an individual point of view, presents it as seen by a par-
> ticular person at a particular point in space and time. (p.92)

The emergence of Greek individuality from Egyptian monumentality is mirrored
in their art forms. In the psychotherapy group the human mirrors offer us multiple
perspectives on ourselves, on how we are seen by others, and let us see the many
facets of human development, our conflicts and attempts to solve them. In the
group I can see that in this way I am like another, but in this way I am not. A
patient who had been in individual analysis said that for her the difference
between the analysis and the group experience was that in individual analysis the
analyst had held up a mirror for her to see a previously unacknowledged part of
herself, and when this had been sufficiently looked at he moved it so that another
perspective appeared. In the group, all the other members presented her with
mirrors so that at any time there were multiple perspectives on the self which
could become overwhelming.

Separateness and individuality, attained through painful conscious and
unconscious developmental struggles, is monitored by changes in self and object
representations and the linking relationships. Each stage of life has its own
threshold, its *limen* in the Latin. This threshold both joins and separates time and
space, inner and outer: door, window, corridor, staircase, mirror, all represent
'liminary' moments (Caws 1981, p.15). In the pre- and post-liminary stage we can
look forward to, and back on, each developmental stage and if our vision is not
mobile the look back can become the fixed gaze in which we are trapped and from
which, like Lot's wife, we cannot turn away. However, the mobile change of group
perceptions can begin to break up fixed and defensive patterns of character
pathology, of narcissistic, masochistic and depressive outlooks. Perhaps these
outlooks would be better termed 'inlooks' or, as I have already mentioned,
inscapes. Sylvia Plath's desolate inscapes were often glimpsed in mirrors,
particularly in the poem entitled *Mirror* (Plath 1981). Eventually she drowned in
the depth of her mind, but recognition, responsiveness and understanding can
reach to the drowning group member and, held in the group matrix, bring her to
firm ground.

You may be surprised to hear that it has been shown that the very presence of a
mirror in a room has a distinct psychological effect (Buss 1980): the person is both
more self-aware of the internal world, its values and standards, and makes more
effort to live up to them, even though they do not look into the mirror. The

presence or absence of a mirror in an experimental set-up has been shown to affect a person's ability to resist suggestion and to withstand pressures to betray their principles, for instance to inflict pain on others in experiments when they are opposed to such behaviour. Seeing oneself on video tapes, however, has the opposite effect, for one is then more likely to conform to social norms and to respond to group pressures (Buss 1980). The mirror effect, therefore, helps us to preserve our individuality in the face of external pressures.

What holds good for waking consciousness does so also for dreaming consciousness. The dream presence of a mirror, particularly if the self is reflected in it, has been shown to indicate the successful integration of a threatening insight, as a helpful presence keeping company whilst the unknown is being faced and accepted (Miller 1948). The dream mirror captures the threatening stimulus and reflects it as an organised image now that the mind can face the previously unacceptable.

Dream mirrors can also be defensive in the same way as an imaginary twin or companion can promise survival, as the double can be blamed and punished as the bad aspect of the self; having a double in an attempted assurance against experiencing loss – we two are as one and need no one else. But the dream mirror that does not reflect the self heralds distress and loss of organisation. Patients wake from such dreams with anxiety and motor unco-ordination (Lewis and Brooks-Gunn 1979).

Some mirror dreams remain superficial, gliding over a narcissistic self-reflecting surface. Others go through the looking-glass into the oedipal world where Alice kills the Red Queen (Feigelson 1975).

I hope that I have brought enough facts to your attention to persuade you of the importance of my topic. Indeed, I fear that already I may have said too much. Can I, before moving on, also recall to your minds the multifold ramifications of mirror magic and rituals; that they are used to foretell the future and by magic means to control it; that the moon and femininity are both mirror images; that mirrors are covered up when there is a death in the house so that the soul will not linger in the mirror, and that the vampire has no reflection because he has no soul.

I now turn to consider developmental studies of mirroring (Bortenfall and Fisher 1978; Lewis and Brooks-Gunn 1979) and what this tells us about human psychology. That only the higher primates are aware that the mirror image is a self-reflection was first demonstrated by Gallup (1970) and Desmond (1980) with chimpanzees, and the latter's technique was then transferred to infant observation. The chimpanzee is made accustomed to his mirror image, in which he takes little sustained interest. He is then anaesthetised and a blob of paint placed above his eyebrow and then, when awake, he is re-exposed to the mirror. If his mirror image informs him of an alteration in his appearance and if he then uses this reflection to explore his own body, not the mirror body, then we can infer that he recognises himself in the mirror. The lower primates, and all other animals, if they pay attention to the reflection at all, will treat it as another con-specific; a budgerigar will sing to it, a stickleback will attack it. I will refer later to the great evolutionary significance of self-recognition and of mirroring responses.

Through observations of children's mirror behaviour we find out about a child's self-recognition, his acquisition of self. As the eminent researchers in this field, Lewis and Brooks-Gunn write (1979, p.17): 'To determine that a reflection is oneself and that the self cannot exist in two places simultaneously – all requirements of self-recognition – knowledge of one's identity as continuous through time and space is necessary. Thus recognising oneself presupposes the knowledge of one's identity'.

It has been shown, *pace* Lacan, that self-recognition does not emerge suddenly at a single point in development, but develops gradually through stages between 6 and 24 months (Bortenfall and Fisher 1978). True, there is a stage of joyful recognition and of play with the mirror image in the first year, but in the second year children withdraw and become 'leery' of their images, becoming painfully self-conscious (Amsterdam and Levitt 1980), and some of that feeling remains with us throughout life, as embarrassment: the fateful division between private and public self-awareness has begun (Buss 1980). The child, capable of being his own spectator, notices that he is visible to others, and this phase of painful self-consciousness might be related to unacceptable genital sensations and consequent body shame.

The paradox of objectivity and subjectivity (Bach 1980): Points of view

Zazzo (1975) has observed that there is a significant period of indecision between 24 and 30 months, during which the child recognises himself visually out there in the mirror but has not verbally, and therefore cognitively, integrated the 'me' out there with the 'me' in here. During this time the child will address his mirror image by his proper name, for instance 'Johnny', whilst referring to his own corporeal, in front of the mirror, self as 'me'. For himself he is a subject; the one in the mirror is both himself and that person whom others address as Johnny, who is a social object. Both terms apply to the same referent but he has not yet succeeded in creating, 'that psychic space called the Self' (Bach 1980) in which multiple subjective and objective perspectives are paradoxically conceived of as transformations of the same invariant person. Thus he has not yet acquired a flexible point of view with which to relate the 'what' out there to the 'who' in here. Lichtenstein (1977) makes the same point, that identity is like a theme with variations throughout life. As persons we constantly develop and transform, but basically the same invariant personal theme of identity has been laid down in a mirroring relationship to mother very early on in life. It is mother who selects only certain patterns of activity to respond to in her child, thus presenting him with an image of himself through her mirroring behaviour. Thus she exercises restraints upon the child's activities and it is only through such restraints that a recognisable identity can emerge. The child can begin to learn who he is through attending to his mother's response to those aspects of his behaviour which make sense to her. Mother inserts meaning and intentionality (Shotter and Gregory 1976) into her baby's behaviour, and so in this way he begins to recognise himself. As Lichtenstein (1977, p.218) says: 'the primary identity is always based on a mirroring experience'. The object is a mirror in which the outlines of its primary identity are reflected. The outlines of the child's own image are reflected by the mother's unconscious needs with regard to the child. This primary identity he likens to an organisational principle which makes the process of psychological development possible. Mahler (1967) makes essentially the same point when she too speaks of the mother's mirroring frame of reference and of her selective response to the child's innumerable responses.

The theme of mirroring entered psychoanalysis through the concept of narcissism (Freud 1914). Let me remind you of the essence of the myth from which Freud adopted the term. The beautiful young Narcissus has reached the age of 16 and is yet untouched by love. He rejects all the approaches of those who would love him and, as punishment for his cruelty, eventually he is condemned by Nemesis to suffer the same fate as others, to suffer unrequited love. Thirsty, one day he reaches a solitary pool in a glade where he lies down to slake his thirst and suddenly espies the beautiful image with which he is immediately enraptured. He does not recognise the image as himself and he is not in love with himself. He pleads for the love of the other and cannot understand why this other, who is so responsive to his every moment, does not come towards him and why he cannot be grasped. Only later does he come to realise that the other is himself and that the image is a reflection; he dies from hunger and thirst and the remains of his body are transformed into the flower Narcissus. Yet this is only one part of the legend; it is not complete without the other sad character, the nymph Echo who loved Narcissus, but who was rejected by him. She, too, cannot break from the paralysis of her desire and she too dies an anorexic death, being transformed into the rocks that surround the pool and which echo the dying youth's laments.

Thus the theme of reflection appears twice: in sound (Anzieu 1979; Major 1980) as echo, in vision as reflected image (Shengold 1974). Each person represents an isolated individual who has no partner for response, for dialogue, for the mutual nourishment of attachment and love.

The blind prophet, Tiresias, had prophesied that Narcissus would live as long as he did not recognise himself and this prophecy came true, for in the act of recognition he became inescapably trapped in self-contemplation. 'Know thyself' was written in the Delphic Oracle; but alongside it was also written 'Nothing in excess' and Narcissus exemplifies the inability to avoid excess, the system that has no restraints.

Louise Vinge (1967) has shown how each age up to the nineteenth century makes it own interpretation of the Narcissus theme: throughout the centuries this tale of Ovid has fascinated psychologists, philosophers, poets and theologians, all of whom find their different meanings in the myth. In the second century the neo-Platonic philosopher, Plotinus emphasised Narcissus as deluded, and taught that man must not repeat Narcissus' error, that of mistaking illusion for reality. The soul must not become trapped in the body, mistaking shadow for substance, for true life is in the soul, which must avoid being trapped in the unreal world of mirrors. But in Medieval texts and from the twelfth century onwards, mirror symbolism becomes more complex and shows an increasing capacity for introspection, and Narcissus is used as a warning not to confuse illusion and reality, neither to be lost in vanity nor to resist the power of love.

Bernard of Ventadour, one of the great Troubadour poets, wrote:

Myself I cannot count as mine,
Nor could I, from the hour I saw,
Within her eyes my image shine, clear in the mirror I adore.
Mirror, in my reflection there
I found deep sorrow lingering, and I am lost,
as was the fair Narcissus mirrored in the spring. (Morris 1972)

Narcissus is a paradigm for the role of mirroring in the evolution of self-consciousness. He first learns to distinguish between his self and his reflection. In discovering that he is different from the image he discovers his own identity, distinguishing his outward form from the life that animates it, the will, the intelligence, the memory; he discovers his capacity for desire and thought. In himself is every faculty that an image cannot possess. So our twelfth-century poet foretells the development of our psychoanalytical developmental psychology. He knows that the individual must move from the narcissistic one-to-one mirroring relationship to that where the other has a reality different to, and separate from, the own self. He knows that this move is reflected in the acquisition of language terms, for the 'I' and for the 'me' and the 'other'. He knows that attention and love have to reach outwards and not inwards and that, for the narcissistic mirror that reflects only sameness, there must be substituted the mirroring that comes from the active contemplation, recognition and exchange between two centres of autonomy and of psychic life. The psychologist of the twelfth century and, indeed, the psychologist of the second century, could easily recognise Lacan's mirror state of development; the child of six months or so, entranced by his embodiment in the mirror image, the specular image that reflects back to him a unified Gestalt of a mobile, graceful, animated body unified within the frame of the mirror.

The important distinction, the difference that is brought out by these myths and these theories, is the difference between the self viewing the self in the mirror and the self actively being mirrored by another responding self. It is the contrast between similarity and difference. It is difference that carries information, and difference is only understandable in a context. Without difference there is no change and no development. Bateson (1972) points out that information is news of difference and for this there must be two entities. The mirror conveys identity; mirroring responses can also reflect identity, but in normal healthy development mirroring reflects differences.

In his exploration of narcissism, Freud (1914), though he took the term from Havelock Ellis (1928), did not offer a dynamic interpretation of the mirror in the legend, the 'third element between the lover and his object' (Lichtenstein 1977, p.212). It was left to Lichtenstein, Winnicott and Mahler primarily to do this. For Winnicott the first mirror was the mother's face, wherein the baby sees himself reflected in his mother's expression, in her eyes, both literally and metaphorically. As Winnicott pointed out, psychoanalysis has neglected the face in favour of the breast, but it is the face that the babe looks at as he feeds and where he first finds himself and learns his first socialisation. Perhaps this is what W.B. Yeats was looking for when he wrote: 'From mirror after mirror, no vanity's displayed, I'm looking for the face I had before the world was made' (Sewell 1953, p.15). Thus narcissism emerges as a quality of the relationship between infant and its environment, 'an interactional synchrony' as it has been called (Sear, Mill and Liendo 1981). With the increasing dynamic interactional model of infancy, the relationship between the figures of Narcissus and Echo and the symbolism of the mirror take on new life. Narcissus and Echo are helplessly trapped in very early types of relationship, with Echo, who cannot speak, the helpless reactor trapped in a masochistic relationship with Narcissus, the neglectful sadist who seeks to find only himself in the mirror, perhaps trying to recapture total love and admiration as experienced when gazing into the eyes of a mother who, herself, enwraps her child in a narcissistic type of object relationship that she cannot relinquish and from which she cannot help him to emerge. Neither Echo nor Narcissus live in a world of responding sounds or sight, and as patients can entrap therapists into realisation of their empty worlds. However, the group analytic situation is intrinsically multi-personal and triadic, and only rarely will a whole group remain entranced and entangled by these forms of projection. The diadic projection receives a triadic form of mirroring, one at a higher developmental level, and a benign cycle of projection and introjection is initiated which can often lead to the freeing up of the closed psychic system and thereby to renewed psychic growth.

The mirror as the 'third element' between the lover and his object

This triangular mirroring is symbolised in the myth of Perseus (Tripp 1970) and the Gorgon, Medusa, the only human member of the three fearsome sisters, who has the power to turn all to stone who see her directly. (Incidentally, the only way to defeat the basilisk is to put a mirror before her, when the sight of her own fearsome ugliness will kill her.) The noble Perseus, the most triumphant of the ancient Greek heroes, is given the task of beheading Medusa and thereby freeing mankind of her dreadful power. He receives aid from the Goddess Athena, Goddess of Wisdom, a piece of her armour so highly polished that it acts as a mirror. Armed with this, and with a leather bag within which to place Medusa's head, for it retains the power to petrify even after death, he approaches her in her sleep and, guided now by her reflected image in the mirror which no longer has the power to petrify, he is able to behead her. He then has to flee her vengeful immortal sisters.

Let us contrast the mirror of Narcissus and the mirror of Perseus. Narcissus' mirror is the surface of the solitary pool of water that he never enters and Narcissus himself has no Oedipal challenges to face; his life has been one of adulation and play. Perseus, on the other hand, has to free his mother from the sexual threat of his stepfather and has to face the hero's journey into the inner depths of the Psyche, symbolised by monsters (Diel 1980). Medusa represents the other, the threat of castration and the face of the bad monster mother of infancy; at another level she represents a deformation of the psyche (Diel 1980), the threat of vain and paralysing blindness, petrification of the spirit and perversity of the imagination. This distorted image of the self, Medusa as a distorting mirror, must be faced before the Psyche can be free and full. The paralysis of horror, which is the response to the Medusa's head, arises from the inability to contemplate objective truth about oneself. 'One attitude only, one single weapon can give protection against Medusa; so as not to be paralysed with horror one must not look upon her face, but must, instead, capture her image in the mirror of truth' (Diel 1980). Athena's shield is the mirror of truth and after he has captured Medusa's image in it, Perseus returns it to the Goddess who will then wear it forever after as an effigy. Now the eternal Goddess shows mankind the liberating truth, the victory over the Medusa, of the mirror of truth over the distortions of the perverted imagination. 'Perseus' shield, is, after all, a symbol of the image into which the poet imprisons a terrible reality and through which alone he is able to save himself from destruction' (Closs 1957).

But from the blood of the Medusa's neck is born Pegasus, the winged horse. Pegasus symbolises the creative imagination that is no longer trapped within the Medusa's body (Diel 1980). As soon as she is dead the true image of life is reborn and Pegasus is released. Pegasus is the horse of the Muses and, as such, represents art and poetic inspiration. We cannot here follow in detail the adventures of

Pegasus beyond his being bridled by the hero Bellerophon with the Gold Bridle of Athena and who, with the aid of Pegasus, is able to overcome many other monsters. The unbridled imagination, controlled, becomes the creative force for the exploration of the psyche.

The analyst as mirror

When Freud (1912) recommended that the analyst should act as a mirror to his patient, showing him only what he brings to analysis, he was, I believe, indicating that the setting of analysis and the transference relationship form the frame (Milner 1952) and the backing of the analytic mirror. In this mirror the patient is helped to look at, and into, himself. That this silver backing which transforms the translucency into reflection is the function of the analyst's selective response to his patient, in effect what we now call his counter-transference, was not then recognised. Freud then was speaking of the transference, not of the counter-transference, and the dynamic aspects of mirroring as an aspect of therapy and as an important aspect of childhood development had not yet been recognised.

We know that Freud himself admitted to a dislike of being constantly looked at by his patients and this, amongst other considerations, led him to construct the situation of the patient on the couch with the analyst sitting behind him. We also know, through a footnote to his paper on the uncanny (Freud 1919), that his own response to his self-image, his self-regard in the physical sense, was derogatory. He describes how once when travelling in the sleeping car of a train and preparing for bed, wearing his dressing gown and a nightcap, he suddenly saw an unpleasant-looking middle-aged man dressed identically enter his compartment. It took him a moment to realise that he was seeing his own reflection in a mirror which had swung out through the motion of the train.

It has occurred to me that the 'private mirror' effect I have already referred to is relevant to introspective therapies not only because we encourage attention to the private self, but because here is another model for the role and function of the therapist, that by his presence he acts as the mirror for the individual or for the group, sharpening inner awareness and increasing the patient's knowledge of his beliefs and values by his very presence. Groups often discuss what difference the presence of the therapist makes, and they usually agree that there is more focus and more seriousness to the session if he is there, enjoyable though the sense of freedom from restraints may be during his absence.

Another way in which the therapist acts as the mirror, but now in an active way, is by his interventions and interpretations, which focus attention on hidden aspects of what is happening and which can frame in a coherent and recognisable form complex and difficult issues. The therapist therefore is not simply a reflecting surface but, by his selection, his wording and his imagery, he holds up a mirror for the individual or for the group to see a particular aspect of themselves. Recently a colleague at the Tavistock Clinic, Mr John Lawrence, told me of a group session during which the atmosphere of the group seemed to spiral downwards into helplessness and hopelessness, with a fear of breakdown and depression from which it could not possibly recover. For a while the therapist felt that he could only acknowledge to himself what was happening and eventually he said to the group that they were experiencing his reflecting on their state of affairs as only making things worse and worse and that they were just feeling that an awful mirror was being held up to them, simply showing them their plight and nothing else. Much to his relief, and no small surprise, following this intervention the mood suddenly began to lift and some of the members began to have real and meaningful interpersonal exchanges. Thus the therapist's comments had acted as mood and image intensifiers, just as the mirror does; his use of the mirror metaphors seemed to free them from being trapped in this mirror world and the released energies and capacities for attention became available for useful work. A Lacanian would recognise this release from the world of imaginary into the world of the verbal and the symbolic.

In group analysis I have come to recognise two radically differing kinds of mirroring phenomena: one is primitive confrontation, destructive and unreflective. It represents an early negative form of diadic relationship. The situation is unresolvable without firm mediation (Pines 1978).

The other phenomenon is exploratory, negotiable and dialogical, between two or more persons who are sharing the same psychological space, one in which different points of view on the same experience can be explored. No mediation is needed.

What is the analytic reconstruction and explanation of this triangulation? Like my colleague Gerald Wooster, I have applied the work of Ernest Abelin (1980) who has carefully studied 'early triangulation' phenomena in infants, combining Piagetian and Mahlerian frameworks, asking: how does the child come to experience himself as an object with his own mind and body? Before this he has been 'egocentric without an ego'. The role of the father, already illustrated by Lacan, is evoked by Abelin. At about 18 months the child becomes aware that he is excluded from his loving, imitative narcissistically mirroring relationships with his mother by his father: he sees father loving mother and, like Narcissus, has to discover that Amor, love, originates within himself, a sentient entity, that love is real, painful and frustrating when it is denied and that it must be directed to, and responded to by, a separate entity. The child's mind has entered into the symbolic realm, where relationships are represented with more or less distortion in the reflective function; reflection begins to replace reaction.

I would now like to present some clinical vignettes, glimpses of how I see mirroring processes at work and at play in therapy (Table 1.2).

Table 1.2 Interpersonal Mirroring Processes

Reflective	Positive	–	Good Qualities Recognised, Accepted
	Negative	–	Bad Qualities Recognised, Accepted
Non-Reflective	Distortive	–	Selective Perception (e.g. Scapegoat)
	Destructive	–	Attack on Unrecognised Aspects of Self in Other

Benign mirroring

Here what we see is the 'to and from' rhythm of dialogue and interaction: this is me that I now see in you, that I can reflect upon, share with you, take back into myself and integrate with my already existing sense of self. What I may see in the other may be pleasant or unpleasant but within a reasonable range of affect the perception is accepted. Much of the ordinary work of the group is carried out at this level. As Caroline Garland has written:

> Group analysis taught me to make use of mirrors, to find one's self in and through others; not just to retrieve the lost or buried parts of the self but to discover some I didn't even know were there; sometimes to bring together elements that had seemed irreconcilable and make them, even momentarily, into a coherent whole. (Garland 1980, p.43)

Thus this form of mirroring in group analysis can be creative: when a person brings together in his mind an image that contains both an aspect of his own self seen in the other person and of his existing self-image, he brings into one mental imaginative space two discrete entities: their juxtaposition creates a new piece of knowledge combining insight and outsight, a new inscape, a new unity out of diversity. 'Actively conceiving two or more discrete entities occupying the same space, a conception leading to the articulation of new identity' has been identified by Rothenberg (1979) as one essential characteristic of the creative process, the other being Janusian thinking, that of, 'actively conceiving two or more opposite, contradictory or antithetical concepts, images or ideas simultaneously' (p.55).

This takes place in the 'mind's eye' and in art leads to the creation of linguistic, auditory and visual metaphors; for example, 'The branches were handles of stars'. For the group members the 'this' of you and the 'this' of me together make a hitherto unseen, new mental image. Elements kept apart come together, creating new knowledge. Though it entails the temporary lifting of boundaries and barriers between persons, this is not regressive or primitive thought; it is a form of secondary process thinking that transcends logic and ordinary modes of thought.

Both group analysis and psychoanalysis are pathways to the release of blocked psychic development and the release of creativity, employing reflective thought, the mirror of Athena. The fundamental technique of psychoanalysis, free association, is a monologue which becomes a dialogue with oneself and which leads to the discovery of the other(s) in the self. The fundamental technique of group analysis, of free discussion with several others, leads to discovering the multiple facets of oneself as reflected in and by others. Both techniques aim at the integration and unification of these diverse factors.

Absence of mirroring

However, some patients are deficient in the mirroring capacity. The self-centred person will only see himself in the group and will try to focus all attention on the self, or else be aware solely of those aspects of the other person that reflect the self image; there is a very defensive and restricted range of empathic exchange and we are in the presence of relatively closed systems. Thus in one group session, a man became impatient of another member's repetitive overconcerns with herself and said to her that to him she seemed to be wasting the opportunities of the group, to have a fixed frame of reference and to see things only from her own point of view. She took no interest in anyone else, never led in another direction; either she had to be the centre of attention or not involved at all. Not put off by her rather mocking reply – did he really so much want and need her attention? – he said that indeed he did, that for him the group works by people being mirrors to each other and that if she was not holding up a mirror to him then something important was missing in the group. In later sessions this particular person was able to say that without her children acting as mirrors for her she would know very little about herself and have no viewpoint.

In contrast, some persons find no self-reflection, either in the mirror or in the eyes of the other. A man says: 'When I look in the mirror I see no one'. An analysand writes a poem about the absence of self-reflection:

In this room there is no mirror
You are there
I am there
There is no mirror in your eye
There is no mirror in this room for the absence in My, I and me
There is no mirror in your eye
There is no mirror in this room
There is no reflection from my soul to say my soul is absent
This is you This is I
Together we are two.
My presence demands two, you and I then three

My willing my wishing cannot make present the other, the I the me,
Myself that is not absent from you or another.

The way that individual people mirror and reflect aspects of themselves in
the analytic group is often easily observed, especially when we are interested
in the process. But other, more obscure, mirroring processes can be identified
in the light of the developmental process of mirroring. In Kohut's (1971)
reconstruction of the developmental line of narcissism, the child who has not
received phase-appropriate mirroring or has been prematurely or
traumatically deprived of an idealising relationship to the parental figures,
will remain fixated at the stage either of the grandiose self or of the idealised
parental images. These psychic sub-systems then play an active part in the
character structure of the individual, their defences and transferences. It
should be possible, therefore, to identify some characteristics of these
patients and their responses to the mirroring potential of the group. Some
pertinent and original observations have recently been made by a group of
Italian therapists headed by Ciani and Fiumara (Ciani *et al.* 1981). They
observed that the patient whose grandiose self is a principal defensive
structure for the maintenance of self-cohesion and who is therefore
dependent on obtaining environmental confirmation through mirroring of
the existence of the grandiose self, will in the group direct his attention
almost entirely to the therapist and ignore the other members. Only the
therapist can have the exalted status of the idealised parent who can then
reflect and confirm the defensive grandiosity. This patient will be greatly
threatened by the regressive group processes, by the fusional processes that
follow on greater boundary fluidity, for such regression threatens the
precarious cohesion of the self. Such patients may suddenly leave the group
as it begins to 'sink into' pre-Oedipal regressive states. Such patients may
defensively play the role of the monopoliser, disrupter, clown or critic. The
demands they make for empathic and non-punitive yet firm responsiveness
by the leader and by the other group members are great, but in my
experience can be met.

Negative mirroring

It is almost a commonplace of experience nowadays to say that something
that we dislike in the other person will represent hidden and unwanted
aspects of ourselves. Time and time again this turns out to be true in the
group: that what we are not turns out in the end to be what we are. So long as
these differences are negotiable, then progress can be made towards the
understanding and integration of these rejected and unwanted aspects of the
self. There comes a point, however, where we clearly have to recognise that
progress of this sort is very unlikely, for there are head-on clashes,

confrontations and rejections: instead of mirroring and reflection, the one person regards the other person's vision as persecutory, defamatory and false, as if it were a searchlight trying to pin the person down and which has to be countered by an aggressive and retaliatory mirroring or by trying to invalidate the vision. The other person is then declared to be totally wrong in his perceptions, or to be projecting aspects of himself into the other, or is treated with contempt and devaluation. Here there is no exchange or learning, no intermediate shared space, no overlap (Winnicott 1971). At this point, I believe that we are in the presence of a form of negative mirroring based on a diadic level of relationship and of a much earlier form of mental development. Without some way of negotiating the differences and creating that intermediate space, we are in the position of Perseus without his mirror. There is no triangulation of space and no capacity for reflection and for meeting on shared ground. There is no acceptance of an aspect of self that is reflected in the other and also of the other in the self. Self and other display quasi-allergic immune reactions of intolerance, irritation and rejection. No progress can be made in situations of this sort until the level of relationship and of mental organisation have been raised to a higher level (Loewald 1980a) where self and other are sufficiently separate not to threaten great danger to each other: the danger of loss of identity or the arousal of defensive destructive fury. Here the role of the therapist or the other group members becomes that of the mediator or the negotiator (Freud 1919) who recognises, defines and maintains both similarities and differences.

The proposition is that looking and being looked at is a fundamental process in personality development, in finding out who one is and who one is not, and is common to all these diverse observations. What they also have in common is a matrix theory (Foulkes 1973) of development, that infant and mother progressively differentiate and individuate within a dynamic interactional psychological force field (Loewald 1980b). This is a basic paradigm of group analysis and which it holds in common with these developmental theories.

Foulkes wrote that a fundamental process in ego development through which the person gets to know himself is by the effect he has on others and the picture they form of him. The prescience of these simple words is remarkable, for they relate to a wealth of more recent observation and theory in infant/mother behaviour. I return to this now within an ethological and evolutionary framework, as set out by John Crook in the book *The Evolution of Human Consciousness* (Crook 1980). Crooks brings out the contingency model of infant behaviour, that the infant soon discovers itself as an active agent, that it produces effects upon itself and upon others. Soon the infant begins to learn to differentiate himself from others by the effect his behaviour produces either upon himself or upon the other. 'When it closes its eyes the world disappears. When it cries a face appears'. Thus gradually we become agents, active centres of self-aware actions, and begin to recognise others as respondents. This differentiation takes place in the context of rhythm and responsiveness between baby and caretaker, linked together by sound and sight, vision and resonance, and by mutually pleasurable mirroring responses. The baby actively seeks out the mother's face in order to make eye contact, which mother responds to with her smile and her baby talk to which the baby in his turn responds with his smile and signs of pleasure which further stimulate mother. Thus the babe has powerful ways of controlling mother through looking, and thereby gains an early sense of security in the exploration of this first social relationship. It is when the babe is most relaxed, after a feed, that he pays most attention to the mother's face, when there is time for socialising before sleep extinguishes consciousness and with it the awareness of separateness.

Babies imitate facial movements very early, for instance sticking their tongues out in response to adults' gestures, 'Imitative mirroring' by adults of babies, copying their sounds and gestures, provides feedback with which a baby later discovers its ability to imitate the adult. Gradually mother and child find ways of establishing their roles, their complementarity, and find how to achieve mutual satisfaction through early forms of negotiation. The infant finds out who he is for his mother, and therefore for himself, by her responses, and finds that he has much power in eliciting smiling or frowning, nice or nasty noises. He gradually becomes a person in a transactional world, self-aware by the effect he has on others which concomitantly informs him about himself: this action brings smiles and nice sounds and gives a nice feeling, whereas that action brings frowns and unpleasant sounds and feelings; and I am the source of both these actions. The infant learns both about himself and about the other in his constant interchanges of gaze and sound interaction with mother. Human interaction is based on this ability to empathise, to feel oneself as another and to understand the transactions in which one is taking part (Miller 1973). Through these constant interchanges we also develop the capacity to monitor reciprocity and, very importantly, to be able to break off contact with a particular partner who does not establish a feeling of trust and mutuality. Sociobiologists emphasise that this ability to monitor partnership reciprocity and to know when to trust or not to trust the other is an important evolutionary mechanism. If you trust wrongly you will be cheated and exploited, lose out on social status, and consequently diminish the chance of obtaining reproductive success. If we could not detect cheats, the best mates would go to them. We need to be able to *see through* others as well as to be seen by them in order to survive and prosper.

Co-operation requires objective self-consciousness (Diekman 1971; Duval and Wicklund 1972), a form of consciousness in which we feel ourselves to be social objects, part of the social world and aware of ourselves as objects, contrasting with subjective self-consciousness when we are fully absorbed in actions where our attention is outwardly directed on to a task and away from the self. Objective self-awareness operates in the co-operative mode; how well or how badly we fulfil a task, such as this lecture, derives its meaning from the social world with its sets of standards that determine my sense of well-being and the regulation of my self-esteem, of my self-regard, that act of looking judgementally at oneself. In this mode of objective self-consciousness we are constantly comparing ourselves with others, learning with and from them; corrective feedback is a built-in mechanism. Foulkes' 'fundamental law of group dynamics' (Foulkes 1948) states that although each member of a group may represent a deviant from the norm of a group, collectively the group will represent the norm and will reflect the climate and culture of the wider society. The analytic group can be a form of democratic control – wiser, more tolerant, more accepting and more insightful than any one individual, including the therapist. Foulkes also said that group therapy is a form of ego training in action, with adjustment as a fundamental mechanism. Now, adjustment does not mean simple adherence to a social norm, but the active striving to adjust oneself to an evolving social norm, the matrix, which makes demands upon the individual for his further development. These ideas of subjective and objective self-consciousness again raise a model of rhythm and flow, of inner and outer selective attention, attention to self and to the other, and of the relationship between self and other with all the mirroring, resonance, transactions and negotiations that a relationship involves. Constantly the individual members of the group are having to make judgements as to whether goodness or badness, desirable or undesirable traits reside in the self or in the other, and attention flows backwards and forwards across the self–other boundaries and across the group space. The meaning of self-in-relationship-to-other is continually shifting as the relationships unfold and the mirroring processes reveal new facets. In some phases the group processes flow with a heightened sense of subjective self-awareness, with a free flow of feelings and of ideas, followed by a phase of scrutiny and of objective self-awareness; these are rhythms of expansion and retraction of consciousness in the subjective and objective modes. That these modes of consciousness may be linked with different types of functions of the two cerebral hemispheres is a tempting possibility to explore, which temptation I shall now firmly resist, but I shall not resist my wish to recall what Donald Winnicott had to say about psychotherapy and mirroring: 'Psychotherapy is not making clever and apt interpretations; by and large it is a long-term giving the patient back what the patient brings. It is a complex derivative of the face that reflects what is there to be seen' (Winnicott 1971, p.117). And, he adds, this task is not easy.

My lecture is now ended; we are released, I hope, from this fascinating world of image and illusion, of reflections and speculations; back through the looking-glass, not to Alice's drawing room with the fire, the sleeping cat and that boring big sister reading her book; but here to the lecture theatre of the Royal

College of Physicians and to our world of group analysis, of companions and colleagues where, in the words of George Herbert, 'The best mirror is an old friend'.

References

Abelin, E.L. (1980) 'Triangulation. The role of the father and the origin of core gender identity during the rapprochement sub-phase.' In R.F. Lax, S. Bach and J.A. Burland (eds) *Rapprochement*. New York: Jason Aronson.

Abrams, M.H. (1953) *The Mirror and the Lamp*. Oxford: Oxford University Press (paperback edition, 1971).

Amsterdam, B.K. and Levitt, M. (1980) 'Consciousness of self and painful self consciousness.' *Psychoanalytic Study Child 35*, 67.

Anzieu, D. (1979) 'The sound image of the self.' *Int. Review Psychoanal 6*, 23–36.

Bach, S. (1980) 'Self-love and object-love. Some problems of self and object-constancy, differentiation and integration.' In R.F. Lax, S. Bach and J.A. Burland (eds) *Rapprochement*. New York: Jason Aronson.

Bandler, R. and Grindler, J. (1979) *Frogs into Princes. Neuro Linguistic Programing*. Moab, OT: Real People Press.

Bateson, G. (1972) *Steps to an Ecology of Mind*. London: Intertext Books.

Bion, W.R. (1970) *Attention and Interpretation*. London: Tavistock Publications.

Bortenfall, B.I. and Fisher, K.W. (1978) 'Development of self recognition in the infant.' *Developmental Psychology 14*, 44–50.

Buss, A.H. (1980) *Self Consciousness and Social Anxiety*. New York: W.H. Freeman.

Caws, M.A. (1981) *The Eye in the Text*. Princeton: Princeton University Press.

Ciani, N., Fiumara, R., Cajaroli, M. and Zanasi, M. (1981) 'The diagnosis and treatment of narcissistic disturbances in group analysis.' *Group Analysis 14*, 3, 178–183.

Cirlot, J.E. (1962) 'Mirror symbolism.' In *A Dictionary of Symbols*. London: Routledge and Kegan Paul.

Closs, A. (1957) *Medusa's Mirror*. London: The Cresset Press.

Crook, J.H. (1980) *The Evolution of Human Consciousness*. Oxford: Oxford University Press.

Deikman, A.J. (1971) 'Bimodal consciousness.' *Arch. Gen. Psychiat. 45*, 481–489.

Desmond, A. (1980) *The Ape's Reflection*. London: Quartet Books, Chapter 8.

Diel, P. (1980) *Symbolism in Greek Mythology*. Shambhala: Boufler and Hotton, 69–83.

Duval, S. and Wicklund, R.A. (1972) *A Theory of Objective Self-Awareness*. New York: Academic Press.

Eleftery, D (1982) from Moreno, J. L. and Elefterhery, D. `An introduction to group psychodrama.' In G. Gazda (ed) *Basic Approaches to Group Psychotherapy and Group Counselling*. 3rd edition. Springfield: C.C. Thomas.

Ellis, H. (1928) 'The conception of narcissism.' In *Studies in the Psychology of Sex. Vol.17*. Philadelphia: Davis.

Feigelson, C. (1975) 'The mirror dream.' *Psychoanal. Study. Child 30*, 341–35.

Foulkes, S.H. (1948) *Introduction to Group-Analytic Psychotherapy*. London: Heinemann Press.

Foulkes, S.H. (1964) *Therapeutic Group Analysis*. London: George Allen and Unwin.

Foulkes, S.H. (1973) 'The group as matrix of the individual's mental life.' In L.R. Wolberg and E.K. Schwartz (eds) *Group Therapy*. New York: Intercontinental Med. Books.

Foulkes, S.H. and Anthony, E.J. (1965) *Group Psychotherapy. The Psychoanalytic Approach.* 2nd edition. London: Penguin Books.

Freud, S. (1912) *Recommendations on Analytic Technique. Standard Edition 12.* London: Hogarth Press.

Freud, S. (1914) *On Narcissism. Standard Edition 14.* London: Hogarth Press.

Freud, S. (1919) *The Uncanny. Standard Edition 17.* London: Hogarth Press.

Gallup, G. Jnr (1970) 'Chimpanzees: self-recognition.' *Science 167*, 86.

Garland, C. (1980) 'Face to face.' *Group Analysis 13*, 1, 42–43.

Glendinning, V. (1981) *Edith Sitwell. A Biography.* London: Weidenfeld and Nicholson.

Goldin, F. (1967) *The Mirror of Narcissus in the Courtley Love Lyric.* New York: Cornell University Press.

Haines, D. (1981) *Greek Art and the Idea of Freedom.* London: Thames and Hudson.

Hamilton, V. (1982) *Narcissus and Oedipus.* London: Routledge and Kegan Paul.

Kohut, H. (1971) *The Analysis of Self.* London: Hogarth Press.

Lacan, J. (1977) 'The mirror stage as formative of the I as revealed in psychoanalytic experience. In *Ecrits*. London: Tavistock Publications.

Leal, R. (1982) 'Resistances and the group-analytic process. S.H. Foulkes Prize.' *Group Analysis 15*, (2), 97.

Lewis, M. and Brooks-Gunn, J. (1979) *Social Cognition and the Acquisition of Self.* New York: Plenum Press.

Lichtenstein, H. (1977) 'Narcissism and primary identity.' In *The Dilemma of Human Identity*. New York: Jason Aronson.

Loewald. H. (1980a) 'Psychoanalytic theory and the psychoanalytic process.' In *Papers on Psychoanalysis*. New Haven: Yale University Press.

Loewald, H. (1980b) 'On motivation and instinct theory.' In *Papers on Psychoanalysis*. New Haven: Yale University Press.

Mahler, M. (1967) 'On human symbiosis and the vicissitudes of individuation.' *J. Amer. Psychoanalytic Assn 15*, 740–763.

Major, R. (1980) 'The voice behind the mirror.' *Int. Review. Psychoananl. Y.* 459–468.

Merleau-Ponty, M. (1964) 'Primacy of perception'. In J. Eddie (ed) and W. Cobb (trans.) *The Prrmacy of Perception and Other Essays.* Evanston: Northwestern University Press.

Meyers, S. (1981) 'Report on the bipolar self.' *J. Amer. Psychoanalytic Assn 29*, 1, 157.

Miller, D.L. (1973) *George Herbert Mead: Self, Language and the World.* Chicago: University of Chicago Press.

Miller. M.L. (1948) 'Ego functioning in two types of dreams.' *Psychoanal. Quarterly 17*, 346–355.

Milner, M. (1952) 'Aspects of symbolism in comprehension of the not-self.' *Int. J. Psychoanal 33*, 181–195.

Morris, C. (1972) *The Discovery of the Individual: 1050–1200.* London: SPCK.

Pines, M. (1978) 'Group psychotherapy with difficult patients.' In L. Wolberg and M.N.Y. Aronson (eds) *Group Psychotherapy*. New York: Stratton Intercontinental Books.

Pines, N. (1950) 'A clinical study of diabetic retinal angiopathy.' *British Journal of Opthalmology 34*, 303–317.

Plath, S. (1981) *Collected Poems*. London: Faber and Faber.

Plotinus quoted in Whyte, L.H. (1979) *The Unconscious before Freud*. London: Julian Freedman.

Rorty, R. (1980) *Philosophy and the Mirror of Nature*. Princeton: Princeton University Press.

Rothenberg, A. (1979) *The Emerging Goddess*. Chicago: University of Chicago Press.

Schafer, R. (1968) *Aspects of Internalization*. New York: International University Press.

Sear, M.C., Mill, M.A. and Liendo, E.C. (1981) *The Sadomasochistic Quality of the Narcissistic Mirror*. New York: Jason Aronson.

Sewell, E. (1953) Quotation in *Paul Valery. The Mind in the Mirror*. Cambridge: Bowes and Bowes.

Shengold, L. (1974) 'The metaphor of the mirror.' *J. American Psychoanal. Asn. 22*, 97–I, 15.

Shotter, J. (1976) from Shotter, J. and Gregory, S. `On first gaining the idea of oneself as a person.' In R. Harré (ed) *Life Sentences*. Chichester: Wiley.

The Times (1981) 20 November. London: Times Newspapers Ltd.

Tripp, E. (1970) *Crowell's Handbook of Clinical Mythology*. N.Y.T.Y. Crowell.

Vinge, L. (1967) *The Narcissus Theme in Western European Literature up to the Early 19th Century*. Lund: Gleerups.

Whyte, L.H. (1979) *The Unconscious before Freud*. London: Julian Freedman.

Winnicott, D.W. (1971) 'Mirror-role of mother – family in child development.' In *Playing and Reality*. London: Tavistock Publications.

Winnicott, D.W. (1971) *Playing: A Theoretical Statement in Playing and Reality*. London: Tavistock Publications.

Wooster, G.W. (1983) 'Resistance in groups as a developmental difficulty in triangulation.' *Group Analysis 16* (1),30.

Zazzo, R. (1975) 'La genese de la conscience de soi (La reconnaissance de soi dans l'image du miroir).' In R. Angelergues *et al.* (eds) *Psychologie de la Connaissance de Soi: Symposium de l'Association de Psychologie Scientifique de Langue Francaise*. Paris: Presses Universitaires de France.

Zinkin, L. (1981) `Mirrors and mirroring in the Group Analytic Process.' *Group Analysis 14* (2) 164.

Further reading

Feigelson, C. (1975) 'The mirror dream.' *Psychoanal. Study. Child 30*, 341–35.

Leal, R. (1983) 'Why group analysis works.' In M. Pines (ed) *The Evolution of Group Analysis*. London: Routledge and Kegan Paul.

Modarressi, T. 'An experimental study of mirror imagery during infancy and childhood. The evolution of self and its developmental vicissitudes.' (unpublished paper).

Pines, M. (1981) 'The frame of reference of group psychotherapy.' *Int. J. of Group Psychotherapy 31*, 3, 275–285.

CHAPTER 2

Mirroring and Child Development
Psychodynamic and Psychological Interpretations[1]

The experimental and observational study of mirroring in children contributes to understanding the developmental lines of

1. self as subject

2. self as object

3. self with object.

To this widely recognised scheme can be added the unusual tangential contribution of Lacan and the French school of

4. self as other.

Categorisation artificially separates the growth of the whole person into part components, the 'person' in relation to 'others'. For some authors, for example, Lewis and Brooks-Gunn (1979), following Cooley and Mead, self and object arise together and are different terms in the same equation. However, for clarity and convenience these categorisations will be preserved in reviewing the evidence on the role of mirroring in child development.

At the outset it is of fundamental importance to recognise that authors use the term 'mirroring' in very different senses. For some, mirroring is used as a metaphor; it represents the social responses of others to the infant, and therefore includes the study of all the components of relationships. For other authors, the study is of infants' actual responses to their own reflection, the mirror image, the 'specular image' of the French school. In this chapter, the use of the metaphorical mirror will be addressed first, and the observations of both clinicians and psychological researchers will then be drawn upon.

1   Published in: (1) *Psychoanalytic Inquiry* (1985) 5, 2, 211–231. (2) Honess, T. and Yardley, K. (eds) (1987) *Self and Identity: Perspectives Across the Lifespan.* Boston, MA: Routledge and Kegan Paul, Inc.

Mirroring as a biological and social phenomenon

The very earliest social responses of caretakers to infants and some of the infants' earliest responses to caretakers have been viewed as 'mirroring' responses at a biological level. The underlying mechanisms have been viewed as imprinting (Lichtenstein 1977), social fittedness (Emde 1983), intuitive parental behaviour (Papousek and Papousek 1979), imitation (Pawlby 1977) and state-sharing (Stern 1983). These observations and concepts are presented in more detail below.

Biological mirroring

Following the suggestions of Emde (1983) and other authors, I propose that mirroring is an important function in the developmental line (Freud 1980) of the process of organisation and coherence that will lead to self-awareness and to the awareness of the relations between self and objects.

Emde (1983) states that it is generally agreed, partly on the basis of the infant's behaviour towards the literal mirror image, that self-recognition emerges at some time in the infant's second year. Emde asks, does this mean that a new psychic organisation, the 'self', emerges for the first time in the second year? Or can we conceive of the self as an ongoing developmental process that gains psychological representation in the second year and hence becomes observable both subjectively and objectively? He proposes that we regard self as a process, a vital set of synthetic functions which increase in depth and complexity as development proceeds through the lifespan, and that prior to the emergence and recognition of self as a psychological process we can conceptualise and observe its development as a biological process. Part of this biological process we can term 'biological mirroring'.

Three biological processes that apply to the organisation and development of systems are necessary for the coherence of the developing and emerging system that we can later recognise as self. These principles are *self-regulation* (the physiological homeostasis and maintenance of individual integrity), *affective monitoring* of pleasurable and unpleasurable experiences and, most important for present purposes, *'social fittedness'*. For this process, the infant is assumed to be pre-adapted to participate in human interaction. Social fittedness involves the actions of both the infant and the caretakers/parents, who intuitively adopt appropriate behaviour towards the infant, such as baby talk or rhythmic soothing, and engage in behavioural synchrony. The aspect that I shall enlarge upon as an example of biological mirroring is the eye-to-eye contact parents adopt with the newborn infant, which has been beautifully investigated and demonstrated by the Papouseks.

The terms 'biological echo' and 'biological mirror' are used by the Papouseks (1979) in their discussion of primary, intuitive parental behaviours, which can be observed cross-culturally, exemplifying Emde's principle of social fittedness. Amongst these primary parental behaviours are facial and vocal behaviours, such as baby talk and exaggerated facial expressions. By speaking to infants in baby talk with its higher pitch, repetitive phrases and free use of nonsense utterances, and by the use of exaggerated facial expressions which offer clear indications of emotional states and offerings of joy, greeting, approval, encouragement or even of amused disapproval, the parent acts as a benign reflection to the baby of its presence within the context of a social relationship. This interaction is described by Winnicott (1971) in his discussion of the mother's face as a mirror to the baby (see below).

The Papouseks have demonstrated, cross-culturally, how visual contact between caretakers and infants is established and that it satisfies a basic need for both parties to get to know, and to be known by, the other. They state that the most important educational principle is, 'to deliver knowledge in appropriate amounts at appropriate times through multiple sensory modalities repeatedly and with respect for the recipient's capacity to process them', and that 'intuitive parenting' seems to guarantee this primary education.

Imitation

Imitative behaviour, also a form of biological mirroring, is another principle of primary intuitive parenting. The capacity for imitation of the adult by the newborn can be seen in the first few weeks of life. Caretakers imitate infants and encourage infants to imitate them. Vocally, they make baby noises and encourage babies to make utterances and then imitate the sounds that come from the infant; they initiate smiling responses and reward the child's smile by demonstrating pleasure when the smile appears; they repeat the infant's gestures; they encourage hitting, grasping, kicking and repeat the movements of the infant; they enter into repetitive sequences, interacting playfully with the infant.

Pawlby (1977) shows that the process begins with the mother being ready to imitate her child: 'Almost from the time of birth there seems to be a marked readiness for mothers to *reflect back* to their infants certain gestures which occur spontaneously within the baby's natural repertoire of activities' (author's italics, p.220). By reflecting back imitatively, mother is acting as a psycho-biological mirror, an active partner in the infant's developing capacity for social relations and the beginning of awareness of self-representation and object representation. But that is not all mother does; she does more than that. Whenever baby is likely to repeat an action two or three times, when sequences are observed, 'a mother may skilfully insert her own copy of that action between two of the repetitions and hence create a simulation of a deliberate act of imitation on the infant's part' (p.220). The mother's intention seems to be to develop and to sustain a meaningful dialogue with her baby and, furthermore, to facilitate the development of a more deliberate imitation by the baby. The mother's answering gesture provides the infant with an interest-holding event which is temporally contingent upon its own performance of a similar event. Thus intentionality and reciprocity are inserted by the caretakers into their beginning dialogues with their infants. They assume that the baby intends to perform a motor action; they reward and praise the infant for random actions and encourage him or her to repeat them: 'Who's a clever baby? Go on, do it again'. They reward the child for actions which are contingent on the child's behaviour and also reassure themselves of their child's capacities for such behaviour and for the establishment of communication between them. Pawlby notes that parental imitation of their children's behaviour seems largely unconscious unless it is actually drawn to the caretaker's attention. Thus imitation seems to be a further example of intuitive primary parenting, of parents as the good mirrors assuring the infant that 'you are the fairest one of all' during that blissful early-world state where there is no other to challenge the state of joyful narcissistic self-experience. Mother is the talking, smiling mirror for her child's earliest self-reflection, creating that sense of primary identity to which Lichtenstein has drawn our attention.

Lichtenstein (1977) invokes the concept of 'imprinting' to describe vital aspects of early infant–mother interaction, defining it as, 'the name given to the process by which the releaser of an innate reaction to a fellow member of the species is acquired'. Here he is using concepts derived from ethology, as described by Lorenz and Tinbergen. According to Lichtenstein, a mother sends 'messages' to her infant that convey a great deal about her unconscious wishes concerning the child. The way she touches, holds, warms the child, the way in which some senses are stimulated while others are not, forms a kind of 'stimulus cast' of the mother's unconscious. He refers to other analysts, such as Mahler (1967), who use the term 'mirroring' for these very early selective responses of the parents to the infant, and agrees that such mirroring experiences are intimately linked with the emergence of both body image and sense of identity. However, he argues that the term overemphasises the visual element of the experience, that the 'image' of oneself that the mirror conveys is at this early stage outlined in terms of sensory responsiveness, not as visual perception:

> These responses as well as the primitive stimuli that elicit them form a continu-
> ous interchange of need creation and need satisfaction between the two part-
> ners of the symbiotic world. While the mother satisfies the infant's needs, in fact
> she creates certain specific needs, which she delights in satisfying, the infant is
> transformed into an organ or an instrument for the satisfaction of the mother's
> unconscious needs. (pp.76–7)

Mother imprints upon the infant an identity theme which is irreversible but capable of variations throughout the life process. Here Lichtenstein, like Emde, is describing the process that gives continuity and coherence to the individual throughout all the momentous dangers from internal and external environments that characterise the human experience from birth to old age.

Where else do we find the concept of mirroring being applied to infant development in the first year of life? In his masterly summing up and integration of research on very early infantile development and relationships, Daniel Stern (1983) writes of ways of 'Being With' another that can be applied to infantile affective experiences, the experience of 'Self with Other'. Some features of that which he agrees can be called 'mirroring' are amongst the most important of these 'being with' experiences.

Stern proposes that the affective experiences of the baby with the other be integrated with the cognitive viewpoint that self and other are indeed differentiated perceptually and cognitively from birth onwards. He argues that Mahler's 'symbiotic' state as the earliest state of post-natal life is not confirmed by research evidence, which demonstrates that the child is 'an avid learner from birth', competent, predesigned to perceive the world in a highly structured fashion and mentally active in organising pre-structured conceptions, of which visual schemata and the recognition of the mother's face are the most important.

In the affective schemata of the mother–infant pair there are three ways of 'being with' the other: 'self–other complementarity', 'mental state-sharing' and 'state transforming'. The 'invaluable concept of mirroring' is in fact predicated on the more basic concept 'state-sharing'. In mental state-sharing and state-tuning, the infant and the mother share similar experiences. State-sharing covers events such as vocalising together, games such as pat-a-cake, interactional synchrony, mutual gazing and interactions between mother and infant such as smiling, where the smile of the one evokes the smile of the other, which in turn increases the pleasure and the intensity of the smiling response, in a positive feedback loop. State-sharing and those aspects of it which can be termed 'mirroring' are, Stern argues, clearly moments of great importance, for they are the first glimpse of having something like a similar experience with another, that is, a glimpse of intersubjectivity: the sharing of mental states creates the possibility of subjective intimacy. During these moments of state-sharing infants are 'engaged' in the slow and momentous discovery that what they already sense is distinctly their own is not unique and unparalleled but is part of shared human experience. They are establishing subjective intimacy. In order to do that the infant must maintain the separate entities of self and other, because the power of state-sharing lies in a sense of what is happening being between two separate persons. However, not all in this process is joyful. State-sharing can also be negative. Mutual gazing and mimicry can be frightening, provocative and at times intolerably invasive in the sense of negative intimacy. This is the first appearance of the concept of negative mirroring, which will be addressed later.

Stern writes that, 'being with experiences are the stuff that human connectedness, as well as normal intimacy and basic trust, are made of at all points of development. The ability to engage in them is amongst the most needed and healthy of capacities'. This again emphasises the great significance of early biological and psychological positive mirroring experiences in the establishment of the basic building blocks of human personality and of human connectedness.

In his contribution to the same volume, Louis Sander (1983) does not actually refer to mirroring. His emphasis is on coherency and unity, on how they are enhanced and maintained in infantile development. I suggest that mirroring is one of the ways in which this coherency and unity is advanced and maintained. If we adopt Stern's concept of 'state-sharing', in which the infant becomes aware that what he/she is already experiencing as his/her experience is then mirrored, that is, shared, by another and this other is experienced as already possessing characteristics of coherency and unity, then the state-sharing reinforces the child's own experience of coherency and unity. State-sharing does not lead to fusion, to loss of boundaries, to a regressive de-differentiation; it is a joyful reinforcement of the sense of individuality, of one who is now 'being with the other', the 'fitting together' which Hartmann (1958) emphasised, as does Emde (1983) when he refers to 'social fittedness'.

The thrust of current research in infant development is on the infant–mother system and not on the isolated individual infant. Previously seen as totally helpless and dependent, the infant seems very different when viewed as an active participant in the 'well functioning' of an organisation that is adapted to its survival, maintenance and development. This systemic viewpoint, which considers both the whole and the parts, sees the parts affecting the structure and function as a whole and the whole concurrently affecting the structure and function of the parts. Development is seen as a creative process in which mirroring has an important part to play through social connectedness – learning and playfulness being inherent in this process.

Within psychoanalytic developmental theory, both Winnicott's dictum: 'There is no such thing as a baby' (meaning that the infant is never seen in isolation, only in the context of a caretaker) and Kohut's description of caretakers as the baby's 'selfobjects' exemplify this systemic viewpoint well.

D.W. Winnicott

Winnicott's famous contribution to the concept of mirroring is presented in his short paper 'Mirror-role of mother and family in child development' (1971). As Davis and Wallbridge (1981) show, we can set this important contribution in the context of Winnicott's emphasis on ego-relatedness and communication, a relationship between mother and baby that arises specifically from the holding environment (see Harwood (1987), Chapter 4). Winnicott states that the function of the environment can be summarised as

1. Holding
2. Handling
3. Object-presenting.

If the infant is held and handled satisfactorily, and with this taken for granted, at some time the baby begins to look around and looks much more at the face than at the breast. (Indeed, it is striking how much less attention has been placed upon the face in the development of object relationships theory than upon the breast.) Winnicott asks the question: 'What does the baby see when he or she looks at the mother's face?'. I am suggesting that, ordinarily, what the baby sees is himself or herself. In other words, a mother is looking at the baby and what she looks like is related to what she sees there. If she looks with love and with tenderness, the baby experiences him- or herself as joyfully alive. If, however, she is depressed and unsmiling, even more so if she does not look back and cannot maintain the reciprocity of looking, the baby experiences him- or herself as joyless, unlively, even absent. The mother's face is, then, all that is seen:

> Mother's face is not then a mirror. So perception takes the place of apperception, perception takes the place of that which might have been the beginning of a sig-nificant exchange with the world, a two-way process in which self-enrichment alternates with the discovery of meaning in the world of seeing things... A baby so treated will grow up puzzled about mirrors and what the mirror has to offer. If the mother's face is unresponsive then a mirror is a thing to be looked at but not to be looked into. (Winnicott 1971, p.113)

David Scharff (1982) has utilised Winnicott's observations in his suggestion that there is a developmental line of gaze interaction, and that the exchange of gazes contributes significantly to sexual and emotional life in the adult:

> Gaze interaction is one physical function for which we can draw a developmen-tal line from infancy to adulthood that illuminates the concepts of growth in ob-ject relations and sexuality. Although in practice it is part of the larger context of holding, handling and vocalising, it can be separated out for purposes of study and illustration. (p.19)

> The adult needs for kissing, smiling, and physical caring or lovemaking have their origins in the shared gaze, touch, holding and vocal 'conversations' of in-fant and mother. The response of each partner to the other is required for a sense of well being. Failures of mirroring in infancy leading to false self problems make it difficult to re-create the mirroring experience in adult sexual life. With-out a capacity for mutual mirroring, exchange is severely hampered. (p.24)

To return once more to Winnicott's short but evocative paper, we find here one of his most important statements about psychotherapy, one that my own clinical experience with narcissistically disturbed and damaged patients repeatedly confirms: psychotherapy is not making clever and apt interpretations; by and large it is a long-term process of giving the patient back what the patient brings.' This has profound significance for psychoanalytic technique and has strong parallels with Kohutian technique (Wolf 1987).

Kohut, self-psychology and mirroring

On the basis of his clinical experience of the transference manifestations of patients with narcissistic personality disorders, Kohut (1971) postulated that there is a, 'normal phase of development of the grandiose self in which the gleam in the mother's eye, which mirrors the child's exhibitionistic display, confirm[s] the child's self-esteem and, by gradually increasing selectivity of these responses, begin[s] to channel it into realistic directions' (p.116).

In Kohut's description of object relations there is the developmental line in which the object, before it is experienced and regarded as a separate object, is experienced as a part of the self. Another person invested with narcissistic cathexis is experienced narcissistically as a selfobject: 'The expected control over such (selfobject) others is then closer to the concept of the control which a grown-up expects to have over his own body and mind'. The object is important only insofar as it is invited to participate in the child's narcissistic pleasure and thus to confirm it:

> Before psychological separatedness has been established, the baby experiences the mother's pleasure in his whole body self as part of his own psychological equipment. After psychological separation has taken place, the child needs the gleam in the mother's eye in order to maintain the narcissistic libidinal suffusion that now concerns, in their sequence, the leading functions and activities of the various maturational phases. (Kohut 1978, p.439)

The concept of mirroring represents one pole of what Kohut came to call the 'bipolar self', the other pole representing the idealised parental imago.

It is rather striking that, despite the popularity of the terms 'mirroring' and 'mirror transferences' as introduced by Kohut, there has been little systematic correlation of clinical and experimental observation of children and their responses within the mirroring relationship (and their responses to the specular image) with the theoretical corpus of what has now become Kohut's self-psychology. Until this is done, the contributions of Kohut to mirroring and child development rest on a somewhat narrow basis. There is no doubt, however, that Kohut's emphasis on the child as the 'gleam in the mother's eye' has led to a great renewal of interest in the concept of mirroring and its application to child development and the clinical situation of psychoanalysis.

The specular image: The French connection

The developmental psychology and psychodynamics of the infant's own mirror image, that is, the child's response to his or her physical reflection in the mirror, the 'specular image', is peculiarly a particular area of interest to, and rich speculation by, the French psychologists Wallon, Lacan, Merleau-Ponty and Zazzo.

LACAN

In his 1936 work (first published in 1949), Lacan put forward the idea of a 'mirror stage', connecting the development of the ego with the mirror stage and the specular image. The following outline of this mirror stage or phase (a preferable term as it denotes an evolving process) is drawn from Lacan (1977), Lemaire (1977) and Laplanche and Pontalis (1973).

Lacan acknowledges the contributions of the American developmental psychologist Baldwin to the study of the child's response to its mirror image. Lacan points out, long before Gallup's more detailed examination of the chimpanzee's response to its mirror image (Desmond 1980), that the primate, apparently well ahead of the child at an early age in instrumental intelligence, quickly loses interest in the mirror image. The chimpanzee, 'once the image has been mastered and found empty exhausts itself in its response'. For its part, the child, far from finding the image empty, responds to it, 'in a series of gestures in which he expresses in play the relation between the movements assumed in the image and the reflected environment, and between the virtual complex and the reality it re-duplicates the child's own body, and the persons and things around him' (Lacan 1977, p.1). Lacan places this stage (phase) between 6 and 18 months and states that it represents an identification, 'the transformation that takes place in the subject when he assumes an image' (p.2), his imago. The child 'jubilantly' assumes his or her mirror image at the infans stage (infans means 'without words'), when he or she is still, 'sunk in his motor incapacity and nurseling dependence'. For Lacan this is the fateful moment when, by identifying with a fiction, the idealised image of himself that he perceives in the mirror, the agency of the ego is cast, the primordial basis of the I that is alienated from the subject; man projects himself into a statue, his 'ideal-I': 'The mirror stage is a "drama", the beginning of the imaginary world, of the succession of fantasies that will eventually lead to the assumption of the armour of an alienating identity which will mark with its rigid structure the subject's entire mental development' (1977 p.4).

Lemaire (1977, p. 177) fills out Lacan's sketch of the mirror phase, describing three successive stages of self-recognition in the mirror:

Phase 1

Child with adult before a mirror confuses reflection and reality. He or she tries to seize hold of the image or to look behind the mirror, but at the same time the reflection is confused with that of the adult.

Phase 2

The child acquires the notion of the image and understands that the reflection is not a real being.

Phase 3

The child realises that this reflected image is his or her own and different from the reflection of the other. Now the intense joy and the classic game of one's own movements seen reflected in the mirror appear.

Parallel to the mirror self-recognition, the child behaves in a typical way towards other children of its own age, who are homologues, more or less of its own appearance. He or she observes these others with curiosity, imitates, tries to seduce or impose upon them by play-acting, is aggressive towards them and cries when another falls. This can be understood as the child situating itself socially by comparing itself with another (Atkins 1983). The phase of what is called 'transitivism' (Buhler 1935) appears. The child who hits will say that it has been hit, a child who sees another fall will cry. This is another instance of the child living in the Imaginary order, of a dual relationship with the merging of self and other: 'It is in the other that the subject first lives and registers himself' (Lemaire 1977, p.177).

Thus the mirror stage is based upon observations of the child's response to the specular image and the child's response to the image of its homologues. In both instances the phase observed can be interpreted as the acquisition of, and the response to, a self-image as a fictional totality, to the action of the imagination and to the merger of this new subjective self, the subject, with whatever closely resembles it. This total representation of the self is at the same time the first stage in human alienation through the identification of the self with an image:

> The self merges with his own image and the same imaginary trapping by the double is seen in relationships with his fellows…the subject is ignorant of his own alienation and that is how the chronic mis-recognition of self and the causal change determining human existence takes shape. (Lemaire 1977, p.178)

How, then, does the human being escape from the trap of narcissism to become involved in what Lemaire calls the 'proper dimension to his humanity', symbolic organisation? According to Lacan, this is what is accomplished in the oedipal phase when the third term, that of language (the law of the Name-of-the-Father), leads to a transcendence of the dual relationship of alienation based upon the imaginary relationship of the child and the mother: 'The resolution of the oedipus constitutes the sense of reality in that it is a liberation from the fascination of the image' (Lemaire 1977, p.179).

With this reality of persons in relationship, truth can enter. The child can now cease to be Narcissus, who drowned trying to reunite himself with his own image. No longer captivated by his or her own image, the child can turn away from his or her reflection to the world of self with others, to be a member of a family and to enter into the social order. The child internalises the Law of the Father, accepts that he or she is a small child who has to wait for biological maturity in order to be able to fulfil his/her wishes and desires, as opposed to his/her previous ambition to seduce the mother and to be for her the unique object of her desire, the phallus. Aggression towards father, who intrudes into this world of desire, leads to the recognition of him, eventually to acceptance of the relationship with him and to internalisation of him, to accepting differences – differences of age, time and generation, differences of bodies.

There is indeed a remarkable strength and even majesty in Lacan's thesis. However, it is based on an intoxicating mixture of sensitive observation and speculation, and I am not aware of any systematic attempt to integrate his theories with the observations and theories of other, more recent, psychoanalytic observers of infants' behaviours towards the mirror image, though Abelin (see below) takes Lacan's mirror stage into account in his reconstruction of early triangulation. Lacan's thesis that mirroring is essentially alienation from self, contrasting with Winnicott's thesis that the child first finds itself in the mirror of the mother's face, points to the contrast between the integrating aspects of socially responsive mirroring and the alienating experience of aloneness with the self that arises with the specular image. This will be further considered as an aspect of negative mirroring (see below).

MAURICE MERLEAU-PONTY

In *The Primacy of Perception* (1964), Merleau-Ponty devotes a chapter to 'The child's relations with others', in which he presents a fascinating and comprehensive integration of the world of French and German child psychologists, of Guillaume, Wallon, Charlotte Buhler and others, with the psychoanalytic observations of Lacan on the mirror stage. He outlines the development of the child from birth to three years, but the section that concerns us here is the stage after six months: 'consciousness of one's own body and the specular image' (pp.125–151).

Merleau-Ponty outlines Wallon's ideas and observations. First, at the age of six months a child situated in front of a mirror, together with a parent, seems to recognise the parent in the mirror reflection prior to recognition of the self-image.

If father and child are together before the mirror, the child smiles at the image of father; if the father speaks, the child turns towards him in surprise. Thus the child recognises father through his mirror image at a stage before he/she grasps the reality of the mirror image as such: 'The image has an existence inferior to that of father's real body – but it does have a sort of marginal existence' (Merleau-Ponty 1964, p.128). It is later, at eight months, that the child clearly shows surprise at its own mirror image. Wallon concludes that the specular image of one's own body develops later than that of the other, and the explanation is that the problem to be solved is much greater in the case of one's own body than that of the other. The child is dealing with two visual experiences of the father: the experience that he or she has of looking at him and that which comes from the mirror. On the other hand, the mirror image is the child's only complete visual evidence of its own body. A child can easily look at feet and hands but not at the body as a whole. Thus it is first a problem of understanding that the visual image of the body, seen over there in the mirror, is not himself or herself since the child is not in the mirror but here, where the child feels him/herself; and, second, the child must understand that, not being located there in the mirror, but rather where he/she feels the self interoceptively, he/she can nonetheless be seen by an external witness of the very place at which he/she feels the self to be and with the same visual appearance as in the mirror. In short, the mirror image must be displaced, bringing it from the apparent or virtual place that it occupies in the depth of the mirror, back to the self, whom he/she identifies at a distance with the interoceptive body.

Merleau-Ponty points out that Wallon does not offer a full explanation of why the child is so amused and fascinated by its mirror image. Here he turns to Lacan and to his thesis that the child identifies itself with the specular image. It is through the acquisition of the specular image that the child notices that he/she is visible for himself/herself and for others, that viewpoint can be taken on him/her, for hitherto the child has never seen himself/herself as a whole. By means of the image in the mirror the child becomes capable of becoming a spectator of itself.

ERNEST ABELIN AND EARLY TRIANGULATION

As mentioned above, Abelin (1971, 1980) provides the most notable example of the integration of Lacanian concepts with those of other developmental psychologists. Abelin, trained in the Piagetian tradition and working with Mahler, is aware of the importance of Lacan's theory of the mirroring phase and links this with the momentous development that can be observed at 18 months during the rapprochement phase of separation–individuation. In Lacan's work it is through the development of the specular image that at 18 months the child becomes aware of the self as an entity which exists in space and can now be observed by others. This is a contribution to the developmental line of the image of the corporeal self, the self as object. Abelin attempts to create a theoretical bridge between the developmental line of the self as object with the developmental line of the self with object and self with others.

Abelin examines the role of object relations and libidinal wishes and attachments in, 'the momentous Copernican revolution of mind' that Piaget demonstrates at 18 months, at the time of the rapprochement phase of separation–individuation. Now the child can imagine the self as being seen from the outside (see Merleau-Ponty, discussed above), where the child is but one cause and effect amongst many others. It is now that the imitation of objects, a biological capacity, is superseded by the capacity for mental representations, of the images of objects, a psychological capacity. Imitation, which is action in time, develops into the capacity for relating to images in space. Abelin (1971) invokes the concept of mirroring for his explanation of the mechanism involved.

From birth he sees the infant as involved in one-to-one narcissistic mirroring with the mother, a relationship which he considers continues as far as the rapprochement phase. In this narcissistic mirroring phase, the infant operates on sensory-motor schema. During the rapprochement phase the child becomes capable of symbolic functions and of representing relations. It is this capacity that is necessary for the reduction of the earlier narcissistic mirroring quality of all relationships. How does this change come about?

Abelin (1971) agrees with Lacan that the role of the father is primary here. Whereas Lacan attributes this development to the symbolic father, to language, to the Law of the Name-of-the-Father, Abelin attributes it to the child's burgeoning awareness of father and mother as a loving pair from which he/she is excluded and which he/she is able to observe only from the outside. The child now has a position in space as a separate entity from which it observes the parental couple in their relationship and occupying the same dimension. Now the infant knows that he/she is excluded from the relationship of father loving mother. Now it knows that it is a self with longings and desires as the affective core, longings which are blocked and frustrated by the rival father. Having a rival means being a rival, a birth into a new experience of self. Knowledge of differences is a different kind of knowledge from the knowledge of sameness. Differences are indicated and demarcated by boundaries, which are obstacles that have to be recognised, negotiated with and, if possible, overcome; if not, there is the experience of failure, of separation and of loss. For Abelin this is the foundation of early triangulation experiences, for the mental representation of relations between self and others, of the capacity for symbolic representations. (He does not discuss Kleinian theory, in which very much earlier oedipal triangulation images and concepts are hypothesised.)

This capacity for early triangulation is the psychological matrix for the representation of sets of images, of reciprocal relations, of the 'reversible group' of Piaget, indeed for the representation of the self as a social being.

As we have already seen when discussing biological mirroring, other observers describe the child as entering into social relationships from the earliest neonatal period, because infants are treated as social beings by parents and caretakers who introduce them to the notions of reciprocity and intention by the way in which they interact with them. Abelin does not discuss these findings, or look for evidence of the child's own capacity to discuss these findings or of the child's own capacity to initiate such relationships and to give them representation. His observations and his theoretical framework are from a different universe of discourse from that of these other observers of early social relationships and have yet to be integrated with them.

Mirroring and early peer-relations

Atkins (1983) argues that psychoanalysis has not yet paid proper attention to the place of 'non-caretakers' in the development of object relationships. However, the close observation of how babies react and respond to the presence of other babies shows that they do indeed interact significantly and that the concept of mirroring can be usefully applied to the understanding of these processes. In this way we can begin to fill in more details of the developmental line of object relatedness in general and peer relatedness in particular.

Atkins invokes the 'gratifying experience of mirroring' to explain this fascinating lure that infants have for one another. Watching the play of two eight-month-old children, he observes smiles, interest in each other and in the other's actions, and he observes actions directed apparently towards the other. Atkins discusses these interactions in terms of the infants responding to some awareness of their similarities to each other, a form of twinship mirroring, which can be analysed in phase-specific sensory, sensorimotor and sensoriaffective integration components.

The infants seem attracted by perceptual similarities, sensing that the other is like oneself. 'Clearly little ones like other little ones – even strangers – even more than they like adults' (Atkins 1983, p.237). They manifest socially directed behaviour, responding to each other's play and gestures as a, 'primitive sign context of motor recognition which, in turn, precipitates, stimulates and furthers' the child's own actions (p.238). The other is distinct, yet like oneself, and I suggest that we can infer that the child becomes more aware of being himself or herself through this similarity and differentiation from the other similar person.

Connecting the 'who' and the 'what'

In a notable series of papers, Sheldon Bach (1980) addresses himself to the relation of the experienced self that is proximal, proprioceptively experienced, the self that is experienced subjectively 'in here', with the self that exists 'out there' in the mirror, in the reflected appraisals of others, which is objectified by others. The synthesis of the subjective and objective self is one of the momentous tasks of the rapprochement phase of separation–individuation.

The subjective self is partly built upon the internalisation of the mother-of-dual-unity; the objective self on the appraisals of the mother-of-separation. The empathic object (Kohut's selfobject that is narcissistically invested) bridges the gap between the subjective self and the objective self, between the subject and object.

In the context of mirroring, Bach refers to Zazzo's (1975) observations that between 18 months and 2 years there is a period when the child can identify the mirror image by the proper name, for example, answer 'Johnnie' to the question: 'Who is that you see in the mirror?', but is unable to use his own name in reference to himself and replies 'me' when asked who he is. This indicates that the child has not yet synthesised the subjective and objective modes of self-awareness:

> He has recognised that for others 'Johnnie' and 'me' have the same reference, but he has not yet succeeded in creating that psychic space we call the 'self', within which our multiple subjective and objective perspectives are paradoxically conceived of as transformations of the same invariant ongoing person. (Bach 1980, p.185)

When the child does achieve this integration, he or she has then created the psychic space of the self.

Bach addresses himself in particular to the boundary area of subjective and objective self-awareness, delicately applying Winnicott's concepts of paradox, transitional space and play to understand the experiences of patients with predominantly narcissistic pathology who are primarily concerned with who the self is, in contrast to the more developmentally advanced patients who are trying to find out what their ego wants: 'In the transference neurotic, thought is trial action, in the narcissistic neurotic, thought is trial identity'. (1984, p.162)

Negative mirroring

Under this heading I include such observations and theoretical constructions as Lacan's, who states that infants' response to their specular images is essentially one of alienation from self, and also the universally recognised developmental stage of the toddler's growing wariness of its mirror image.

From about 14 months onwards, the response of the child who has previously shown delight and enthusiasm at the presence of its mirror image begins to change. It now begins to become wary and to withdraw when placed in front of the mirror. Self-recognition seems soon to lead on to self-consciousness, that is, to a form of painful self-awareness and embarrassment. How is this development to be understood? One approach is that of Amsterdam and Levitt (1980), who argue that at the beginning of the second year of life three key events occur which appear to be critical to the onset of painful self-conscious behaviour:

1. The beginnings of representational thinking, which allows the body self to be taken as object.

2. The infant's struggle to obtain upright posture and locomotion.

3. Intentional reaching for and self-stimulation of the genitalia.

The argument is that the child, through recognising itself in front of the mirror, is also aware that it can be seen by others. Further, that this occurs at a time when he or she is becoming aware that pleasurable sensations which arise from within, in response to his or her own genital stimulation, are now unacceptable to the adult world. Though they think that shame and painful self-consciousness may arise in connection with excretory functions, Amsterdam and Levitt argue that the mother is more likely to encourage and to approve of excretory functions, whereas few mothers can observe their children's masturbatory behaviour with unselfconscious approval, at least in Western societies. Thus the child must begin to learn to inhibit genital sensation and exploration in the presence of others at precisely the same time as he or she also experiences affective self-consciousness before the mirror. Painful self-consciousness seems to occur when the body is experienced as a shameful object and this is a major narcissistic injury in the mother–infant relationship. Because of mother's disapproval and prohibition of genital play, the child's bodily display is no longer responded to by the approving gleam and reflection in mother's eyes.

An alternative interpretation of the above observations has been put forward by Paulina Kernberg (1984). She invokes the child's increasing awareness of differentiation from mother. Up until now, if the attachment between mother and child has been firm and the mother's attunement to her child's behaviour sensitive and appropriate, then she has on the whole acted as a mirror to her child, enhancing the child's sense of self and bringing meaning to the object world. During this period the child's behaviours in front of the mirror can be seen as 'echoing' the attachment behaviours between child and mother. Because of this, the child's reaction to the mirror includes his or her reaction to the mother whether or not she is actually present with the child in front of the mirror. At this later stage of rapprochement, from 14 to 24 months, the child is increasingly aware that the reflecting mirror is not mother. Children therefore show a type of stranger reaction to their own images, reflecting their unstable sense of self. The toddler is aware of separateness, is perplexed by it, occasionally fascinated but very often withdrawing from this confusing situation. Later, between 24 and 36 months, the child seems to have gained a more secure sense of self-awareness and can again look at itself in the mirror, though now in a more sophisticated manner, sometimes with admiration, sometimes with embarrassment. Now the child is more in possession of a sense of self-constancy and object-constancy, and with this capacity for self-constancy it contains the mirroring function that previously was mother's.

Conclusion

I have attempted to show that the concept of the 'mirror', understood both literally and metaphorically, provides an invaluable contribution to our understanding of the developmental lines of 'self as object', 'self with object' and 'self as other'. The mirroring concept is used in many different ways by both psychologists and clinicians and we must remain cautious in transferring knowledge between different contexts. However, it has been suggested that there are grounds where such cross-fertilisation would be of significant value.

References

Abelin, E.L. (1971) 'The role of father in the separation-individuation process.' In J.B. McDevitt and C.F. Settlage (eds) *Separation–individuation.*' New York: International Universities Press.

Abelin, E.L. (1980) 'Triangulation, the role of the father and the origins of core gender identity during the rapprochement subphase.' In R.F. Lax, S. Bach and J.A. Burland (eds) *Rapprochement.* New York: Jason Aronson.

Amsterdam, B.K. and Levitt, M. (1980) 'Consciousness of self and painful self-consciousness.' *Psychoanalytic Study of the Child 35*, 67–83.

Atkins, R.N. (1983) 'Peer relatedness in the first year of life: the birth of a new world.' *Annual of Psychoanalysis 11* 227–244.

Bach, S. (1980) 'Self-love and object-love: some problems of self and object constancy, differentiation and integration.' In R.F. Lax, S. Bach and J.A. Burland (eds) *Rapprochement.* New York: Jason Aronson.

Buhler, C. (1935) *From Birth to Maturity.* London: Kegan, Paul, Trench, Trubner.

Davis, M. and Wallbridge, D. (1981) *Boundary and Space: An Introduction to the Work of D.W. Winnicott.* London: H. Karnac.

Desmond, A. (1980) *The Ape's Reflexion.* London: Quartet Books.

Emde, R.N. (1983) 'The prerepresentational self and its affective core.' *Psychoanalytic Study of the Child 38*, 165–191.

Freud, A. (1980) *Normality and Pathology in Childhood. The Writings of Anna Freud, Vol.6.* London: Hogarth Press.

Hartmann, H. (1958) *Ego Psychology and the Problem of Adaptation.* New York: International Universities Press.

Harwood, I. H. (1987) 'The evolution of the Self: An integration of Winnicott's and Kohut's concepts.' In T. Honess and K. Yardley (eds) *Self and Identity.* London: Routledge and Kegan Paul.

Kernberg, P. (1984) 'Reflections in the mirror: mother–child interaction, self-awareness and self-recognition.' In R. Tyson (ed) *Proceedings of the Second Congress of Infant Psychiatry.* New York: International Universities Press.

Kohut, H. (1971) *The Analysis of the Self.* New York: N.Y. Int. Universities Press.

Kohut, H. (1978) 'Remarks about the formation of the Self.' In P. Ornstein (ed) *The Search for the Self.* New York: International Universities Press.

Lacan, J. (1977) *Ecrits.* (transl. A. Sheridan). London: Tavistock Publications.

Laplanche, J. and Pontalis, J.B. (1973) *The Language of Psychoanalysis.* London: Hogarth Press and Institute of Psycho-Analysis.

Lemaire, A. (1977) *Jacques Lacan.* London: Routledge and Kegan Paul.

Lewis, M. and Brooks-Gunn, J. (1979) *Social Cognition and the Acquisition of Self.* New York: Plenum Press.

Lichtenstein, H. (1977) *The Dilemma of Human Identity.* New York: Jason Aronson.

Mahler, M. (1967), 'On human symbiosis and the vicissitudes of individuation.' *Journal of the American Psychoanalytic Association 15,* 740–763.

Merleau-Ponty, M. (1964) *The Primacy of Perception and Other Essays.* Chicago: Northwestern University Press.

Papousek, H. and Papousek, M. (1979) 'Early ontogeny of human social interaction.' In M. von Cranach, K. Foppa., W. Leperies and D. Ploog (eds) *Human Ethology.* Cambridge: Cambridge University Press.

Pawlby, S.J. (1977) 'Imitative interaction.' In H.R. Schaffer (ed) *Studies in Mother–Infant Interaction.* London: Academic Press.

Sander, L.S. (1983) 'To begin with – reflections on ontogeny.' In J.D. Lichtenberg and S. Kaplan (eds) *Reflections on Self Psychology.* Hillsdale, NJ: Analytic Press.

Scharff, D.E. (1982) *The Sexual Relationship.* London: Routledge and Kegan Paul.

Stern, D. (1983) 'The early development of schemas of self, other and "self" with other.' In J.D. Lichtenberg and S. Kaplan (eds) *Reflections on Self Psychology.* Hillsdale, NJ: Analytic Press.

Winnicott, D.W. (1971) 'Mirror-role of mother and family in child development.' In *Playing and Reality.* London: Tavistock Publications.

Wolf, E. (1987) 'Some comments on the selfobject concept.' In K. Yardley and T. Honess (eds) *Self and Identity: Psychosocial Processes.* Chichester: Wiley.

Zazzo, R. (1975) 'La genese de la conscience de soi (La reconnaissance de soi dans l'image du miroir).' In R. Angelergues *et al.* (eds) *Psychologie de la Connaissance de Soi: Symposium de l'Association de Psychologie Scientifique de Langue Francaise.* Paris: Presses Universitaires de France.

CHAPTER 3

Psychic Development and the Group Analytic Situation[1]

The psychoanalytic situation and the group analytic situation are both powerful situations of social interaction that may in many ways replicate some characteristics of the situation in which we as human beings found our personal origins. What the nature of these similarities is forms part of this paper: I shall discuss recent theories of early human development based on infant–mother interactions.

The nature of the differences in the therapeutic outcomes of individual psychotherapy and group psychotherapy has been aptly caught in an aphorism by Michael Balint. In this memorable sentence he puts clearly the paradox that faces us: 'After psychoanalysis the patient is often less neurotic but not necessarily more mature: after group psychotherapy he is often more mature but not necessarily less neurotic' (Balint 1961, p.46). What I hope to do is to approach this paradox by considering some aspects of personal development and relating them to issues of group development, and to consider some approaches to the maturity to which Balint was referring. Maturity of the personality necessarily brings us to considerations of the self concept, its origin and development, and for our purposes we shall be considering maturity of the social, emotional and intellectual components of personality.

I shall take as my starting point the concepts of cohesion and coherence. The term 'cohesion' is one which we are already familiar with in group psychotherapy. It was popularised by Irving Yalom (1975), who defined it as, 'the attractiveness of a group for its members', and who emphasised that this was a therapeutic factor of primary importance and that a group had to be cohesive in order to become therapeutically effective. For Yalom, the cohesion of the group is represented by its attractiveness to its members; it is the invisible force that holds group members

1   Keynote address to the Canadian Association of Group Psychotherapy, Banff, 29 October 1983. Published in: *Group* (1985) 9, 1, 24–37.

together in the face of emotional conflicts and the frustrations of the therapeutic situation which can lead to a deep acceptance of each other and the formation of meaningful relationships. A cohesive group develops an identifiable social structure. Membership of a cohesive group has clearly defined and rather impermeable boundaries. The group members have the opportunity to become significant others with whom the work of emotional growth can be accomplished. Kellerman (1981) has devoted a whole volume to the exploration of this concept of group cohesion, but there is not a single reference to group coherence in the index and only a few in the text, notably by John Hartman (1981). However, Hartman treats cohesion and coherence as similar concepts, whereas I consider their differences significant; similarly Yalom does not deal with the concept of group coherence.

We are also familiar with the term 'cohesion' through the work of Heinz Kohut (1971, 1977) and the Chicago school of self psychology (Gedo and Goldberg 1973). There the term is used to describe a developmental process in which previously discreet aspects of self representation, ego nuclei, coalesce together so that the individual experiences spatial and temporal continuity, a self that holds together in the face of stress and regression. In this school the achievement of the stage of self cohesion marks a developmental threshold; prior to this 'the centre does not hold' and the world can fall apart into borderline and psychotic experiences of disintegration. After the firm establishment of self cohesion, emotional conflict will lead to neurotic developments but central self representation will hold together. We will come later to a further consideration of what this 'centre' represents.

The term 'coherence' is less frequently used than cohesion. However, once your attention has been alerted to this term you will find it quite frequently used, and indeed my impression is that its use is increasing, reflecting a greater interest in organisational principles in the development of the personality, which is a matter to which we shall be returning later. Anzieu, a leading French analyst of groups writes: 'A human being can exist as a subject only if he feels physically and psychologically coherent' (Anzieu 1984). Meanwhile, let me refresh your memories as to some dictionary definitions of these terms (cohesion and coherence) taken from Webster's *Dictionary of Synonyms* (1951):

> Coherence usually implies unity, firstly of immaterial, of intangible things, such as the points of an argument, the details of a picture, the incidents, characters and setting of a story; or secondly, of material and of objective things that are bound into a unity by a spiritual, intellectual or aesthetic relationship, as through their clear sequence or their harmony with one another; it therefore commonly connotes an integrity which makes the whole and the relationship of its parts clear and manifest.

The dictionary illustrates this with a quotation by the philosopher Alexander, who points out that both science and fine art possess the appearance of beauty because of a shared inner coherence.

Cohesion more often implies, 'unity of material things held together by a physical substance such as cement, mortar, glue or by a physical force such as attraction or affinity'. Cohesion, therefore, unlike coherence, does not represent a principle of organisation, nor of differentiation. A 'sticky', resistant phase of a group exemplifies strong cohesion; Bion's Basic Assumption theory brilliantly describes such phenomena, as when a group sticks together, does not develop and where individuals merge in the common enterprise of resistance to change. These resistance structures are powerful cohesion-builders and regulators of change. In psychology and ethology such cohesive terms as 'bonding' are used to describe the forces that will hold infant and mother together, as in the work of John Bowlby. Cohesion, then, is a physical analogy.

I am attracted to the term 'coherence' because it brings out the concept of, 'the unity of parts brought together in harmony with one another'. There is an organisational process at work, in contrast to the process being involved. Hartman (1981) uses the term 'adhesion' to cover similar ground. As he says, clay that sticks to the shoes does not become a unity where as clay in the hands of the sculptor does.

In this respect it seems to me to be of great interest to look at the etymological roots of the very word 'group' itself. Again, according to the dictionary (*The Shorter Oxford English Dictionary* (1973)) there are two roots, one Germanic and the other Latin. The more ancient Germanic origin of the term 'group' is derived from the word for 'crop', that is, the gizzard of a bird. Apparently the derivation of the word 'group' from 'crop' is that within the crop of an animal is to be found an agglomeration of substances that have been swallowed and which have lost their discrete nature and have clumped together to form a fibrous mass. Here we have the concept of a group which is undifferentiated, which has no formal characteristics and does not represent a higher form of social organisation. The word of Latin origin for 'group' has its origins in the concept of 'grouping', as in a painting. Here objects are grouped together in order to display a harmony, and this is evidence of a higher form of psychological organisation that has placed them together in order to produce an aesthetic satisfaction. The word 'cohesion' therefore seems to be applicable to the ancient Germanic concept of the agglomerated mass, the undifferentiated group, and the term 'coherence' to the group which follows organisational principles, whether it be small or large.

Where we seek to follow processes of development, tracing out the evolution either of an organism or of an organisation, a number of organisms combining together to form an organisation, we are dealing with organising processes that are lawful and therefore understandable. We are in the realm of coherence rather than cohesion. You may recall the phrase that a baby is, 'an organ within the maternal organisation', as Heinz Lichtenstein (1977, p.72) has pointed out, and of Winnicott's (1964) dictum that there is no such thing as a baby, for the baby is always located in a setting of a caretaker, of mother or her human or non-human substitute. Here the life setting of the baby is always seen to be organised.

So if we follow the pathway of coherence in infant development, we may come to see something relevant to the developmental processes of analytic forms of therapy, both individual and group. Incidentally, I have said analytic forms of group therapy to distinguish the more unstructured analytic small-group setting from the more structured forms of group psychotherapy, those that will follow the organisational principles laid down by the group leader or conductor and which therefore do not evolve as organisations through the exploration and discovery of self-organisation capacities on the part of the group members. The more structured group has, of course, a very definite and valued place in the spectrum of group therapies and is adapted, for instance, to the needs of some particular populations in their own organisational settings. Theme-centred groups which discuss the issues that confront all the members, as in groups of parents of handicapped children; homogeneous groups whose members share the same life difficulties; groups of persons facing transitions in their life situations; these task-limited and task-orientated groups can and will evolve in the direction of becoming more efficient and more effective at their task, given skilled leadership. They will, however, differ significantly from the open-ended non-time-limited analytic groups of the sort that my colleagues and I practise following the group analytic principles of S.H. Foulkes (1975).

Foulkes conceived of a number of therapeutic factors which he called 'group-specific' to differentiate them from those therapeutic factors which are common both to individual and to group psychotherapy. For example, some of these group-specific factors are socialisation, the group as a forum and the group as a place for exchange. He also indicated that we need to pay particular attention to such phenomena as mirroring and resonance which show themselves in the group and which I shall look at later, again in a developmental perspective. However, what I propose to focus on now is what S.H. Foulkes called the group matrix, the concept that is intrinsic to group analytic theory and practice but which is difficult to pin down to a precise meaning (Roberts 1982; Van der Kleij 1982). Perhaps its very value lies in this feature, that it is trying to describe an elusive and evolving phenomenon. It is indeed an evolutionary concept referring to the developmental history of an analytic group and is based upon the communicational network which is laid down by its participants over time. On the basis of this communicational network, a form of psychological organisation develops in a group based upon mutual experience, relationships and understandings. The shared history of the interpersonal relationships in the group and the shared work in deriving meaning from their work together lays down this dynamic group matrix. An analytic group seems to follow a spiral course, returning again and again to some of the same eternal human issues of love, hate, of hopes and disappointments, of dependency and interrelatedness, of individuation and togetherness, of the relationships of the self and other in childhood and in the present. As these issues return in the evolutionary spiral, there will often be a better grasp by the members of the meanings of these issues, based on their common history and understanding, though spirals can be regressive as well as progressive. The analytic work of the group can lead to the recognition and acceptance of patterns of relationship, both in the present and in the past, that will lead to an appreciation of the organisation of the personality from its childhood origins in the family setting and to seeing how the group setting, through transference and transposition, repeats some of the early developmental experiences, and also how the evolving context of the group gives to its members an opportunity to transcend and to transform these powerfully laid down early patterns. Foulkes called this 'ego training in action', based on an ongoing corrective interaction with others. The group process will sanction the more constructive and socially acceptable behaviours of its members and will not sanction the more socially disruptive aspects. If the group deteriorates into a socially conformist and non-evolving organisation which fails to serve the development of personal maturity and of individuation, this would represent a cohesive closed system, not open to growth through learning from experience. The role of the conductor is to support and to represent learning from experience and to oppose these powerful cohesive resistance structures. Here I think it may help to clarify Foulkes' notion of the developmental aspects of the dynamic matrix if we think about the group in terms of an increasing coherence, an integrity that makes the whole and the relationship of its parts more clear and manifest, and that the achievement of coherence in the group process which enables its members to re-trace the developmental path of coherency which I am discussing is only partly conscious. It is to the nature of the unconscious aspect of coherency that I now turn.

My attention was first drawn to this concept by some passages in the writings of the psychoanalyst Hans Loewald (1980) in which he pointed to some passages in Freud where Freud draws the contrast between the repressed and the coherent unconscious. This is a little-noted aspect of Freud's theory and it is interesting to follow the evolution of Freud's idea about coherency, the ego and unconscious processes (Freud 1921). In *Group Psychology* he wrote: 'In the course of our development we have effected a separation of our mental existence into a coherent ego and into an unconscious and repressed position which is left outside it; and we know that the stability of these new acquisitions is exposed to constant shocks' (p.131). Here Freud equates the coherent ego with a conscious ego and that which is unconscious and repressed is not coherent. However, when, in *Beyond the Pleasure Principle* (Freud 1920) he discusses the repetition compulsion, Freud points out that it is not the repressed that demonstrates resistance in the course of therapy; resistances arise from a repressing source that originates from the same higher strata and systems of the mind which originally carried out the repressions. As these resistances and the motives for them are unconscious, Freud points out that we should not make a contrast between the conscious and the unconscious but between the coherent ego and the repressed. Much of what is unconscious is organised and therefore is properly ascribed to the ego organisation. In *The Ego and the Id* (Freud 1923) Freud concludes that we cannot derive neurosis from a conflict between the conscious and the unconscious and we have to substitute for this antithesis another – the antithesis between a coherent ego and the repressed which is split off from it. Repression works against coherent psychic organisation; psychic processes remain unorganised. Thus the unconscious does not coincide with the repressed; all that is repressed is unconscious but not all that is unconscious is repressed. A part of the ego undoubtedly is unconscious and coherent. Thus there is an unconscious coherency and an unconscious repressed and incoherent part of the mind. Repression works against coherency and organisation. What, then, works for coherency and organisation?

Leowald used this distinction as his model for an explanation of change in the psychoanalytic situation (Loewald 1960). The previously unorganised repressed ego becomes reorganised as the coherent unconscious ego through the forces of the transference, through the psychoanalytic process, through internalisation. His model of the psychoanalytic process is that it is like a psychological force field where patient and analyst can be seen, respectively as more and less differentiated poles of this field. In this way the process of therapy represents the reorganisation of the dynamics of this field so that the previously more unorganised and primitive poles, represented by the neurotic aspects of the patient's unconscious, now approximate more to the more highly organised and coherent aspects of the analyst's unconscious. Loewald shows how in this way, the analytic situation reproduces the matrix of infantile development, the mother and infant, respectively representing the differentiated and undifferentiated poles of a psychological force field.

I believe that this model can also be applied to later developments, to the relationship of ego and super ego. The healthy ego must be open to exchanges, to learn by experience. It has, in effect, to say 'yes' to new experience. Some aspects of the super ego, particularly the more rigid and primitive ones, are based on the fantasised consequences of experience rather than openness and exchange. The super ego says 'no' to further exchanges. It represents a cohesive rather than a coherent organisation. When we can open up these areas dominated by the super ego to renewed dialogue, negotiation and experiences, the ego principles can reclaim those territories: 'Where super ego was, ego shall become'.

This concept of a dynamic psychological force field, taken into the sphere of group dynamics by Kurt Lewin (1951), was used as a basic tool of social psychology, and Foulkes acknowledged Lewin's influence in this respect. The notion of the 'life space' can explain a great deal of the process of psychological conflict and the capacity for change. Taking the group analytic group as a psychological force field, as the group develops in organisational complexity and the group members become able to perform for themselves those functions the group conductor had previously carried out for them – such as the functions of reflection, of search for meaning, for the resolution of emotional conflict for the maintenance of boundaries – so the dynamic force field of the group matures and becomes more informed with coherency.

I have been using the term 'coherency' to characterise the fitting together of parts that make a whole. The work of Bion and Winnicott, who introduced the concepts of containment and of holding in the infant–mother relationship and how this is replicated in the psychoanalytic situation, is also, I believe, concerned with the attainment and maintenance of coherency. (These concepts of containment and holding have already been brought into connection with Foulkes' concept of the matrix by my colleague, Dr Colin James (1984).)

The more that we see human development taking place within a matrix, within a setting, one that sets its mark, that imprints itself on the developing organism, and the more that we see the infant's early relationships as being determined by such factors as rhythm, synchrony and interplay, so the concept of a dynamic field of interaction becomes a leading developmental paradigm. The analytic group as a dynamic field of interaction is a potential situation for the resumption of interrupted or disharmonious development. However, you may be beginning to wonder if I am advocating the deliberate evocation of harmony, a structured essay in a corrective emotional experience. Indeed I am not, and in this context it is worth recalling those observations that show that analytic groups, and also larger communities, may go through what have been termed 'utopian' (Hartman and Gibbard 1973) stages when conscious harmony reigns and class distinctions are abolished. In the therapeutic group this happy state is achieved through the expulsion or dethronement of the therapist. Blissful prospects entice the group members, who hope that this stage of affairs will endure. The phase, alas, is usually short-lived. It has followed a 'successful' rebellion and precedes the renewal, the fresh outbreak of conflict, in which the previously oppressed often become the oppressors of others. The group is cohesive: the members do not reflect upon and work through their current state and see it in perspective. Anzieu and the French school also refer to this state as the 'group illusion', that defensive attitude of a group that is enjoying a sense of unity and is avoiding the recognition of painful underlying conflicts. They are also studying myths as a basic underlying aspect of group mentality, of group cohesion. What I am referring to as the 'fitting in' of a developing coherence in the unconscious group matrix does not have these surface characteristics. This is shown by the increasing appropriate and sensitive understanding that becomes available to the group in response to the problems and conflicts that members bring to the group setting.

I would now like to draw your attention to some views of child development with regard to this concept of coherency. There has been a definite shift within the views of some psychoanalytically informed observers to studying interactional patterns rather than studying the single child. Patterns of organisation are invoked to explain developmental phenomena, to explain how the apparently helpless neonate and infant becomes capable of self organisation. Increasingly we see that, despite the enormous physical and emotional immaturity of the infant, of human biological helplessness, this capacity for self organisation is evident from very early on in neonatal life.

Good mothering seems to consist of the ability to recognise and to enhance the infant's capacity for self organisation, and human beings need to be addressed in terms that fit the evidence of an increase in complexity, of establishments of capacities which lead to becoming a self organising system. Here we need developmental models rather than homeostatic and cybernetic models, for these describe the regulation of established systems rather than the development of a system. We need models of systems open to inputs of information and of organisation which can lead to the development of new, more complex levels of organisation, so that the infant can both regulate its own physiological and psychological processes and become capable of interacting harmoniously with other persons.

One of the leading writers in this field, Joseph Lichtenberg (1982, 1983), in a recent summary of the implications of neonatal research for psychoanalysis has stated:

> From the beginning both newborn and mother are primed with complex reaction patterns to participate in a social interaction rather than act as two individuals sending discreet messages. Their attachment is based on their mutual reciprocity of two partners each prepared to act on and react to, the other. The researches emphasise participation within organisational forms rather than viewing each partner as sending discrete messages.

The thrust of neonatal research is that:

> Psychoanalysis possibly over-states the separateness of man, his degree of independence from his animate and inanimate surroundings so that the interactional context which is essential in the study of the growing child need not be entirely replaced by a model of intrapsychic regulation and conflict; the interac-

tional concept retains throughout life a considerable degree of validity as a psychological context.

The interactional concept and the psychological context are where group analysis is rooted.

You may think that both Lichtenberg and I are over-stressing the obvious, that infant and mother relate together as an evolving system within the organisation of the family. Yet what is obvious to us now was not obvious just a few years ago, and we may ask ourselves why is it so important, and indeed so difficult, for psychoanalytically trained researchers and therapists to accept and to use the interactional model. If we are not able to do so we may not be able to act effectively as group conductors, able to see and to appreciate the contextual qualities of the group situation and to distinguish the 'group-as-a-whole' situations from the group of separate and relating individuals.

I believe the reason lies in the area of scientific paradigms, those major shifts in perspective that can be seen retrospectively but which are difficult to grasp and to organise whilst the shift is actually taking place. Loyalties to models go deep, as they represent some of the foundation blocks of our ways of seeing the world. In this paradigm shift from the view of the individual to the view of the group there are very powerful questions indeed. It brings up the nature of the relationship of an individual to a group and the nature of individuality *per se*. Under our Western eyes we tend to see and to value the individual's uniqueness and individuality. This history of Western civilisation over the past eight or nine hundred years, particularly since the Renaissance, has been that of the emergence of an individual in increasingly secular and democratic societies, in contrast to the previous immersion of the individual in religious and strictly hierarchical societies where the prime relationship was that of the individual to his God rather than that of man to man. Indeed, the word 'consciousness' only appeared in our Western language some 300 years ago and prior to that Man was only able to turn to his conscience rather than to his consciousness, for by awareness of his conscience he became aware of transgressions in his relationship to his Maker. The word 'consciousness' is a secular term, part of the freer society that developed with the Enlightenment.

Our emphasis on individualism has led to doctrines of individual psychology where the individual is seen to be driven by his own inner forces, instinctual drives which are mediated by internal structures derived from interaction with society. This leads to theories of the personality structured into Id Ego and Super Ego, primary and secondary processes and to viewing social life as an interaction between discrete individuals. Group psychotherapy itself has indeed been seen in the light of these individualistic models. Members of the group are said to adjust to each other on the basis of the trade-offs which they construct; inner objects are projected and externalised, transference relationships established and common group tensions, for instance as described by Ezriel's (1950) model, seem to me to be much like that of a skilled snooker player. The good interpretation clears the table with all the balls falling skilfully and very impressively into their respective holes. The therapist then receives the applause of his amazed audience or, if not from them, he gives himself considerable inner recognition and satisfaction. There seems to me a tendency to over-apply object relations theory, a picture of the inner world as containing representations of internalised object relationships to the group field, and in this way to preserve, paradoxically, the concept of a strongly delimited and delineated individual. Foulkes himself did not accept this model of internal object relations, for what he saw being internalised were processes of relationships and interrelationships and for him the nature of the individual was much more elusive and changeable than in some of these psychoanalytic models.

In our modern psychology, psychological life appears as an interior event in a world defined by physics and with a body defined by physiology, as has been pointed out by Romanyshyn (1982) in his fascinating exploration of the historical development of modern psychology *Psychological Life: From Science to Metaphor*. Our world picture is still Newtonian and Cartesian, a world of vertical depth where we look deep inside the individual to uncover his drives and motivation; this is the world of individual psychoanalysis, of vertical depth, the depth of repression. What other way is there of understanding psychological life? As Foulkes emphasised, in group analysis we are concerned with the horizontal dimension of transference, of what goes on between people in the here and now. Romanyshyn discusses 'lateral depth': the depth that lies between people and which becomes visible through images, reflections, responses. Merleau-Ponty (1964) said, 'I borrow myself from others; man is a mirror for man', and in group analysis we are indeed in a world of human mirrors, of reflections and perspectives of ourselves obtained through our evolving relationships.

The paradigm shift from a vertical 'individual-centred epistemology' to a horizontal or lateral one of fields, of systems, gives rise to a 'roomier epistemology', one in which we can study systems, relationships and the evolution of individuals within these systems. Personal redefinitions can be more easily achieved given this more flexible outlook on the part of the group conductor.

I have already suggested that personal maturity (social, emotional and intellectual), as a member of an analytic group, develops in the context of the maturation of the group as a social system (conceptualised by Foulkes in terms of the group matrix). I propose now to look at some other aspects of human development that are also embedded in the social matrix with particular reference to language and to intelligence. In Foulkes' theories the process of communication is identical with the process of therapy. Patients learn to articulate, to express themselves in language that has to be understood by their fellow members, and gradually their symptoms, their reasons for coming to the group, become disentangled and their relationship problems become located in the group process and become recognisable by all the members of the group who are involved in the evolving pattern of relationships with any one particular patient and with each other. The group gradually learns to extend its range of interpersonal understanding and responsiveness, and much of this work can be conceptualised as acquiring and extending the concept of dialogue.

Our patients sit and talk to each other in a manner that has been called 'group association' and 'free floating discussion'. What does this consist of? It consists of one person starting, others listening, commenting, interrupting, associating; another person takes over from the first, brings out his problems or preoccupations. Our group members acquire skills in listening, in responding, in social interactions, whether or not we consciously hold the acquisition of such skills as therapeutic in our technical aims. Let us therefore look at the childhood roots of acquiring a concept of dialogue.

One of the principal researchers in this field, Schaffer (1979), has characterised all social interactions as dialogues, for they all involve highly intricate, closely synchronised sets of behaviour patterns contributed by two or more individuals. These dialogues are generally characterised by an impressive 'smoothness' and are conducted according to sets of rules that are more often than not far from explicit. How are the conditions for dialogue set up in infancy and how might these conditions be re-experienced in the group analytic situation?

First, it is the dialogue, not the monologue, which is the basic speech unit; for the primary function of speech is to communicate. Language arises against a background of already well-established ways of shared meaning between mother and child. So much of mother–infant interactions involves taking turns – now me, now you – and the phrases 'pseudo-conversations' and proto-conversations' (Leal 1983) have been used to describe these sequences which are prior to the use of words. Turn-taking is, of course, a diadic phenomenon and there is much evidence to show that depressed, anxious and insecure mothers impose a false rhythm on to their children and dislocate the natural rhythm that would be more appropriate to the child's development. However, mothers do not only 'take turns' with their children in these non-verbal modes of communication. Before the child has acquired the concept of verbal language she will interpret and respond to the child's gestures, vocalisations and babblings by attributing meanings and intentions to the infant, thereby inserting meaning into the developing dialoguer (Shotter and Gregory 1976). She responds to a child 'as if' the child had intentionality and purpose, and in this way she begins to develop the child's capacity for intentionality which, as we shall see, is a vital element in the creation of genuine dialogue. She talks to the child and assumes that the child wants to talk back to her, and thereby she connects what might be random gestures with meaningful ones of her own. By being meaningful to her they become meaningful to her child and thereby to the pair. We know how often this process of inserting and acquiring meaning in the mother–child dyad may be disturbed by the attitudes of the mother, according to her fantasies about her child, her own self-experience, her moods and preoccupations. Many parents are lacking in sensitivity to the child's signals and misinterpret them.

It is relevant here to remind ourselves that Jerome Frank (1973) many years ago indicated that the 'installation of hope' is a therapeutic factor of great magnitude and this, I think, can be seen as the insertion of optimistic meaning into the dialogue between therapist and patient and therapist and group. You yourselves will, as I have often been, be impressed by the very sensitive capacities of group members to respond optimistically, hopefully, and creatively to the despairing self-destructive attitudes of their fellow group members, and thereby they install hope into the transactions. The significance of hope is strikingly illustrated by the researches of Broussard (1976), who has shown that mothers who regard their newborn infants as being 'better than average' will have children whose mental health is much better than children whose mothers responded pessimistically rather than optimistically at the age of 4 and 11 to the question: Is your child better than average at birth?'. The labelling of the child by the mother has a profound effect on future mental health, and the installation of hope in the group situation is a therapeutic factor of high significance which can go some way towards undoing the effects of early pessimistic labelling.

Major developmental steps towards acquiring the concept of dialogue, that is, becoming aware of the process that has already been taking place from birth onwards, seem to take place towards the end of the first year once the capacities for reciprocity and intentionality are acquired.

The notion of reciprocity refers to the realisation that a dialogue needs to be sustained by both partners, that both are equally responsible for steering its course and that the roles that they play are not only integrative but can also be interchangeable.

The child begins to learn now, as he continues to learn throughout the games of infancy and childhood, that the giving and receiving, talking and listening, chasing and being chased are two sides of the same coin. He learns reciprocity together with ideas of complementarity, synchrony and role reversal, essential steps in social maturation (Schaffer 1979).

The other component, intentionality, which, as I have already suggested, is inserted by the mother into the child's random activities, develops within the mother–child dyad and is shown by the child's capacity to direct both its own activities and those of others. The child progresses from crying as an involuntary and automatic expression of distress to a cry that demonstrates his need to another person to come to his aid. He now cries to show that he needs his mother to deal with his discomfort. He needs and can gain adult attention and, of course, how the adult responds to demands lays down much of his emerging sense of self. If I as an infant experience myself as someone whose distress is meaningful to my caretaker, I thereby internalise relationships with a good mother who relieves distress. The basic building blocks of self and object representation seem, as Kernberg, Lichtenberg and others have shown, to consist of a self representation, an object representation and a linking effect.

On the basis of this reciprocity and intentionality, the child begins to enter more fully into the social world with ideas about its own competence and its own place in the social world. The dialogue develops so that social and cognitive capacities develop to the point that the child can enter fully into the interactive sequences of peers and adults which will then be characterised by the reciprocity of roles and of intentionality.

I would like to be able to go further with the research on child development that demonstrates how much cognition as well as affect develops within the social matrix, but I shall refer you instead to Margaret Donaldson, who has presented the case in her book *Children's Minds* (Donaldson 1978).

It seems clear to me that the group situation both depends upon and fosters these processes of dialogue in a way which is quite different from the interchange of dyadic psychotherapy or the more structured group situation where the responses of the therapist or of the other group members are dictated more by the programmes of theoretical understanding and intentionality of the therapist. In the analytic group the persons take part in group dialogue that is part of the give and take, the social form of reciprocity that characterises all form of human behaviour from infancy onwards. It is very striking in this respect to note the finding that the timing of mother–infant interactions seems to have a very close resemblance to the timing of adult turn-taking in conversation. Thus this element of rhythm, turn-taking and sharing seems to characterise the developmental line of social interaction and response.

I now want to return to the question of maturity and to Balint's paradox that the person who has been in group therapy may be more mature but not necessarily less neurotic. I question the suggestion that you can be more mature without being less neurotic as there is an internal contradiction here, which I shall go into whilst acknowledging there is something of substance in what Balint says.

How, then, can we characterise maturity? Freud gave us the lead when he said that the ability to work and to love are the foundation stones of healthy adult life when you are released from neurotic restrictions; many would now add to these the capacity for play. Maturity seems to me to be a process, the capacity and the ability to create and to use life experiences through which the process of growth of self and the continuing relationship to other proceeds. To quote Loewald

(1960, p.230): 'Mature object relations are not characterised by a sameness of relatedness, but by an optimal range of relatedness and by the ability to differentiate objects according to their particular levels of maturity'. So here we are looking at the capacity to range at different levels in appraisal of, and responses to, other persons. The analytic group offers just this opportunity through emotional resonance: to relate to a number of persons who are at different levels of maturity. Each member of the group has a different psychic structure; all different in regard to their aims and desires and in the attitudes they take towards these needs. In a well-balanced therapeutic group we will have put together persons who will resonate at different levels to the dynamics of the situation and gradually the members will be exposed to a great range and variety of human experience and responsiveness. This will sometimes produce antagonism and rejection, as people come up against attitudes in other persons that represent quite different solutions to universal and shared problems in their social lives. Indeed, some of the most effective work in groups involves the exploration and understanding of just these differences and their eventual resolution. Thus the range of the object-related responses must constantly extend to encompass the development of the group and of the other persons within it. The range of what is encompassed in the process of emotional growth must also include a growing sensitivity to oneself, to one's own inner life which one partially encounters through externalisations involving other persons. There is a constant to-and-fro psychic movement; the basic rhythm of group sessions is a 'now me, now you' process held within the context of the 'us-allness' of the whole group. In this the group presents and represents the basic rhythm of human emotional life, that of resonance, of dialogue, the rhythm from which we create our own humanity from its roots in the infant–mother pair from which we move to a triangle of the third person, the toy, the sibling and the other parent.

Let us look more closely at this basic to-and-fro movement.

Seeing oneself in others and seeing aspects of others in oneself is to recognise similarity. Accepting similarity means opening oneself up to the world of others, both the outer world of the actual other but also to the inner world of internalised relationships. The process may involve seeing that, 'I am like you, that you are like an aspect of one of my parents and therefore there is an aspect of myself based upon my identification. I extend myself into the world and I do this through dissolving the differences between myself and another'. Identification dissolves some of the boundaries between self and object and therefore opens the person to new experiences, new recognition and appraisals of the building bricks of identity (Loewald 1980).

Identity, the autonomous structure of the self, the sameness that persists throughout the life cycle, has been profoundly influenced by identification but represents the outcome of a process of giving up these identifications, a destruction and restructuring of these identifications of childhood. Identity is based upon internalisations which are different from identifications; identifications preserve the identity and merger of self and other whereas self identity involves the renunciation of the identification unity. Internalisation as a building block of identity follows the process of destruction and reconstruction of the self–other unity of identification. This is a process that Kohut called 'transmuting internalisation' (Tolpin 1971) or, as Loewald (1980) describes it, is a process of transforming relationships into, 'an internal intrapsychic depersonified relationship which increases and enriches psychic structure' (p.83). Identification with the object is renounced so the individual is enriched by the relationship he has had with the loved object, also the hated object. When the object tie has been renounced the person is no longer burdened by identification with, and a fantasy relationship to, the other. From this comes a freedom from object ties and an inner freedom, achieved by this process of internalisation, that is a necessary condition for growth to maturity.

The ancient world knew this polarity as the distinction between Apollo, standing for individuation, and Dionysus, representing merger and engulfment. Mental life, says Loewald, is so constituted that it oscillates between the two poles of identity and identification. Internal identity makes object relations in the true sense possible because here one separate person is relating to another person recognised as separate. The other pole of identification dissolves the differences between self and object. A therapeutic group is *par excellence* a situation that offers its members an opportunity to move between these polarities of identity and identification, and the group context can hold individuals whilst they renounce old identifications and old solutions and move on to new ones. This context, the analytic situation, will hopefully maintain the values of open communication, of devotion to understanding in the face of difficulties and a commitment to the growth of individuality through the recognition of similarity and differences. The internalisation of this context, the analytical atmosphere which is there to be taken for granted and whose reliability is in the trust of the group conductor, is, I believe, a fact of profound importance. It provides the background in which the foreground of the therapeutic work can take place; it represents the holding and containing which make psychic development possible.

However, there is an even earlier aspect of this rhythm of back and forth in a context of group relationships. Before language is established as the medium of communication in the child, a language of reciprocity of gestures and games has been built up between infant and caretaker. Infants actively explore the world, initiating processes which require responses of another. There is a gestural dialogue, a play of contingency through which the infant discovers that he is an active agent, initiating processes that bring about responses that give pleasure. Through these interactions with the significant other, the infant begins to discover that he is a self and he is a self in relationship with another. He plays games which involve a reciprocal feedback; the human infant has been described by J. Watson (1967) as genetically equipped for games of reciprocal feedback. Here is the very basis of emotional resonance, of the growth of mutuality and the expectation that others will be available to ourselves for the completion of our own actions. For the happy infant these games and interactions take place in an atmosphere of security, where the pleasure of the other in responding is experienced and internalised. The child takes into himself through the myriad of interactions with the mother the sense of who he is for her; what is internalised is not an object but the relationship with the object, the images and affects that mark their meaning for each other.

If a group is given the opportunity for, and the task of, achieving spontaneous communication, the characteristic rhythm of contingency analysis seen in early childhood may be re-experienced. Conversations in the group centre upon emotions. My own expression of personal feeling will be followed by another person's response: 'When you said that you felt that, then I felt this. I know what it feels like for you because this is what it felt like for me when...'. At this now adult level the members are engaged in emotional exchange rhythms which form the very matrix from which the differentiation of self from other emerged. As Rita Leal (1982) has put it, group analysis works because it is a, 'process of mobilising natural elements, life's own maturational forces in the service of adult creative growth'. Here again the emphasis is on maturational growth. The rhythms of group discussion renew contact with self and self with other in a setting which has been described by de Maré (1990) as a 'movable context'. By this he means that the other persons with whom a member is in a relationship do not maintain a fixed and predictable response to that person. All group members are in the process of change, of adaptation to the dynamics of the situation and to the new encounter with self. The response to this task is what Foulkes called 'ego-training in action', that is, the constant need to adapt to this movable context. Individuals pose their neurotic problems to the other members of the group, who will long continue to fit into the expectations that are held out for them. The transference rigidity of the neurotic problem becomes exposed as figure against ground of the evolving group situation. Sooner or later the neurotic aspect of a person's behaviour will not receive the sanction of a group which will begin sensitively and accurately, to a remarkable degree, to differentiate between the neurotic and healthy aspects of each of its members. It is in this way that the group begins to integrate and synthesise the more mature aspects of each of its members, at all levels. By this I mean that a group can accept and welcome emotional insight and expressions which originate from very early areas of experience and differentiate them from attempts to impose infantile methods of control. The way Foulkes wrote about it was thus:

The sound part of individuality is both supported in the group and as a therapeutic culture develops the further growth of healthy individuality is approved and supported by the group as a whole. Neurotic process, that is symptoms and neurotic aspects of individuality, diminish as the individual meanings become communicated and understood, both by the patient and by the other members of the group. As the process of communication moves individuals and the group as a whole from the exchange of un-understandable experiences, communicated by symptoms and by neurotic behaviour patterns, to shared, articulate, understandable communication, so there is a freeing of individual potentialities which can be used now in the creative development of the group process itself and of the individual's own personal growth and change. (p.30)

References

Anzieu, D. (1984) *The Group and the Unconscious*. London: Routledge and Kegan Paul.

Balint, M.E. (1961) *Psychotherapeutic Techniques in Medicine*. London: Tavistock.

Broussard, E.R. (1976) 'Neonatal prediction and outcome at 10/11 years.' *Child Psychiatry and Human Development 1*, 16–23.

Donaldson, M. (1978) *Children's Minds*. London: Fontana/Collins.

Ezriel, H.A. (1950) 'A psycho-analytic approach to group treatment.' *British Journal of Medical Psychology 23*, 59–74.

Foulkes, S.H. (1975) *Group-Analytic Psychotherapy. Method and Principles*. London: Gordon and Breach.

Frank, J. (1973) *Persuasion and Healing*. Baltimore: Johns Hopkins University Press.

Freud, S. (1920) *Beyond the Pleasure Principle. Standard Edition 18*. London: Hogarth Press.

Freud, S. (1921) *Group Psychology and the Analysis of the Ego. Standard Edition 18*. London: Hogarth Press.

Freud, S. (1923) *The Ego and the Id. Standard Edition 19*. London: Hogarth Press.

Gedo, J.E. and Goldberg, A. (1973) *Models of the Mind*. Chicago: University of Chicago Press.

Hartman, J.J. (1981) 'Group cohesion and the regulation of self esteem.' In H. Kellerman (ed) *Group Cohesion*. New York: Grune and Stratton.

Hartman, J.J. and Gibbard, G.S. (1973) 'A note on fantasy themes in the evolution of group culture.' In F.S. Gibbard and R.D. Mann (eds) *Analysis of Groups*. San Francisco: Jossey Bass.

James, C. (1984) 'Bion's containing and Winnicott's holding in the context of the group matrix.' *International Journal of Group Psychotherapy 34* (2), 201–13

Kellerman, H. (ed) (1981) *Group Cohesion*. New York: Grune and Stratton.

Kohut, H. (1971) *The Analysis of the Self*. New York: International Universities Press.

Kohut, H. (1977) *The Restoration of the Self*. New York: International Universities Press.

Leal, R. (1982) 'Resistances and the group analytic process.' *Group Analysis 15*, 2, 97.

Leal, R. (1983) 'Why group analysis works.' In M. Pines (ed) *The Evolution of Group Analysis*. London: Routledge and Kegan Paul.

Lewin, K. (1951) *Field Theory in Social Science*. Edited by D. Cartwright. New York: Harper.

Lichtenstein, H. (1977) *The Dilemma of Human Identity*. New York: Jason Aronson.

Lichtenberg, J.D. (ed) (1982) 'Infant research: the dawn of awareness.' *Psychoanalytic Inquiry 1*, 4.

Lichtenberg, J.D. (1983) *Psychoanalysis and Infant Research*. Hillsdale, NJ: The Analytic Press.

Loewald, H.W. (1960) 'On the therapeutic action of psychoanalysis.' *International Journal of Psychoanalysis 41*, 16–33.

Loewald, H.W. (1980) *Papers on Psychoanalysis*. New Haven: Yale University Press.

de Maré, P.B. (1990) 'The development of the median group.' *Group Analysis 23*, 124.

Merleau-Ponty, M. (1964) *The Primacy of Perception*. Evanston: Northwestern University Press.

Roberts, J.P. (1982) 'Foulkes' concept of the matrix.' *Group Analysis 15*, 2, 111.

Romanyshyn, R.D. (1982) *Psychological Life: From Science to Metaphor*. Milton Keynes: Open University Press.

Schaffer, R.H. (1979) 'Acquiring the concept of the dialogue.' In M.H. Bornstein and W. Kessen (eds) *Psychological Development from Infancy*. Hillsdale, NJ: Lawrence Erlbaum.

Shotter, J. and Gregory, S. (1976) 'On first gaining the idea of oneself as a person.' In R. Harre (ed) *Life Sentences*. New York: Wiley.

The Shorter Oxford Dictionary (1973) London: Oxford University Press.

Tolpin, M. (1971) 'On the beginnings of a cohesive self.' *Psychoanalytic Study Child 26*, 316–352.

Van der Kleij, G. (1982) 'About the matrix.' *Group Analysis 15*, 3, 219.

Watson, J.B. (1967) 'Memory and "contingency analysis".' In Infant Learning. *Merrill-Palmer Quarterly 13*, 55–76.

Webster's Dictionary of Synonyms (1951) Springfield, MA: G.C. Merrian.

Winnicott, D.W. (1964) 'The baby as a person.' In *The Child, the Family, and the Outside World*. London: Penguin Books.

Yalom, I.D. (1975) *The Theory and Practice of Group Psychotherapy*. New York: Basic Books.

CHAPTER 4

Group Analysis and Healing[1]

The problem of the doctor's relationship to the concept of a natural healing power is perhaps the greatest of all problems that have occupied the physician for thousands of years. Indeed, one could designate it as *the* problem of medicine, since the aim and limits of therapeutics are determined by its solution. Almost every physician takes a position: indeed *must* take a position in regard to it (M. Neuberger, in Menninger 1977).

To ask who needs to be cured, what it means to be cured, who can cure and why, is to ask about the values, the beliefs and the structure of the society in whose frame of reference these questions are being posed (Pouillon 1972).

This paper was stimulated by the theme of the 1986–7 14th London Workshop of the Group-Analytic Society: 'Aspects of Healing in the Context of Group Analysis'. The word 'context' means to weave together. 'To heal' means to bring about wholeness. Thus there is a strong meaningful connection between the two words. They are both holistic terms.

In group analysis our aims are to weave the individuals into a group, a group as a whole in which each individual contributes a distinctive element to the texture, to the patterning of the group. The essence of our therapeutic intent is to activate and maintain the development of the wholeness of the group. How do we do this? The therapist establishes the basic group analytic situation, maintains the boundaries of time, space and person, accepts the contributions of the members, looks for underlying themes that unconsciously hold the group together and has a basic attitude towards the process of therapy. The therapist does not arrogate to him- or herself the prime position in the group or see him- or herself as the only valid source of knowledge. The therapist is, in S.H. Foulkes' terms, the first servant of the group, for a basic element of group analytic technique is our trust in the developmental capacities of the group, a belief that there is a maturational capacity, a potential, in the group for widening and deepening each person's knowledge of him- or herself and of others.

1   Published in: *Group Analysis* (1989) 22, 4, December, 417–429.

All healing methods reflect the underlying philosophy of the healer. With the group analytic therapist this involves a personal amalgam and integration of the psychoanalytic model of the mind, together with sociological and anthropological perspectives on the human condition. The group analyst has to have a working knowledge of psychoanalytic theory but also to accept fully the social structure of the human being who is, as Foulkes put it, 'permeated through and through by the colossal forces of society', so that even the most basic forces that drive us are developed and take shape and form within the human context.

The group analyst takes the historical view of the development of society and its individual members, and views human nature neither as a predominantly genetic, biological phenomenon with its philosophy of unchanging basic drives, nor as a character structure that is relatively independent of the forces of family and culture. Thus the group analyst is open to sociological and anthropological viewpoints as well as those of the individual psyche. Intrapsychic reality is a reflection of interpersonal reality; the social fact precedes the psychological.

Human beings are linked into networks by language, and each of us is a nodal point within that network. Primarily aware that we are individuals physically separate from each other, we have to struggle to recognise that our notions of individuality are both true and yet not true. The boundaries that differentiate us from, and link us to, other persons are not only physical, they are mental. As Foulkes and many others have pointed out, 'mind' is that which takes place between people and does not exist within the individual. Mentality is social. We all live suspended in a linguistic, symbolic universe, hence our great need to study carefully and to understand our systems of communication, our language. As a psychotherapy, group analysis expands and explains the space between people. What, then, is the language that we use in therapy? What are the meanings of terms such as 'illness', 'cure', 'disease' and 'treatment'?

The anthropological psychiatrist Kleinman (1980) analyses concepts of disease and illness as follows: '*Disease* is a malfunctioning of biological and/or psychological processes. *Illness* is a *psychosocial experience* that gives meaning to perceived disease' (p.72; original emphasis). Disease is the basic process. Illness is the shaping of disease into behaviour and experience in the context of a particular society. Thus illness is a complex cultural response; a *shaping* of disease as an adaptive response to the disease process. Let us for the moment accept that disease affects individuals, that the disease process originates within, or enters into, the individual organism. Illness, however, affects others as well. The ill person becomes the patient and others must respond. Illness behaviour can only be understood by reference to a specific context of norms, symbolic meanings and social interactions of a particular society.

What Kleinman has to say about sickness is of great interest to group analysts. He says that sickness represents a *semantic network*, a culturally articulated system that interrelates cognitive categories, personal experiences, psychological states and social relations. This comes close to the concept of *matrix* described by Foulkes as: 'the common shared ground which ultimately determines the meaning and significance of all events and upon which all communications and interpretations, verbal and non-verbal, rest. This concept links with that of communication' (1964, p.292). Healing, therefore, involves semantic networks and the matrix. Semantic sickness networks draw on beliefs about causality and significance to make available particular treatment options that enable instrumental and symbolic therapies to be used together. Thus there is a meaning to whatever interventions the healer makes in relationship to the patient, whether it be a drug, an injection, the laying on of hands, an interpretation or a reassurance. Within the context of group analysis, healing represents the application of a new semantic network to the experience of the patient whose illness has already been expressed within the network valid for his or her own personal previous experience and culture.

Persons designated as healers are present in all societies. Each society, each culture, has a set of organising principles that overlie those actions taken by healers to intervene in disease processes. There is always a philosophy of healing, expressed in a variety of symbols, languages and images. Thus spiritual models aim to restore an individual to a harmonious relationship with God through the use of prayer and the laying on of hands.

The view that the healer takes of the world reflects the healer's view of society and so is constantly changing over historical time. Rush (1981) concludes that all healing philosophies involve the restoration of a proper relationship, whether it be with a deity or to a balance in the body. The latter can be chemical or mechanical, arrived at through the removal of factors that disturb the body, such as germs or toxins, in order to restore a state of internal and external harmony of the forces, energies and processes that we now recognise make up homeostatic balance. The underlying root metaphor that unites all philosophies of healing is the restoration of harmony, of a right relationship, balance and equilibrium. The healer has to bring about an attunement of mental and bodily processes, a dynamic condition in which the organism is in a process of restoration.

Healing is not a concept used by Sigmund Freud or by most schools of psychoanalysis. Few analytical textbooks take up the subject of healing. An exception to this is Menninger (1977), who not only pays attention to healing but invokes what he calls the 'intangibles' of the therapeutic relationship and of therapeutic processes. By the intangibles, he means love, faith and hope. These, he says, are crucial determinants of effective healing – indeed, they are sublime expressions of the life instinct. Of love, he writes that: 'This intangible thing, love, enters into every therapeutic relationship. It is an element of which the physician may be the carrier, the vessel. It is an element that binds and heals, comforts and restores, which works what we have to call miracles' (p.365). Therapeutic love manifests itself as '*agape*', the Greek word for a selfless concern, a love that is neither sexual nor possessive. This manifestation of love is, according to Menninger, accompanied by a more libidinal involvement, usually unconscious, discounted and denied by therapists, which the patient, who has a great unconscious need for love, will take advantage of and respond to as libidinal. '*Agape*', also a 'love feast' held by early Christians in preparation for the Lord's Supper, might be a metaphor for group analysis. As for faith, this is essential for a therapist, that he or she has faith in what he or she does, that he or she can make illness meaningful and that he or she can help the patient recover, restored to a state of wholeness and health. We need to believe that illness is reversible and amenable to planned interventions.

Feelings about hope are very mixed. The cynics regard hope with fear, as an illusion and a snare. Menninger (1963) defined hope as, 'positive expectations in a studied situation which go beyond the visible facts' (p.386). But hope is the strongest antidote that we have to that state of demoralisation which is part of every depressive situation, all states of hopelessness. That the hope should not be facile and over-optimistic, that it should be based upon a well-grounded foundation of learning and experience, is essential to the planned therapeutic endeavour that psychotherapy represents.

Some further words of Menninger's (1977) should also be listened to: 'The establishment or re-establishment of relationships with fellow human beings is the basic architecture of human life – one of the forces making for recovery' (p.294). This is a basic restatement of our group analytic position. Finally, Menninger says: 'To live is to love, and a healthy life is one in which we are able to work, to play and to be in balance'. Here he harkens back to the therapeutic wisdom of the Greeks, of repair and self-regulation of the organism. This is similar to what Foulkes (1948) had to say in his first book on group analysis: 'The healthy organism functions as a whole and can be described as a system in dynamic equilibrium. Dynamic means that it is never in a state of rest, has constantly to adjust actively to the ever-changing circumstances, milieux, conditions in which it lives' (p.1). Foulkes does not write about healing, but clearly he talks about wholeness, which, as we know, is a closely related concept. Of this he has to say that: 'Creative activity seems to be an inevitable ingredient, a hallmark of healthy life' (p.1). Dynamic equilibrium therefore means active and creative maintenance of a good balance. Such a state is described as being well, healthy, feeling happy, contented. The influence of Kurt Goldstein and of Gestalt psychology is clear. For Foulkes, group analysis is an approach to the wholeness of persons achieved in the group analytic setting, and this basic philosophy of mind and of the healing process is at the forefront of his writings. Psychoanalytic research explores the intrapsychic, the realm of psychology; a group analysis encompasses psychoanalysis as it studies family, society: the context in which the individual develops as figure against ground.

C.G. Jung, always more holistic than Freud, departed radically from the medical model quite early. Jung (1916) wrote: 'There is a widespread prejudice that analysis is something like a cure to which one submits for a time and then is discharged, healed. That is a layman's error left over from the early days of psychoanalysis' (quoted in Gordon 1979, p.209).

Gordon (1979) points out the difference between the words 'curing' and 'healing' and that this distinction should be retained, for in our work we hope that both curing and healing take place. The goal of analysis is primarily the facilitation of the process of healing defined as evolution towards greater wholeness, for the subject, a more active process than curing. The distinction that Gordon makes is linked to the distinction that Jung made between ego processes of integration and individuation:

> Integration refers to the *cohesion* of ego and this depends upon the bringing into consciousness of the contents that have previously been unconscious because they have been repressed, rejected and refused. Such integration of unconscious contents leads then to the extension and expansion of the ego. Integration is thus in the service of adaptation and of the experience of the person and the *cohesive* identity. (p.209, author's italics)

Individuation is a far wider and more comprehensive process. It involves the self and refers to the relationship between ego and self:

> The process of individuation encompasses the processes of individualisation though it moves a person beyond this essentially ego building process and on towards the search for values, meaning and self-transcendence. Individuation, being the more comprehensive process, tends usually to encompass integration; but it reaches beyond it to an individual's relationship to his innermost self. (Gordon 1979, p.209)

Whereas integration is a process of greater cohesion, individuation, the more comprehensive process, appears to me as a process of coherency.

Jung's concept of the self was formulated to account for the experiences of symbols of completeness and totality and also accounts for the drive towards wholeness, be it through fusion, union, projective identification, ordering, synthesising or any other method at any stage of life. Michael Fordham has described the self as, 'a dynamic system that de-integrates and integrates in a rhythmic sequence' (quoted in Gordon 1979, p.210). The process of de-integration, in Fordham's view, uncovers the primitive psychic experiences, the introjects of Freudian theory. These archetypal forces are projected into and on to actual persons through relationships, and through the introjective and projective experiences of those relationships the archetypal figures become 'tamed', the introjects are less primitive and psychic development can proceed. Gordon also writes of D.W. Winnicott's 'third area of the psyche', the 'area of experience', the transitional space, the space that, 'exists as a resting place for the individual engaged in the perpetual task of keeping inner and outer reality separate, yet inter-related' (1971, p.2). It is through this third area of experience that the process of de-integration can be contained, tamed and gradually integrated into the ego. When inner and outer reality are contained in this third area they can be experienced and experimented with there, in the form of dreams and fantasies as the object for the work of the imagination. We have become accustomed to considering the group situation as representing this third area of experience as a transitional space.

To summarise, Gordon suggests that cure is concerned with ego growth, which depends on the integration of unconscious drives, affects and fantasies. Healing, on the other hand, is a process in the service of evolution of the whole personality, towards ever greater and more complex wholeness. This is potentiated by the process of individuation, which facilitates the de-integration of the self, hence the emergence of ever new and complex patterns of experience – and the capacity of the conscious ego to expose itself, to relate to, and eventually to integrate the de-integrates that are at first so powerful and often even numinous. This then furthers creative living and development. Gordon's differentiation between ego growth and individuation, between curing and healing, can be related to the differentiation between processes of cohesion and coherency (Pines 1986). Cohesion is the more primitive process, the process of binding together of parts to maintain unity, being stuck together as with glue. Coherency applies to an organisation that has the capacity to maintain integration through its own internal processes. It refers to the fitting together of parts, to the attainment and maintenance of harmony and unity, and is an active process that involves higher levels of functioning than the concept of cohesion. The attainment and maintenance of coherency in ourselves is one of the essential goals of our psychological processes. The danger of disruption of coherency, of a loss of the sense of the unity and meaningfulness of the self, is one of the greatest threats to our own self concepts.

Heinz Kohut's (1981) system of self psychology is a psychology that significantly differs from the 'classic' psychoanalytic model of psychic development, the nature of the psyche itself and of the structure of the mind. The self is regarded as an indivisible psychic life, not a psychic apparatus constituted by various instances that are bound together by mechanisms. It cannot be approached and understood by a mechanistic psychology, by a topographic theory nor by a structural theory. It is defined by three principal needs: the need for cohesion, the need for firmness and the need for harmony. The greatest emphasis is on cohesion, the maintenance of unity, whilst the greatest threat is that of fragmentation. Fragmentation pathologies take the form of dispersions, of lack of harmony between the poles of ambitions, talents, skills and ideals. Here we see the introduction of the values that have already been pointed out in Jung's psychology. For Kohut and self psychology the goals and values of the self are integral and essential components and always have to be taken into account in an understanding of any individual.

In Kohut's work there has been an enormous expansion of the importance of empathy. The 'vicarious introspection' of empathy enables the therapist to know much more of what the patient is saying, of what he or she is experiencing, than an interpretive approach which attempts to show him the truth that underlies his self-deceptions. For Kohut (1981) empathy is the essential and vital link between the self and its self objects and, 'empathy encompasses all the modalities of help that one self can bring to another in the quest for integration, identification and individuation' (Ricoeur 1986, p.441). The aim of therapy, which is also the aim of healthy development, is the attainment of attunement and consonance, harmony, 'fitting together'. This aim of harmonisation, attunement and consonance belongs to a different philosophical approach from that of the Enlightenment, which emphasised first and foremost the power of knowledge which opposed the resistance of darkness. Empathy, argues Ricoeur, is linked more with concepts of pity, compassion and sympathy.

Kohut identified forms of transference which relate to the narcissistic area of the personality, which manifests itself through mirroring, idealising and twinship transferences. It is through the establishment and the working-through of these transferences that a cure takes place. The cure is essentially the filling-in of defects of self-structure that have arisen during faulty development. The working-through, termed 'transmuting internalisation', takes place through the repeated optimal frustrations that are an inevitable part of any analytic, or of any human, relationship. The infantile and archaic desires for omnipotence and idealisation are constantly meeting partial frustrations, though these frustrations are met within a setting of empathic resonance and responsiveness. It is through these optimal frustrations that the self has to rediscover that the other is not omniscient or always responsive, does not represent the archaic, idealised object; neither can one in relationship to the other relive the wish to be an omnipotent self; nor the other be a twin who will prevent the self from having to confront a different other, an other who is truly other than one-self in every way.

The effect of analysis is that the person develops 'autonomy through heteronomy'. It is through the impact of the relationship with the other that one can become truly one-self, and this process goes back and proceeds optimally when there is a high degree of attunement and consonance between therapist and patient. As Foulkes has written:

> Mirror reactions are characteristically brought out when a number of persons meet and interact. A person sees himself – often a repressed past of himself – reflected in the interactions of the other group members. He also gets to know himself – and this is a fundamental process in ego-development by the effect he has on others and the picture they form of him. A certain degree of disillusionment about one's self, of deception as regards others, needs to be integrated into the self's education. (1964, p.110)

We need to learn that narcissistic wounds are indeed parts of life that can be healed.

For we group analysts who live in the face-to-face world of speaking and listening, of looking and being looked at, the experience of a face, the notions of peace and justice, of attunement and harmony, are integral to our way of working. We accept and recognise conflict, work with it through inevitable imperfect recognition and acknowledgement, through meditation and integration of partial conflicts, into a concept of the greater whole that encompasses them. By looking for group-related themes, by attending to group development, by recognising and acknowledging the growth and development of the matrix of the group, through helping to establish and to strengthen the semantic network of verbal interchanges, so the wholeness of the group situation develops. As this is recognised, both consciously and unconsciously, is absorbed and lived with by its participants, we can specify processes of projection, introjection, identification, internalisation, as mechanisms through which the process is manifest, but these all need to be seen as mechanisms that contribute to wholeness rather than aims and ends in themselves.

As we know, many of Foulkes' ideas come from holistic and Gestalt developmental physiology and psychology. It is notable, therefore, that Kohut takes his definition of normality from biology, where the normal is that which functions in accordance with its design. The way in which the therapist helps the patient to attain that level of normality is through the technique of self psychology. As Kohut (1981) puts it, there are two stages to the technique. First comes empathic immersion, leading to an understanding by the therapist of the patient's nuclear self, which encompasses ambitions, ideals, talents and skills. Then, when the therapist has sufficiently understood the patient, he or she proceeds to explanations, which can be dynamic, genetic or directed to the transference, and can lead to insight and the capacity for a higher level of awareness and integration. Though it is often argued that self psychologists minimise the importance of aggression, Kohut states – and I am in complete agreement with him through my own personal experience – that when a patient feels safe through the process of successful understanding by the therapist, there is a negative transference that can be even more intense and meaningful than that to which we are accustomed in classical analysis. The aggressive nature of this phase of the transference can take two forms:

1. That directed towards objects that block the way to the goals of the nuclear self, an aggression which ceases when the goal has been reached.

2. An aggression directed at frustrating self-objects, experienced as permanently and totally frustrating, leading to an endless need for revenge and to the most painful attacks which are manifestations of narcissistic rage.

Self psychology's cure comes from structural changes, the person developing compensatory structures for those which were undeveloped in infancy and childhood. Through developing these compensatory structures, a firm self can arise. Self psychology is very relevant to group analysts because of its concept that the self-object, the other, is always integrally part of the self's development. It is not a matter of instinctual discharge upon objects, or even a need for ego-relatedness. The organism's need for affiliation and achievement is absolutely intrinsic and basic. As this is activated and nurtured, or hindered and distorted in transactions with the environment, so development evolves or is blocked.

Recent work in child development confirms these ideas. When the infant's needs are appropriately gratified, a greater interest in, and spontaneous interaction with, the surrounding environment takes place, during which new learning occurs. Gratification is much greater than frustration in the development of mind and self. This is a radically different position from that of Wilfred Bion and Hanna Segal of the Kleinian school, which sees frustration as the difficult and rocky path to symbol formation, concept formation and the development of mind. The Kohutians have a notion of 'optimal responsiveness' that goes hand in hand with the notion of 'optimal frustration'. Their ideas are closer to those of Winnicott and a facilitating environment – closer, it seems to me, to the observable realities of childhood development.

Gross and minor failures of responsiveness are inevitable and lead to the frustrations and disappointments that are part of everyone's lot and which are built into our psyches as experiences of narcissistic pain and mortification. These are the wounds that group analysis can help to cure and thereby release the self-healing capacities of the organism. But they are not the bases of the psyche; the foundations are laid down by optimal frustration on a basically harmonious and empathic responsiveness, experienced in infancy and re-found in the group analytic situation.

Conclusion

I conclude with three quotations. The first is from Shainberg (1983):

> In their contact with one another, all men find a meaning. The one-ness be-
> tween people is a fundamental state, not an accomplishment. What is necessary
> for the one-ness is the right person(s) and the right environment where there is
> space to be ourselves, to find ourselves, to express ourselves without being hurt.

The second is from a little-known Swiss psychoanalyst, Heinz Trub, quoted by
Friedman (1985):

> The roots of neurosis lie both in the patient's closing himself off from the world
> and in the pattern of society itself and its rejection and non-confirmation of the
> patient. Consequently, the analyst must change at some point from the consoler
> who takes the part of the patient against the world, to the person who puts be-
> fore the patient the claims of the world. This change is necessary to complete
> the second part of the cure, the establishment of real relationships with the
> world that can only take place in the world itself. On the analyst falls the task of
> preparing the way for the resumption of direct relation of the interrupted bio-
> logical relationship between the individual and the community. The patient
> must go forth whole in himself, but he must also recognise that it is not his own
> self but the world with which he must be concerned. This does not mean that
> the patient is simply integrated or adjusted to the world. He does not cease to be
> a real person responsible for himself: but at the same time he enters into a re-
> sponsible relationship with his community. (p.33)

Before reading Friedman's own final paragraph, recall the words: 'If you have to
choose one of two alternatives, always look for the third'. Friedman (1985) writes:

> The third alternative to the sickness of conformity and the sickness of rebellion
> is the community that concerns others. Such a community gives each person a
> ground of his own, a ground from which he can touch the others touching, a
> ground in which mutual confirming and meeting can take place in spiralling
> circles that bring more and more of each person's touch-stone, whether born of
> trauma or of ecstasy, into reality of life together. This is the secret of the bond
> between person and person. (p.218)

Paul Ricoeur sees the Belgian philosopher, Eugene Levinas (1969), as the source
of a philosophical position that is consonant with self psychology. For Levinas,
the self maintains its existence by defining itself as living, enjoying itself. As
Aristotle said: 'Enjoyment seeks self identification in every way'. The self has to
affirm itself so as to evaluate an object and the relationship to the other is
mediated by the experience of the face. For Levinas the experience of the face of
the other declares to us: 'Thou shalt not kill'. The face of the other teaches justice
and peace. As opposed to Hegel's master–slave philosophy, Levinas teaches that

the relationship between the self and the other is that of master–disciple. It is by entering into language, through listening, that we are bound to the other.

References

Foulkes, S.H. (1948) *Introduction to Group-Analytic Psychotherapy.* London: Heinemann; reprinted London: Karnac (1983).

Foulkes, S.H. (1964) *Therapeutic Group Analysis.* London: Allen and Unwin; reprinted London: Karnac (1984).

Friedman, M. (1985) *The Healing Dialogue in Psychotherapy.* New York: Jason Aronson.

Gordon, R. (1979) 'Reflections on curing and healing.' *Journal of Analytical Psychology 24,* 3, 207–217.

Jung, C.G. (1916) 'The transcendent function.' *Collected Works.* Vol.8. London: Routledge and Kegan Paul.

Kleinman, A. (1980) *Patients and Healers in the Context of Culture.* Berkeley: University of California Press.

Kohut, H. (1981) *How Does Analysis Cure?* Chicago: University of Chicago Press.

Levinas, E. (1969) *Totality and Infinity.* Pittsburgh: Dusguane Universities Press.

Menninger, K. (1977) *The Vital Balance.* Harmondsworth: Penguin Books.

Pines, M. (1986) 'Coherency and its disruption in the development of the self.' *British Journal of Psychotherapy 2,* 3, 180–185.

Pouillon, J. (1972) 'Doctor and patient. Same and/or other?' *Psychoanalytic Study of Society 5.* New York: International Press.

Ricoeur, P. (1986) 'The self in psychoanalysis and phenomenological philosophy.' *Psychoanalytic Inquiry 6,* 3, 437–458.

Rush, E. (1981) *Toward a General Theory of Healing.* Washington, DC: University Press of America.

Shainberg, D. (1983) *Healing in Psychotherapy.* New York: Gordon and Breach.

Winnicott, D. (1971) 'Transitional objects and transitional phenomena.' In *Playing and Reality.* London: Tavistock Publications.

CHAPTER 5

Group Analytic Psychotherapy and the Borderline Patient[1]

My frame of reference for understanding the nature of the borderline syndrome includes four predominant aspects:

1. The threat of loss of cohesion of the self-representation and self-organisation, which places the syndrome on the continuum of self-organisation proposed by Kohut (1971).

2. The organisation of the underlying personality structure, the nature of which has been considerably elucidated by Kernberg (1975).

3. The model of the inner world, the internal representation of self and other (Jacobson 1965).

4. The realm of narcissistic development and psychopathology (Akhtar and Thompson 1982).

My perspective as to the aetiology and meaning of the syndrome is that there is a structural deficit in personality development that arises from disturbed interpersonal processes at an early developmental stage. This disturbance has led to a structural deficit in the personality and to an arrest in the evolution of the separation–individuation process (Mahler, Pine and Bergman 1975), a process that, when it proceeds normally, leads to the capacity for full autonomy of the individual and for the emergence from childhood into adulthood with the capacity for self-containment, for stability in time and space, and for volition and relatively mature mental functioning. These attributes of the self are matched by a recognition that they are to be expected and respected in others and that there are

1   Published in: (1) Roth, B., Stone, W. and Kibel, H. (eds) (1990) *The Difficult Patient in Group: Group Psychotherapy with Borderling and Narcissistic Disorders*. American Group Psychotherapy Association Monograph Series. Maddison, CT: International Universities Press, Inc. (2) *Analytic Psychotherapy and Psychopathology* (1984) *1*, 1, 57–70.

certain types of exchange that are possible between independent entities in the world. There are clearly defined boundaries to individuals, interpersonal space exists between them, and they can leave, separate, be lost and return to the field of interaction of the self and others. Affects that are aroused by these experiences are admitted to consciousness, recognised and, even if painful, allowed to remain in consciousness until the natural processes of affect change have occurred.

According to the interactional model exemplified in the work of Margaret Mahler (Mahler *et al.* 1975) and in the theoretical schema proposed by Hans Loewald (1973), individuals merge from the matrix of the mother–child relationship, itself placed in the context of the family and culture, as autonomous entities, persons who have internalised the capacities that will enable them to carry out functions of the self for which previously they were dependent on the environment. This capacity for self-organisation goes profoundly into the depths of the personality, organising even what otherwise might be regarded as basic instinctual drives. These drives are themselves fashioned and formed from the start, even before birth, by the actions, attitudes and capacities of the family situation into which the individual is born (Erikson 1950; Foulkes, 1948; Loewald 1980). This is not to say that I subscribe to the approach that attributes the aetiology of the borderline syndrome to innate qualities such as a heightened oral–sadistic phase or the constitutional envy of the neonate, notions I regard as a contemporary version of the doctrine of original sin.

Experience has led me more and more to try to understand the phenomenological world of the borderline patient. I have been led to this both by my own experience and by the growing literature that emphasises the need for understanding the 'state of mind' of the other. The experiential world of the borderline patient is significantly different from that of the 'ordinary' neurotic patient or of the 'ordinary' normal person. By this I mean that the person who lives in a world in which the background of experience includes a deep sense of safety, in which fragmentation or loss of cohesion of the self is not a constant threat, will find it difficult to empathise with the experience of the borderline patient. We find it difficult to identify with the desperate efforts to maintain the integrity of the self against attacks from without and within that the borderline patient experiences, and more than difficult to sympathise, let alone empathise, with the narcissistic defences of arrogance, contempt and attacks on others that we see so frequently, or to follow the patient into the agonising depths of helplessness, hopelessness and self-abandonment. Nor do we find it easy to follow the oscillations of feeling states so characteristic of these patients – elation quickly followed by despair, friendliness by rage, warmth by destructive coldness. The only key that we have, I believe, to maintaining a relatedness with the patient is through a deep understanding of the dynamics of the personality structure. This understanding enables us to maintain the necessary distance from the patient, to maintain an interpersonal space and a capacity for relating and reflection that are constantly under attack but that are essential if any therapeutic gains are to be made.

Let us return for a moment to the realm of narcissism and to the concept of the narcissistic relationship. Freud (1914) held that object relationships can be of two types: the anaclitic (with a separate and supportive other) and the narcissistic. In the narcissistic object relationship we relate to the other primarily through those qualities which represent aspects of our own selves. We relate to the other as who we were, as who we are or as who we would like to be. Though narcissistic elements must enter into many aspects of our personal relationships, there is a clear distinction between persons who have a sense of being in their own right, and who can relate to others as separate centres of autonomy and volition, and those whose relations to others are based primarily on a narcissistic need. Kohut (1971) has assigned the term 'selfobject' to the type of relationship whereby the other is needed to maintain the coherence and cohesion of the self and is invested with narcissistic rather than object libido. It is as if the object is needed to fill a gap, to plug a hole in the self-organisation, and that without it vital energies and resources will simply flow out of the self into the world, leaving the self to collapse and disintegrate, unable to maintain its integrity. In fact this aspect of being false, of being pseudo, permeates the life of the narcissistic or borderline patient. There is a pseudo-self, a pseudo-cohesion, a pseudo-object relationship-type pattern, and often a sense of pseudo-vitality and initiative.

Now, we know that within the realm of narcissism we will always find grandiosity and idealisation, qualities that may be attributed either to the self-representation or to the object representation. We know too that their opposite, destructive narcissism, will annihilate the recognition of good qualities, whether in the other or in the self. Thus both the positive and negative narcissistic forces can be essentially sterile and maladaptive. No progress and no change can occur in these states in which narcissistic self- and object relationship processes and fantasies are constantly being churned over, externalised and reinternalised. Real change can come about only through the 'metabolisation' of the self as real self and the other as real other. Aliment, nutriment of bodily and of psychic nature, must come from without the self and must enter through the external boundary of the self. I propose now to turn to considerations that relate to boundary functioning, external and internal, of the borderline and narcissistic personalities.

The function of an external boundary of a living system is to maintain the differentiation of that system from the outside world and to allow for the exchange of vital supplies and the products of metabolism that permeability so essential for the life and growth of the organism. But the external boundary when defended by narcissistic fantasies, as it were by a narcissistic 'boundary object'

(Grotstein 1980), is in fact a barrier rather than a boundary. Because the person needs to maintain the self structure and because, as we shall see later, there is such a vast failure of internal structure to maintain the integrity and cohesiveness of the self, enormous efforts are made to guard the external boundary. It represents a Berlin Wall, a Spartan shield, to contain and to defend an unhealthy internal system that cannot allow free exchange with the outside world. This barrier is manned and guarded by the narcissistic defences of grandiosity, contempt and arrogance – by dragon's teeth. What little exchange with the outside world there is is organised with paranoid scrutiny of what emerges and what enters through the barrier of the self into the internal space. It is as if access to the vulnerable self is guarded by heightened levels of defensive aggression, as if all the psychic orifices based on the bodily openings are armed with teeth. There is a greatly heightened attention cathexis at the boundary, with close scrutiny of what goes in and out, desperate attempts to guard against intrusion and invasion and also to protect the external world from destruction by dangerous inner contents. Because so little exchange occurs with the outside world there is an inner sense of starvation and of profound emptiness and discontent that erupts periodically in rage and profound experiences of envy of those who seem to possess the missing qualities of the self. The person is inordinately sensitive to impingements in unwanted and unexpected ways on to the boundary of the self, and desperate attempts at healing are made by the mobilisation of primitive countercathected forces. The white cells, the psychic phagoctyes of narcissistic rage, rush to the breach in the stimulus barrier to plug the gap and to counter-attack by invasion of the other. This is a regular sequence, as the immediate response to hurt in the self is to try to force, to hurl through massive projective identification, one's bleeding, wounded experience into the mind of the other.

An alternative response is to withdraw from any contact with the world of others, including their inner representations, and to try to fill the empty self with substances or experiences that will restore some sense of cohesion and fullness. In females this can lead to bulimia or less episodic forms of overeating. Typically this consists of food, drink, drugs, excitement, sexuality, forms of sensorimotor stimulation which at their most primitive level will take such forms as self-mutilation, pathological forms of masturbation, rocking and head-banging. Often the precipitants of these responses are, as already noted, the impingement of the other in a painful way upon the self. It is characteristic of patients whose psychic economy is based on narcissism that they cannot bear the sense of loss of admiration, love, attention or approval. They need these narcissistic supplies to maintain the false inflationary narcissistic economy whereby the psychic supply is constantly increasing and thereby losing its value. Another great loss to the patient is with regard to mirroring (Pines 1980; Zinkin 1973), a process whereby others are significant only insofar as they reflect back those images to which the individual is addicted for the maintenance of a desired self-image. There are clear links here to Lacan's mirror stage of development (1977).

I turn now to a consideration of the internal boundary. As the infant grows, so gradually does his inner world become more complex and more differentiated. This notion is inherent to the psychoanalytic structural model and is beautifully illustrated by Kurt Lewin's model of the life space (Schellenberg 1978), in which he shows experimentally how in the course of development the inner world of a child comes more and more to be differentiated and filled with representations both of the self and of the other. Increasing complexity and internal differentiation lead to the capacity for specialised functions and for the taking over by the child of functions previously performed by significant others, principally the mother, but within the context of the economic unit of the family, typically supported by the father. Within this inner space, through the process Kohut has aptly named 'transmuting internalisation', the growing organism acquires self-maintaining and adaptive capacities (Tolpin 1971). We know that there are crisis points in this development, well illustrated in Mahler's separation–individuation schema and in Erikson's epigenetic schema (1959), in both of which there occurs a sudden, as it were, quantum leap from one stage to another. The child who becomes the toddler, who can explore space, who can experience separateness from the mother physically and begin to grasp the separateness of self from other in the inner map of the mind, is in a position enormously different from that of the infant, whose self-concept has not yet been differentiated, clearly and stably, from its concept of the mother. Such achievements as object-constancy, stability of internal representations and development of the symbolic function are clearly crucial here.

In the inner world of the borderline patient is found the experience of a failure to differentiate clearly the self-representation from that of the object; there is a state of blurring, of fusion and confusion. The threat of separation brings about a 'separation anguish' that threatens the whole sense of stability and the existence of the individual. But the consequences of this failure of structural organisation and differentiation go much further. My image of the person who is psychically built like this is that of a ship without bulkheads, without watertight compartments to keep the vessel buoyant even when one compartment is breached and flooded. Without such compartments the entire vessel is quickly flooded and goes under. There is the danger also of internal catastrophe: an explosion or fire will spread rapidly through the vessel and destroy it. The inner state of these patients is similar; affect storms flood the entire personality, which quickly sinks beneath the waves. Damage to the self, and to self-esteem, is reacted to by the whole organism, which does not contain its own capacities to heal, to soothe or to control the damage. The level of experience of this hurt, and the consequent rage or despair, is very primitive. At a fantasy level it resembles the primitive contents of the body of the infant and of the mother. Higher levels of soothing, patience, comfort, distraction, reparation, rejoicing and rejoining scarcely exist.

The borderline patient has not developed certain higher-level structures and functions of the mind. One of these functions that is essential for psychic growth is what Schaffer (1968) has called 'reflective self-representation', by means of which we know we are the thinkers of our own thoughts (Bach 1980). When this is established we have the capacity to objectivise thought and to know that a thought is a thought; we are in a position to know and to say 'I think, I believe, I feel, I remember, I see,' and so on. If this capacity for reflective self-representation is suspended or unavailable, the thinker vanishes but the thought remains. The thought is now a thing, an event, a concrete external reality, for there is no thinker to know it for what it is. This self-representational function can be temporarily suspended, as in the daydream which allows for the gratification of tension. We are constantly moving in and out of higher levels of consciousness, but this is something of which we can be aware; we know the difference between one and the other. Our borderline patients, however, do not always know the difference between the daydream and higher levels of consciousness, do not know the difference between thoughts they are thinking and thoughts that come to them, as it were, out of inner and outer space.

We can also relate the psychic experience of the borderline patient to a failure in symbolic functioning. The etymology of the word 'symbol' shows that it is a construction of two Greek roots: '*sym*' (together with) and '*bollon*' (that which has been thrown). Thus 'symbol' conveys the idea of things which have been put together in what is now a container of meaning. Implicit in this is the concept of putting together what has been torn apart or lost. Thus reparation, putting together and finding of the lost object are implicit in the concept of symbolisation. This has been linked to the capacity to achieve the depressive position (Segal 1957) – that is, to experience separation, frustration and reparation. The lost object is replaced by the symbol. The development of the symbolic function also enables the infant to experience itself as being in the world, as one part of a process that needs another part to bring it to completion. This is clearly linked to the capacity for reflective self-representation, to see oneself as the 'I' in a world in which there is also a 'you' and therefore, taking them together symbolically, a 'we'.

By contrast to the proper development of the symbolic function, in the narcissistic personality there is no real other, and therefore only pseudo-symbolisation, a pseudo-relationship and a pseudo-symbol of the other, who in fact represents only an extension of the self.

Reverting to the concept that when reflective self-representation is missing the thought is experienced concretely as a thing that may emerge from either inner or outer space, we can speak of diabolic functioning rather than symbolic functioning. The word 'diabol', as opposed to 'symbol', refers to something which has been thrown across ('*dia*') or jumbled up rather than having been brought together to make a coherent and meaningful whole. Thus what appears 'diabolically' may appear on the surface to be like a symbol but in fact is not conducive to object formation or object use. It can be experienced only in terms of violence, of accusation either from the self against the other or from the other against the self, and represents an improper projection, an excessive projection, rather than one that is part of a normal projective and introjective process. These important distinctions have been made by Gemma Fiumara (1977).

I wish now to turn to the theory of treatment and to try to show something of the place in group analytic psychotherapy in the treatment of the borderline and narcissistic personalities. As far as individual psychotherapy goes, there is a spectrum of opinions ranging from despair to optimism. It is clear that if the theoretical aetiology is a solely intrapsychic one based on instinct theory, as in the Kleinian approach, individual psychotherapy in the standard setting, with great emphasis on the maintenance of boundaries and of the ground rules of psychotherapy, is indicated. Despite this theoretical assumption, I think there are very few even among the Kleinian school who would affirm that individual psychoanalysis with the more disturbed of these patients can be carried out with the standard technique. It is possible to have a different approach to a solely intrapsychic view of aetiology; there can be a modification of technique with the prime aim of containment and holding of the patient so that the metabolism of primitive affects, fantasies and ideation becomes possible through the transference relationship and the effect of mutative interpretations. Here the relationship aspect comes to the fore, as opposed to the more purely interpretive approach.

The group analytic view of treatment

It is not possible to treat a group made up entirely of borderline patients. A group must have the capacity to operate at the higher levels of functioning lacking in borderline patients, but available to the neurotic, to the normal person and to the therapist. A group of borderline patients will scarcely represent the norm of society from which each is a deviant, which for Foulkes (1948) was the basic law of group dynamics. Foulkes seemed to be thinking not so much of a group of psychotics or borderline patients as of a group composed of neurotic personalities. It is perfectly possible, using our model, to include in a group one or two persons functioning at a much more primitive level than others, for the capacity of the group to maintain higher-level functioning would be well established and, indeed, there are considerable advantages for the group as a whole if there are persons in it who are determined to bring the group into contact with the powerful and primitive forces of the psyche. A growing amount of written evidence, however, shows the attempt to run completely borderline groups is doomed to disaster.

Kutter (1982), working in Germany, described his group of borderline patients as having progressed to self-destruction as a group. The group was very active, chaotic and frightened: destructiveness and premature self-revelation were characteristic. Cohesion was never long-lasting and was often broken up by destructive attacks. Primitive mechanisms, predominantly splitting and other mechanisms consequent on it, characterised both the individuals in the group and much of the group dynamics. Members would come to the session as if to a place of security which they tried to make good, and yet each time split-off destructive parts projected into the others and prevented the establishment of good relationships and mutual understanding. Whenever a problem was brought in by one member, the others felt that this was too demanding; everyone had pressing problems. The group as a whole, unable to stand up to this enormous internal pressure, gradually began to disintegrate: its remnants seemed to the therapist to resemble a dismembered torso. Both the therapist and the group were progressively devalued, and the former was constantly seen as cold, rejecting, dogmatic and repressive. Dreams of concentration camps, and of frightening and destructive bodily and sexual fantasies, recurred; through associations it was possible to see that the members felt that the group, personified in the therapist, resembled a weak father kept under control by a powerful mother; the father was seen as a complete failure, unable to protect his children from the devouring destructive mother. The group felt like unwanted, abandoned and rejected children. After 98 sessions, the group dissolved.

In retrospect the therapist saw the patients as regressed to an oral stage of drive organisation and as unable to deal with their emotions in a constructive manner. From the beginning they split off unintegrated destructive forces and projected them on to the group. There was no mutual empathy, and ruthless questioning about each other's vulnerabilities took its place. The group increasingly became for its members a frightening destructive object, a perilous hole into which they might fall; the therapist was seen as weak, disappointing, unreliable and irresponsible. As they did not feel that there was any protection by authority, the members could experience each other only as mutually exploiting objects. Eventually they had to protect themselves from these experiences by leaving the group and projecting the damaging parts of the self on to it. Kutter saw them as operating at a level on which they wanted to destroy everything because of their envy of the therapist, an envy that led to the fear of abandonment and of retaliatory rage by the rejecting mother.

On the basis of this report and my own *a priori* theoretical position, I strongly advocate the creation by the therapist of a standard group analytic setting. Here the group circle stands as a symbol of containment and of wholeness. Its external boundary, which is created by the therapist in that he offers the space and the time and the situation for persons to become members of the group as a living boundary, is maintained by the therapist's therapeutic functions and by the collaboration of the group members. They maintain the boundary by their presence, their reliability, their punctuality and, where the group is run by a therapist in private practice, their payment of fees. The patients contribute their labour and their money, and the therapist contributes his skill in exchange for this. Thus a mutual system, not of exploitation but of division of labour, begins to build up. Continuing with this mode, within the group processes of exchange, support and acceptance go on between the peer members of the group, who themselves begin to create the group matrix (Roberts 1982; Van der Kelij 1982).

The concept of the matrix is basic to the group analytic model. It represents the growth of culture, of patterns of communication and meaningful understanding which have been established in the group and which can be drawn on by all the members because they themselves have had a part in its creation. It is as if there is an opportunity for therapist and patients together to create this new entity, the group, which has never existed before; it therefore becomes 'their' group, the subjective object, the 'environmental mother' of Winnicott (1964). Winnicott proposed that for the infant there is an environmental mother before there is an object mother – that is, before the mother is represented in the child's mind and objectified out of the infant's subjective experiences. If we recall the defects in boundary functioning that I described earlier, the failure of healthy maintenance of separation and individuation from the outside world by a boundary that allows relatively free exchange across it, the borderline patient is unable in many ways to contribute to the establishment of this healthy boundary functioning in the group, but is also able gradually to accept and to internalise the boundary functioning created by the healthier members of the group. The borderline patient will characteristically test out this boundary again and again for its strength, its acceptance and its reliability, as he will distrust and fear the group as a potentially bad maternal situation, the black hole into which the individual will fall endlessly, to use Kutter's model. What he has to find out is that he can gradually exchange this 'diabol' for a true 'symbol' of caring, patience, understanding and holding.

The borderline patient functions much of the time at the level of projection and introjection, in primitive forms of externalisation, which in the narcissistic mode of existence leads to no exchange and therefore to no change. What becomes available in the group is that these processes of projection and introjection are raised to a higher level because the other members of the group are able to maintain this higher level, to offer understanding and support, and then to metabolise these processes in a mutative exchange of psychic products.

Naturally this is difficult to achieve in the face of the enormous and destructive attacks of the frightened patient. Here the therapist's function is extremely important. Often he has to act as the container of these enormous tensions and to act as a negotiator, a person who mediates between the opponents in these destructive relationships. But the therapist, too, has basically to trust to the capacity of the group to maintain high levels of psychic functioning such as love, caring, the search for truth and the maintenance of integrity.

A basic feature of therapy, and in particular of group therapy, replicates as essential maternal function; the infant relates to the mother solely as a part object to begin with, but the mother, the good loving caring mother, relates to that infant as a whole person, a whole object, with love, respect and understanding, from the first and indeed from before the first, when the infant is still but a fantasy, a symbol in her mind. Thus there is a constant process of transformation of part-object processes into whole-object responses. It is very important, therefore, that the therapist relates to the group as to a whole entity, sees it as whole, and is able to tolerate and understand its growth while at the same time seeing its individual members as whole persons in their own right, though carrying roles in the group that represent part-person activities. If a person appears to be acting as a focus of communication for these affects and fantasies, it is the therapist's function to help free the person from being used in this way – that is, as a focus of destructive activities rather than as a nodal point in a communications network (Pines 1983).

Thus the therapist constantly relates to the individuals in the group as to whole persons, trying to show them their place in the pattern of the group as a whole. This is not possible if the therapist is devoted to transference-based interpretations at the part-object level, interpretations which have as their basis the group's relation to the therapist. The therapist who does this, wittingly or not, inevitably fragments the group's efforts to become a whole and to relate to each other as whole persons. I have heard therapists describe sessions in which severely disturbed patients seem desperately to be trying to create a living entity out of the group and have to fight off the therapist's demands, which seem to me narcissistically based, that they pay attention to him, to his function and to his interpretations. The therapist needs constantly to listen to his patients, to follow, to care and to be interested in their efforts to grow, to understand and to create a viable group. When this ongoing group process takes place, then we have both matrix, a basic maternal function, and pattern, a basic paternal function, as demonstrated by Cortesao (1971).

Earlier I mentioned the extreme oscillations to which borderline patients, with their lack of inner structuration, are prone. These patients will constantly bring their states of despair and emptiness to the group, and it is remarkable how a well-functioning group can bring them back to a higher level of functioning and establish meaning for them in what seems a meaningless state of despair.

Gradually the wild oscillations begin to cease, as the patient can begin to use the group as a structure and the process of 'transmuting internalisation', which has failed in these patients, begins to develop.

We must not neglect the opposite process: for any change in psychic structure to take place there must be a de-differentiation of the existing structure. This is a process whereby parts of each individual are given up to form a group mixture. Out of this predominantly benign mix a redifferentiation can take place, with each member now containing something new from the intercourse of the group. Here again it must be a genuine intercourse, a real meeting of feelings, thoughts and fantasies, and not solely a contest between therapist and patient.

Other deficiencies in the patient that can be remedied include a weak capacity for reflective self-representation, for in the group there is a constant demand for reflection and an offer by other members of the group to act as mirrors for each other (Pines 1980). Time and again one hears members saying to each other that they now see something of themselves in the other they had not seen previously. On the basis of this understanding they are able to improve not only their relationship with the other, but also their relationship to the self; they can now see at a distance something of themselves to which previously they had been blind. This allows for introjection and reintegration of split-off, repressed and unconscious parts of the self.

In a properly conducted analytic group, the patients will make reasonable demands on each other for reciprocity and for exchange. They will demonstrate, over time, capacities for altruistic caring, for non-possessive love and for healthy confrontation, all of which have been absent or seriously defective in the childhood of borderline patients. But these patients are not simply the passive recipients of this bounty; they are also active contributors in the processes that bestow it.

References

Akhtar, S. and Thompson, J.A. (1982) 'Overview: Narcissistic personality disorders.' Amer.J. Psychiat. 139, 1–20.

Bach, S. (1980) 'Self-love and object love: some problems of self and object constancy.' In R. Lax, S. Bach and J. Burland (eds) Rapprochement: The Critical Subphase of Separation–Individuation. New York: Aronson.

Cortesao, E. (1971) 'On interpretation in group analysis.' Group Analysis 4, 39–53.

Erikson, E. (1950) Childhood and Society. (Rev. ed. 1963) New York: Norton.

Erikson, E. (1959) Identity and the Life Cycle. Psychological Issues Monograph I. New York: International Universities Press.

Fiumara, G. (1977) 'The symbolic function, transference and psychic reality.' International Rv. Psycho-Anal 4, 171–180.

Foulkes, S.H. (1948) Introduction to Group Analytic Psychotherapy. London: Heinemann. Maresfield reprint, 1984.

Freud, S. (1914) *On Narcissism. Standard Edition 14*: 67–102. London: Hogarth Press (1957).

Grotstein, J. (1980) 'A proposed revision of the psychoanalytic concept of primitive mental states.' *Contemp. Psychoanal 16*, 479–546.

Jacobson, E. (1965) *The Self and the Object World*. London: Hogarth Press.

Kernberg, O.J. (1975) *Borderline Conditions and Pathological Narcissism*. New York: Aronson.

Kohut, H. (1971) *The Analysis of the Self*. London: Hogarth Press.

Kutter, P. (1982) *Basic Aspects of Psychoanalytic Group Therapy*. London: Routledge and Kegan Paul.

Lacan, J. (1977) 'The mirror stage as formative of the I as revealed in psychoanalytic experience.' In *Ecrits*. London: Tavistock.

Loewald, H.W. (1973) 'On internalization.' *International J Psycho-Anal 54*, 9–17.

Loewald, H.W. (1980) *Papers on Psychoanalysis*. New Haven, CT: Yale University Press.

Mahler, M.S., Pine, F. and Bergman, A. (1975) *The Psychological Birth of the Human Infant*. London: Hutchinson.

Pines, M. (1980) 'Reflections on mirroring.' *Internat. Rev. Psycho-Anal 11*, 27–42.

Pines, M. (ed)(1983) *Evolution of Group Analysis*. London: Routledge and Kegan Paul.

Roberts, J.P. (1982) 'Foulkes' concept of the matrix.' *Group Analysis 15*, 111–126.

Schaffer, R. (1968) *Aspects of Internalization*. New York: International Universities Press.

Schellenberg, J.A. (1978) *Masters of Social Psychology*. New York: Oxford University Press.

Segal, H. (1957) 'Notes on symbol formation.' *Interna. J. Psycho-Anal 38*, 391–397.

Tolpin, M. (1971) 'On the beginnings of a cohesive self.' *The Psychoanalytic Study of the Child 26*, 316–352.

Van der Kleij, G. (1982) 'About the matrix.' *Group Analysis 15*, 219–234.

Winnicott, D.W. (1965) 'The development of the capacity for concern.' In *Maturational Processes and the Facilitating Environment*. London: Hogarth Press.

Zinkin, L. (1983) 'Malignant mirroring.' *Group Analysis 16*, 113–125.

Further reading

McDevitt, J.D. and Settledge, C.F. (eds) (1971) *Separation-Individuation: Essays in Honour of Margaret S. Mahler*. New York: International Universities Press.

PART 2

Psychoanalysis and Psychotherapy

CHAPTER 6

Dissent in Context
Schisms in the Psychoanalytic Movement[1]

As I began to think over this question of schisms in the psychoanalytic movement, I noted the 'D words', words with the prefix that signifies separateness between two opinions. The words are: to disagree, diverge, dispute and dissent. We dispute and debate; hopefully we dialogue. Dialect represents a local language; the Russian philosopher, Bakhtin, (Holquist 1990) warned us of the dangerous consequences of one dialect insisting upon legislating itself as the only officially sanctioned language. He tells us that the many tongues of 'heteroglossia' represent the full human condition, the diversity of minds, always at risk from the 'monoglossia' of a ruling power that legislates its own dialect above that of all other discourse.

I shall consider the events in the history of the psychoanalytic movement when debate and dialogue have contained dissent and, when not contained, become schismatic.

When dispute and dissent are contained we are in the realm of the 'C words', of communication, concordance, conciliation and convergence. However, we should also remember collusion and contrivance!

The root of the word 'schism', so familiar in the history of religion, means to shed, separate, to split. Schism evokes ideas of hatred, struggles for purity fuelled by the need to expel impure elements within and locate them without. A schism, an unbridgeable gap, appears when the disputants cannot tolerate the overlap of their areas of belief. As the anthropologist Edmund Leach (1976) points out, a boundary separates two zones of social space-time which are normal, timebound, clear-cut, central, secular. But the spatial and temporal markers which actually serve as boundaries are themselves abnormal, timeless, ambiguous, at the edge, sacred. In the Euler diagram there is always some uncertainty about where the

1   Opening paper for the Congress of the International Association for the History of Psychoanalysis, Berlin, 21 July 1994.

edge of category A turns into the category not-A. But this ambiguous area of overlap is the area of the numinous, the mysterious, fundamentally of creativity arising from the intercourse of ideas.

Psychoanalytic dissidents have been boundary markers for concepts that at one time or another have not been acceptable to the psychoanalytic movement, to the main body of psychoanalysts. When at first Freud himself embodied psychoanalysis, they were in dispute with him personally, members of his psychoanalytic *circle* before there was an organised psychoanalytic movement, a *school*. Each dissident has a particular significance: their deviant and dissident ideas at that particular cultural-historical time have later often been incorporated, though not openly, within the psychoanalytic movement.

Ellenberger (1970) argues, and I find this acceptable, that both Adler and Jung were not so much deviationists but persons who for some years joined with Freud within the psychoanalytic movement, bringing their own originality and creativity, but who eventually found it necessary to follow their own paths. Adler was an active Jewish socialist, a social reformer, eager to change society and to help children by guiding their parents with psychoanalytic knowledge. Thus he originated the child guidance movement and helped towards creating a social niche for child analysis. His early formulations on the place of aggression, feelings of inferiority, of reaction formation and character formation, are implicit in the psychoanalytic theory of personality. Stepansky's (1983) study of the links between Adler and Kohut will be discussed later.

Jung's place is major. Suffice it here to say that his concern with the psychology of the self is now also the concern of the psychoanalytic movement as a whole. But his significance is much greater than that, and I shall return to him later.

Psychoanalytic dissidents pushed the boundary of theory and technique, spatially and temporally. Shortened methods were advocated by Stekel, Rank, Alexander and Lacan. Others, eager advocates of reforming society through psychoanalytic understanding, significantly influenced by Marxism, pushed the boundaries of psychoanalysis beyond personal therapy and theory of the individual towards social reform: Adler, Reich, the Fenichel group of Marxists, active in pre-World War II Europe, though going underground after 1933. This Marxist-influenced movement died when exported to England and to North America, but blazed up again after World War II in the aftermath of the French student rebellion of 1968, most noticeably and quite surprisingly in Switzerland! Exported to South America by Marie Langer, this movement found fertile soil.

Freud, Jung and Adler in context

Peter Homans (1989) analyses the deeper meaning of the schism between Freud and Jung in the following terms: Freud insisted that psychoanalysis was primarily a scientific method of investigating and treating the individual unconscious through the psychoanalytic situation; that psychoanalysis was a radical development of modern science. He devoted much of his work to asserting the claims of psychoanalysis to be recognised as science: he greatly feared that psychoanalysis could be either regarded as a form of religion or attributed to the influence of Jewish thought. Freud's need for Jung as his anointed successor, for the adherence of the Bleuler Christian Zurich group, was fuelled by these needs and fears.

Homans (1989) presents Jung as Freud's 'other', who represented important things that he both hated and loved, sometimes with overwhelming intensity. The most important and anxiety-making of these was Jung's conviction that psychoanalysis might really be a new vision of a way of being in the world, a new form of *culture-making*, that through psychoanalysis modern science had rediscovered the unconscious as a universal stratum of mind, the repository of cultural symbols that could revitalise the mental and moral impoverishment of modern man. Homans calls this the 'Deep Past' Theory of the origins of depth psychology, its inseparable link with the symbolic structures of both Western and Eastern cultures.

In Ernest Jones' influential presentation of Freud's work and through Strachey's 1974 *Standard Edition* we can see this imperative, that psychoanalysis be recognised and accepted as fully participating in modern science and also the massaging of the history of psychoanalysis to strengthen this claim. Many of the factors that Jones sifted out of the history of psychoanalysis have been recognised and restored by later workers.

Psychoanalysis has been greatly weakened by this misguided effort to locate it in relative cultural isolation, for to do so is to remove it from cultural embeddedness in the earth and it is weakened, as was Anteus, by this removal. Our Association exists to restore that vital context, to bring figure and ground together through the different disciplines of history, sociology and the philosophy of ideas.

If we accept the thesis that depth psychology of the twentieth century, of which psychoanalysis is the principal movement, represents a creative response to the nineteenth-century sense of cultural loss of a shared set of symbolic structures – religion, political structure; to the unease of Western society undergoing rapid socio-economic changes, the industrial revolution; that these changes broke down the significant cultural attachments of the earlier society; that this led to an 'introspective revolution'; that depth psychology was needed and welcomed because it represented a new form of coherency, a new basis for enlightenment attachment and comradeship for psychologists and psychiatrists at the turn of the century; then we can see the inherent necessity for diversity in the growing psychoanalytic movement.

During this conference we shall be identifying various 'faultlines', places where fissures can lead to schisms, examining the inherent, ever recurrent tensions in our field. Sometimes these faultlines are bridged, knitted together, through the growth of knowledge, through debate and the marshalling of evidence. A great potential fissure is the relationship of the intrapsychic to the interpersonal and the social. This led to the schism first with Adler, then with others. Another faultline is the border of neurosis and psychosis which led to the exploration of the pre-oedipal.

Freud and Adler

Paul Stepansky (1983, 1989) has reconstructed a possible group dynamic in the Viennese Psychoanalytic Society and the developing psychoanalytic movement to explain Adler's strong position until he resigned in 1911. For several years Freud had tolerated Adler's clearly divergent views, though he expressed his personal antipathy and distrust of Adler in his personal correspondence. The argument is that Freud needed to avoid a split, that he wished to see his Viennese Society as a circle, a forum for free exchange of views in which independently minded workers, of whom Adler was the most prominent, could belong. The minutes of the meetings of the Psychoanalytic Society show how much Adler's views provoked discussion, given consideration and much support. His views on masculine protest, inferiority complex, neurotic character formation and ego defence are well known. There are similarities between his 1911 presentations and the later theories of the neo-Freudians, Karen Horney and Harry Stack Sullivan. Stepanksy also shows that after Adler's defection Freud incorporated some aspects of his ideas into his own theories and therapeutic technique, and that some of Franz Alexander's later ideas about the Total Personality and the Delinquent Character are influenced by Adler.

Adler, who began as an active social democrat, emphasised social factors in the development of neurosis; the effects of faulty education and lack of affective concern by the adult environment on the helpless infant. He spoke up for recognising the effect of social institutions and economic conditions on the opportunity for instinctual gratification and did not, as Freud and other analysts claimed, propose a separate aggressive drive. Rather he spoke of aggression as a defence response, an attempt to attain a degree of masculine mastery over the environment, a debate which continues today in Kohut's assertion that drives represent the disintegration products of a whole self that has not received appropriate empathic responses from the self-objects, the human environment.

Stepansky argues that Adler, who had the support of such respected representatives of Viennese internal medicine as Federn and Hitschman, though later they rejected him, was needed by Freud. Freud held power as the originator of the psychoanalytic movement but Adler represented social power, the recognition of the medical establishment. When in 1910, after the Nuremburg Congress, which Freud called the Nuremburg 'Reichstag', the International Psychoanalytical Association (IPA) was formed, psychoanalysis became an organised movement, a school, no longer a circle. As Freud wrote in a letter to Ferenczi: 'the Nuremburg Reichstag closes the childhood of our movement. I hope now for a rich and fair time of youth'. Psychoanalysis had moved from an informal to a formal organisation. Freud had appointed Jung to the Presidency of the IPA to secure the support of the Zurich group and to ensure the continuation of psychoanalysis after his death. The Viennese felt themselves abandoned and neglected and it was to conciliate them that Freud appointed Adler as the President of the Viennese Society. With the founding of the IPA psychoanalysis now had the kind of institutional growth that provided a structural foundation for the crystallisation of rival groups, Freudian and Adlerian. Adler's views and the support of his group could now be damaging to the organisation, its growth and its expansion as a unified coherent set of concepts into the wider society. A unified language must therefore be prescribed. The time for debate and dissent was over.

Stepansky shows that Kohut has made many similar assertions to Adler's, for instance that sexual drive derivatives represent 'disintegration products' of the healthy, whole self in response to environmental conflicts and failures. That Kohut's ideas have obtained a considerable following within organised psychoanalysis which, despite the strong opposition raised against it has not been forced into a schismatic move, can be attributed to the evolution of a 'research tradition' within psychoanalysis, which did not exist in 1911. New psychoanalytic ideas can be presented to, discussed and tested by, a large psychoanalytic community capable of productively containing the resulting tensions.

Trigant Burrow

The case of Trigant Burrow represents again the faultline of the intraspychic and the interpersonal. The expulsion of Trigant Burrow from the American Psychoanalytic Association (APA), of which he had been President, is a little-known corner of psychoanalytic history. Burrow was a respected psychiatrist, who spent one year, 1909, in analysis with Jung and was one of the founders of the APA.

Burrow had an original and creative mind, and wrote about the infant's primary identification with mother during the organism's 'primary subjective phase', an early exploration of primary narcissism. After 13 years of psychoanalytic practice, Burrow became increasingly aware of the social implications of neurosis: 'Society has its elaborate system of defence-mechanisms, its equivocations and metonymies, its infantile make-shifts and illusions'. His exploration of the social led him to recognise psychoanalysis itself as an enormously powerful social situation, that the dynamics of transference are in many ways not individual but universal, a product of the authority structure in the analytic dyad. In 1918 he accepted the challenge of his analysand, Clarence Shields, to reverse roles, and found himself faced with the very authority problems that had previously belonged to his patient. (There are parallels with Ferenczi's mutual analysis.) He then began his lifelong exploration of the nature of relationships between individuals, of *horizontal* depth, and in 1923 began work with groups. Elected President of the APA in 1925, he continued to take an active part in it, and attended the Bad Homburg Congress. In several long letters to Freud one can see his continued commitment to psychoanalysis, his attempts to interest Freud in the social implications of neurosis, including the collective reactions of psychoanalysts themselves as, 'a special form of social unconscious'.

In 1933, though a founder and former President, he was dropped from the membership of the reorganised APA. He accepted this rebuff with dignity and continued his exploration of group dynamics.

Burrow pushed the boundaries of psychoanalysis to include the social, and thereby became something of a scapegoat within an American psychoanalysis reorganising itself to become a strong and cohesive body establishing psychoanalysis as the prime form of psychotherapy. There was then no place for his viewpoint that included the social within the individual.

Fortunately the climate has changed and it is now legitimate for psychoanalysts, myself included, to practise group analysis and to offer a frame of reference which incorporates the vertical intrapsychic dimension and the horizontal interpersonal dimension. The realm of the 'inbetween', perhaps best known through Winnicott's work on transitional space and transitional object, is recognised as a legitimate field for psychoanalytic exploration. The work of Hans Loewald is a significant bridge between the intrapsychic and the interpersonal. His formulation that the therapeutic action of psychoanalysis is achieved through the experience of the analyst as a new object who enables interrupted developmental sequences of childhood to be resumed during analytic work, has been widely accepted.

Loewald's (1980) work represents the successful bridging of what might otherwise have been a schism. The tension aroused within the psychoanalytic movement, particularly in North America, by the school of Kohut and self psychology might in earlier times have led to a schism, but the growing maturity of the psychoanalytic movement and our capacity to recognise the different developmental lines of our theories has enabled us to encompass more divergency than previously.

Some dynamics of schism

A school developing sectarian propensities shows such features as:

- First, that it is a system of knowledge that possesses a high religious-emotive content, that promises answers to crucial existential questions.

- Second, that the members of the group are marginal socially, economically or psychically. They turn to theory for an interpretation of their condition and enter the group in order to transcend that condition, involving their whole lives with the fate of the group. The response of the outside world, whether the message of the group is accepted and incorporated into the ways of thinking and acting of the social and professional groups to which they aspire to belong, greatly affects the group.

- Third, the type of relationship to the leader of the group and the intensity of relationships with this leader affects the relationships between the followers, as Fritz Redl (1942) showed many years ago. Through all the transference and counter-transference relationships that existed between Freud, his own analysands and those of the other leading analysts and their analysands, this intensity was greatly increased. These centripetal forces bind a group together, isolated from the wider community. The centrifugal forces that maintain communication with that wider community are the plurality of political religious and scientific beliefs of the individual members and the fact that many of them wish to continue to be accepted as full members of the other communities. This intellectual pluralism has kept open the boundaries between psychoanalysts and their surrounding communities, but has inevitably led to divergences within the psychoanalytic movement itself. Hence the Freudo-Marxists, the Ego-Psychologists who wish to make psychoanalysis a general psychology, the Cultural Freudians, the paediatrician Winnicott, the ethologist John Bowlby, the French linguistic philosophers. Our Tower of Babel continues to grow laterally if not vertically, and we have to learn the heteroglossia that characterises a healthy intellectual community.

The growth of the psychoanalytic movement and the schismatic process

1. First we have Freud, leader of the circle, held together as a cohesive group embattled with what they regarded as a hostile world. This 'heroic myth' has been challenged, as much research has shown. The reception of psychoanalysis was not as hostile as Freud asserted.

2. Later, when the circle became a school, deviancy led to expulsion. The succession of deviants led to the formation of the Secret Committee, designed both to take the strain away from Freud himself but also to make sure that the leadership of the psychoanalytic movement was in safe hands.

3. The Committee was dissolved when, through the wider spread of psychoanalysis after World War I, other centres began to establish their autonomy. With the increase of size and complexity of the group of psychoanalysts, new structures were needed to regulate the practise of psychoanalysis and to create an agreed training procedure. This move by the centre was opposed by a significant peripheral group, the North Americans.

4. National centres established in Berlin, Budapest and London, developed their own characters. Berlin undertook rigorous trainings, with many prominent analysts strongly influenced by Marxism. Budapest, under the leadership of Ferenczi, became a centre for experiments with technique, exploring the pre-oedipal, and recognising and accepting regression and empathy as vital factors in the psychoanalytic process. We can see the present day influence of this in the attention given to empathy and intersubjectivity under the stimulus of self psychology and research into child development. London, before the arrival of Melanie Klein in 1926, was already exploring child analysis along different lines to those that Anna Freud was establishing in Vienna. British psychoanalytic culture, the intellectual climate which later fostered the work of Bowlby and Winnicott and provided fertile soil for Melanie Klein, had begun to appreciate and work with concepts of object loss in the aftermath of World War I when enormous numbers of families experienced bereavement. The Tavistock Clinic as a centre of psychodynamic exploration provided a forum for cross-fertilisation between psychotherapists of different approaches, such as Jungians, Freudians and some Adlerians, whereas the Psychoanalytic Society, under the powerful control of Ernest Jones, struggled to maintain psychoanalytic purity. The struggle that developed over the work of Klein deserves separate treatment and will be dealt with later on.

It is important to recognise that throughout the 1920s and 1930s attempts were made to maintain a dialogue between London and Vienna. The correspondence between Ernest Jones and Freud reveals how both of them attempted to keep lines of communication intact; exchange lectures were arranged between Vienna and London to bring these personal exchanges between Freud and Jones into the societal sphere. The same process of attempting to maintain a dialogue between dissidents, who might eventually become schismatics, occurred between the leaders of Viennese psychoanalysis and the Budapest and Berlin Fenichel group of Marxist psychoanalysts. Russell Jacoby (1983) has shown that every effort was made to keep Fenichel within the psychoanalytic community; the earlier expulsion of Reich was not to be repeated.

Edward Shils (1975) has shown that societies are structured as central and peripheral zones. The central is the realm of the governing values, beliefs and symbols of the sacred. In the movement from the centre, where authority is possessed, to the periphery, over which authority is exercised, the strength of the central value system is attenuated. Peripheral areas, the colonies of believers, can either remain orthodox or become centres of initiative which may or may not wish to keep their link to the sacred centre. In North America we saw the orthodox, reinforced from Europe, struggle to maintain control over the heterodox: pure psychoanalytic societies versus those that affiliated with universities and medical schools.

Prior to World War II, and resumed after it, was the secessionist movement of North American psychoanalysis. American insistence that psychoanalysis was a branch of psychiatry and therefore a branch of medicine, led to a pyrrhic victory. Medicalised psychoanalysis reigned supreme for some 40 years before being overthrown by American psychologists who demanded the right to a psychoanalytic training on a par with that of medical doctors.

In Latin America the Marxist influence reasserted itself through Maria Langer and her supporters in the Argentine Society. Re-imported to Europe in the aftermath of the 1968 student movement, this led to the schism of the 'Plataforma' and the 'Documento' movements. The Zurich Institute was disorganised and reorganised to accommodate this upsurge, which has led to a split in the Zurich Society and Institute, as it also has in Buenos Aires.

The loyal opponent: Ferenczi

Adler, Jung and Rank, left the psychoanalytic movement. However, Ferenczi, Freud's most loyal opponent, did not become leader of a schism and left a rich legacy, increasingly appreciated. His work, writes Gedo, is a seminal event in the intellectual course of psychoanalysis that provided the impetus to the movements initiated by Melanie Klein, Object Relations Theory and Kohut's self psychology. Ferenczi understood the need for tact, empathy, for flexibility with more disturbed patients; the crucial significance of emotional trauma. Increasingly divergent from Freud's theory and technique, he remained loyal. Was it their deep personal relationship, his great need for love and approval; did the shared cultural history of Austro-Hungary provide a basis for dissent without secession? Did the more radical peripheral Hungarian analysts need the legitimation of the symbolic centre of Vienna? Probably all these factors played a part in maintaining the links between Vienna and Budapest.

How do the dynamics of psychoanalytic institutions affect schismatic processes?

In 1945 Clara Thompson (1958), flushed with the success of forming the William Allinson White Institute of Washington, wrote that many of the qualities of a close family group, qualities both good and bad, are to be found within psychoanalytic institutions: 'All satisfactions and evils of family life are revived again' (p.787). Psychoanalytic groups fight persecution from without and persecution from within. Keeping psychoanalysis pure leads to small groups centring round leaders who claim to represent the essence of Freud's teachings. Subgroups develop which fail to communicate, resort to projection to maintain their identity. Problems from unresolved transferences and unconscious dependency lead to the need for authoritarian personalities, leaders who will produce rivalry and opposition or appeasement. Both tendencies represent unresolved infantile dependencies; because of these, power positions are sought and also create fears of leaving home. Thompson considered herself lucky to have had her training far from home, in Budapest, and thereby to be relatively free of such dependency problems to a local training analyst. She was concerned with the mini schisms within psychoanalytic institutions, features which develop within all psychoanalytic and, I must also say, group analytic societies. These schisms grow because of the intolerance of diversity in psychoanalytic institutions. The notorious difficulty that psychoanalytic institutes have in managing theoretical diversity, to which the history of schisms in psychoanalytic institutes testifies, has been surveyed by Kenneth Eisold (1994). He suggests that this intolerance of diverse points of view is an 'institutional social defence': the essential uncertainty and ambiguity of psychoanalytic work leads to needs for certainty, to dogmatism. The nature of psychoanalytic work is that analysts work independently, outside organisations, engaged in intense and difficult pairing relationships with patients. At the same time they are quasi-independently parts of organisations, psychoanalytic societies and institutes which have strong systems of lineage. To be part of such an institution is to belong to a subgroup.

Eisold (1994) argues that the therapeutic instrument of psychoanalytic work, being the self of the analyst, involves a continued assault on the emotional lives of therapists. They must, therefore, tolerate an enormous amount of ambiguity:

> Under conditions of isolation, uncertainty and stress analysts turn to their theo-
> ries, for release from such stressful ambiguities, and their theories are their links
> with the community. Our theories are internalised in training from other per-
> sons who are inevitably idealised and this is part of the gradual formation of the
> psychoanalytic identity. (p.45)

Theory serves two purposes, enabling the analyst to maintain a sense of balance in relationship to the patient, but also sustaining the relationship with colleagues, forming 'schools'. Schools are formed by subgroups, leading to factionalism which can facilitate differentiation and stimulate dialogue, but which also brings the danger of developing an analytic 'pseudo-identity', being an adherent to a particular school. Schools can become increasingly rigid, intolerant of compromise: they will locate negative attributes in other factions, misidentify others as inadequate or misled; their theories are not granted the status of reasonable alternatives to their own. The dichotomy of true and false arises.

The consequences of the intense pairing relationships that characterise psychoanalysis

Intense pairing relationships of analysts and patients represent unconscious threats to the organisation, which responds by developing rigid boundaries to contain the powerful centrifugal forces of the pairing couple. Overbounded institutional systems develop excessive, impermeable boundaries, rigid hierarchies, inflexible roles and task assignments.

The close tie with the patient and the loose tie to the organisation, the inevitable ambivalence in the pairing situation, may lead to splittings, projections into the organisation, which then is felt as intruding into the pair relationship; then the organisation becomes the object of attack. Group formation pools defences against these internal attacks, leads to targeting of other groups, leaving analysts feeling secure in the strength of their own subgroup and in the truth of its theories.

Thus Thompson's dictum that psychoanalytic institutions reproduce both the good and evil qualities of the close family group, and Eisold's examination of the effect of the pair relationship and of training on the dynamics of organisations clarify the powerful forces that have to be contained within institutions and the psychoanalytic movement as a whole.

The capacity for tolerating diversity in psychoanalytic institutions

The outstanding and best documented example, after the early minutes of the Viennese Society, is that of London's Controversial Discussions. Here I draw on Riccardo Steiner's (1985) deeply thought-out views of what prevents a crisis from becoming a catastrophe. The schism between the Kleinians and the Freudians was averted and a greater degree of tolerance of opposing views established.

I have already mentioned that Ernest Jones maintained a serious debate over the increasing differences between Vienna and London that followed the arrival of Melanie Klein in 1926. With the support of Jones she established a considerable following, and Jones wrote to Freud that, 'we need a penetrating critic from Vienna to come and criticise our work'. Waelder came, saw, spoke but did not conquer. Jones and Riviere visited Vienna but did not convert.

The arrival of the Viennese refugee analysts in 1938 greatly increased the internal tension in the British Society, properly dealt with by instituting debate and dialogue, the Controversial Discussions.

Steiner (1985) suggests that the anxiety aroused by Klein's work was because she had plunged psychoanalysis back into the unknown, into the dark realm of the primitive, of psychotic and not 'merely' neurotic anxieties. I have already said that the 'faultline' between neurosis and psychosis is a recurrent theme in psychoanalytic schisms. The institutional response to Klein's exploration of psychotic anxieties resonated at that level, 'a psychosis of transference at the collective level' (p.57), with paranoid anxieties and splitting defences. This could have led to schism but did not.

Steiner suggests that the very issue of debate, Klein's development of the infantile depressive position, inserted into the British Society the values and attitudes that held it together and avoided splitting. In the depressive position the capacity develops to balance destructiveness with reparation, to integrate positive and negative experience and, crucially, a new ability to use time. The Controversial Discussions gave the British Society a container in space and time, a defined and bounded area for agonistic debate under increasingly responsive and democratic procedures. Jones gave up his overlong authoritarian Presidency of the Society, not succeeded by his favourite son Edward Glover, who was feared by the Kleinians as a destructive critic. What held the group together through this difficult time was the development of what Steiner calls, 'a minimum code of reciprocal acceptance'.

The dynamics of innovation

Psychoanalytic knowledge is transmitted through personal relationships, training analyses, revered teachers. Innovations therefore arouse primitive anxieties, threatening established linkages; certainty is thrown into doubt, what is presented as new can arouse fear, suspicion and envy. My colleague, the group analyst and large-group theoretician, Patrick de Maré, links the envy of the new idea to the envy of the newborn into a kinship group. A kinship group has a common ancestry and consanguinity – family, clan, tribe. When kinship is in strife – Cain and Abel – there is no bifocal vision. The image of the other in the minds of disputing parties arouses destructive impulses, the result has to be submission or conquest. In early developmental terms there is no triangulation, no position from which one can view the claims of both disputants. A third party can bring about dialogue, as the presence of the Middle Group of British analysts made dialogue between the Kleinians and Freudians possible. This viewpoint, not dominated by family dynamics, comes from kith, neighbours, members of another clan.

Together kith and kin meeting in large-group settings, such as this congress, can share differing viewpoints and create new visions. The 'impartial fellowship of Koinonia' can replace the authoritarianism and restriction of knowledge of the kinship group. Cultural change within institutions cannot be brought about in small committees, which is why we need large congresses where, as Freud wrote to Groddeck, 'my lions can roar'. In our large-group gatherings we look outwards towards each other and hopefully what we see in the face of the other, as Levinas (Davis 1997) movingly describes, is one of acceptance and responsiveness, the face that accepts and responds to utterance with dialogue.

I end, as I began, with Bakhtin, with his distinction between the univocal and the dialogic. The univocal is the voice of Authority, of the Father. It is the voice of transmission of fixed, unmodifiable meaning, not modified by contact with new voices. Its demand for acknowledgement is independent of persuasive power. There is no play at the borders that could allow for gradual transitions or for creative variants. Entering consciousness as an indivisible mass, it cannot be divided into parts accepted and others debated. It is a cohesive mass of ideas.

By contrast, the dialogic has another voice, the voice that Freud so well represents in his writings, that is internally persuasive and which allows dialogic interanimation. The words of the persuader awaken new and independent words, create a discourse which reveals ever new ways to mean which can yet belong to the main body of ideas.

When both voices co-exist in dynamic tension there cannot be schisms.

References

Davis, C. (1997) *Levinas: An Introduction.* Oxford: Polity Press.

Eisold, K. (1994)'The intolerance of diversity in psycho-analytic institutions.' *International Journal of Psychoanalysis 75,* 787.

Ellenberger, H.F. (1970) *The Discovery of the Unconscious: the History and Evolution of Dynamic Psychiatry.* London: Penguin.

Holquist, M. (1990) *Dialogism: Bakhtin and His World.* London: Routledge.

Homans, P. (1989) *The Ability to Mourn. Disillusionment and the Social Origins of Psychoanalysis.* Chicago: University of Chicago Press.

Homans, P. (1995) *Introduction. Jung in Context.* Chicago: University of Chicago Press, second edition.

Jacoby, R. (1983) *The Repression of Psychoanalysis: The Political Freudians.* Chicago: University of Chicago Press.

Kutter, P. (ed) (1992) *Psychoanalysis International. Vol.1: Europe.* Stuttgart-Bad Canstatt: Frommannholzboog.

Leach, E. (1976) *Culture and Communication.* Cambridge: University of Cambridge Press.

Loewald, H. (1980) *Papers on Psychoanalysis.* New Haven: Yale University Press.

Redl, F. (1942) 'Group emotion and leadership.' *Psychiatry 5,* 573–6.

Shils, E. (1975) *Center and Periphery: Essays in Macrosociology.* Chicago: University of Chicago Press.

Steiner, R. (1985) 'Some thoughts about tradition and change arising from an examination of the British Psycho-Analytic Society Review Controversial Discussions (1943–44).' *International Journal of Psychoanalysis 12*, 1, 27.

Stepansky, P. (1983) 'Perspectives on dissent: Adler, Kohut and the idea of a psychoanalytic research tradition.' *Annual of Psychoanalysis 11.*

Stepansky, P. (1989) *In Freud's Shadow: Adler in Context.* Hillsdale, NJ: Lawrence Erlbaum.

Strachey, J. (ed)(1974) *Standard Edition Psychological Works of Sigmund Freud.* London: Hogarth Press.

Thompson, C. (1958) 'A study of the emotional climate of psychoanalytic institutes.' *Psychiatry 21*, 45–51.

Further reading

Aron, L. and Harris, A. (1993) *The Legacy of Sandor Ferenczi.* Hillsdale, NJ: The Analytic Press.

Fleming, J. (1976) 'Report of the ad hoc committee on Los Angeles.' *Bulletin of the American Psychoanalytic Association 24*, 4, 910–915.

'Freud–Klein controversies fifty years later.' Symposium in *Int.J of Psychoanalysis* (1994) 75, 2. 335–402.

Gitelson, F.H. (1983) 'Identity crises: splits or compromises – adaptive or maladaptive.' In E. Joseph and D. Widlocher (eds) *The Identity of the Psychoanalyst.* New York: International Universities Press.

Haynal, A. (1993) *Psychoanalysis and the Sciences. Epistemology – History.* London: Karnac Books.

King, P. (1983) 'Identity crises: splits or compromises – adaptive or maladaptive.' In E. Joseph and D. Widlocher (eds) *The Identity of the Psychoanalyst.* New York: International Universities Press.

King, P. and Steiner, R. (1991) *The Freud–Klein Controversies 1941–45.* London: Tavistock/Routledge.

Kurzweil, E. (1989) *The Freudians. A Comparative Perspective.* New Haven: Yale University Press.

Moser, A. (1992) 'Psychoanalysis in Switzerland.' In P. Kutter (ed) *Psychoanalysis International. Vol.1: Europe.* Stuttgart-Bad Canstatt: Frommannholzboog.

Quen, J.M. and Carlson, E.T. (1978) *American Psychoanalysis: Origins and Development.* New York: Brunner-Mazel.

Timms, E. (ed) (1992) 'Franz Wittels. From the memoirs of a Freudian.' In E. Timms and R. Robertson (eds) *Austrian Studies III. Psychoanalysis in its Cultural Context.* Edinburgh: Edinburgh University Press.

Weisz, G. (1975) 'Scientists and sectarians: the case of psychoanalysis.' *Journal of the History of the Behaviour Sciences 11*, 350–364.

CHAPTER 7

Change and Innovation, Decay and Renewal in Psychotherapy[1]

How, I ask myself, am I to celebrate a 15th anniversary? Fifteen years is too old for a Barmitzvah address, that mixture of congratulations and warnings fit for the onset of puberty; perhaps an early coming of age would be more appropriate; for an institution 15 years' duration is already quite lengthy. Having been given a free hand by the organisers to choose my own subject, I thought my somewhat elaborate title appropriate for the celebration of an organisation that stands for innovation and change in the understanding and treatment of disorders of mental and emotional life. My intention is to present psychotherapy as an historical process, a process of development but also of decay in our understanding of the mind. We so often take progress and development for granted, that what we do today must be an advance of heretofore, that we build on the solid foundations left to us by our forefathers. Might this not, however, turn out to be a wish fulfilment, an illusion, a family romance of psychotherapy in which we count ourselves lucky to be the inheritors of royal mantles? A harder look at our own history may give us a different picture, then we can heed the warning given to us by Santayana, for those who do not understand history are doomed to repeat it.

So I turn to the history that I know best, which is my own personal history in psychotherapy.

In 1953, during my psychoanalytical training, I was invited to select two books as gifts to myself from the Ella Freeman Sharp Memorial Fund. The two that I chose reflect the two tracks that I have followed in my career and represent the vantage point, the binocular vision, from which I attempt my survey. You will, I hope, gather what that position is from my description of these two volumes.

One book was *Trends in Psychoanalysis* by Marjorie Brierley, published two years earlier in 1951. Marjorie Brierley had a very high reputation as a

1   The Arbours Lecture, 11 February 1986. Published in: *British Journal of Psychotherapy* (1987) 4, 1, 76–85.

theoretician in the British Society. The book is a closely argued set of reflections on the development of psychoanalysis by a wise woman whose breadth of knowledge and of vision is evident. Naturally she discusses Kleinian psychology, particularly the concept of internal objects, and points out how Melanie Klein often uses perceptual rather than conceptual terms in her series, and thereby mixes the language of fantasy and of abstract terminology. Whilst appreciative of Klein's contributions, Brierley doubts whether Klein and her followers through their preoccupation with internalised objects have not perhaps become mystics who have developed a magical technique to deal with these objects. She suggests that neither should we be bound by the Old Testament according to Freud, and that we cannot profit by a gospel of the good object. To that I add the dogma of the Exact Interpretation as laid down by Edward Glover (1931).

I had not opened Brierley's pages for many years until preparing this talk and I was impressed by what I had read many years ago and had quite forgotten. She stands for the study of the whole psyche, of the total personality, for psychoanalysis as a neo-realistic humanism. She points to the weakness of the psychoanalytic theory of affects, saying that we must not only register and interpret affect in object and impulse terms but must analyse the affects themselves, that insofar as we are able to unravel the complex skein of a composite affect so we lay bare a fragment of developmental history. It is essential to enable the patient to feel the feeling as originally entertained about the introjected objects and this we can achieve through our empathy, our direct contact with the patient's affects. She points towards our need for a much greater grasp of the phenomenology of psychological experiences. How weak affect theory is, is illustrated by the recent belated recognition of the importance of the differentiation of the affects of guilt and shame, a subject to which Joe Berke (1989) has significantly contributed.

The other track that I have followed is illustrated through my second book choice. This was not the work of cool meta-psychology blended with scientific humanism by a proper member of the English school of psychoanalysis. It was written by a Danish/Austrian painter turned psychoanalyst and child analyst, Eric Erikson (1965). The book *Childhood and Society* had a profound impact upon me but Erikson's influence was in no way reflected in psychoanalytical training at that time. His work was considered deviationist, lightweight, not proper psychoanalysis. His urging for the concept of identity, the forerunner of today's focus upon the self, found favour neither with Anna Freud nor with Melanie Klein. The psycho-social had no place with the psycho-sexual and his great broad sweeps of childhood development in relation to different cultures was not at that time welcome. But my interest *was* in the social as well as in the individual and this dual track interest found a natural home in the group analytic movement, at the Cassel Hospital then under the inspiring leadership of Tom Main.

This, then, is my vantage point: the dynamic of psychic and social, of individual and group. Let me remind you of the framework given to us by a contemporary of Marjorie Brierley, John Rickman, a leading member of the Psychoanalytic Society between the two Wars and one of Bion's closest and earliest collaborators. Rickman, anthropologist, psychiatrist, Quaker, a fine integrator of the human sciences with psychoanalysis, pointed out (1957) that in the human sciences we deal with numbers. In psychology there is a one-body psychology, a two-body psychology, a three-body psychology, and so on. Classical psychology isolates the individual into a one-body framework confined to a laboratory context. Psychoanalysis is a two-body psychology working in the setting of a relationship between two persons, but in that same setting of the two bodies there is always a third or more. Thus psychoanalysis is a bridge between sociology, the study of the many. Fritz Redl (1966) was making the same point in his own way when he said that if you look under the psychoanalytic couch there is always a group hiding beneath it. In the analytic setting we have the analytic space, the transitional area of Donald Winnicott in which we pursue the eternal task of keeping the inner and outer worlds related and yet separate, and preserving a space for play, for illusion and for creativity. There are always pressures to push us to one side or to the other, to go back to the pure one-body psychology or outwards to the three-body psychology, but if we give way to those pressures we lose the essential dynamic tension that is psychoanalysis.

I wonder if John Rickman knew the words of Emerson that for me bear a striking resemblance to his one-, two- and three-body framework. Emerson (1920) wrote: 'I had three chairs in my home, one for solitude, two for friendship, three for society'.

I shall be returning to this question of the basic models of psychotherapy. In developing my theme, 'Change and Innovation, Decay and Renewal in Psychotherapy', we will have to consider the nature of the institutions through which psychotherapy is taught and the ways in which change can enter into these institutions, the conditions of resistance and acceptance that they manifest. Our host, The Arbours Association, has in the course of my own professional lifetime become a recognised and respected institution that now celebrates its 15th anniversary, but I can well remember the time when it was comparatively friendless, regarded with some suspicion and when there was very little understanding of its ways of working. When we have to deal with institutions we meet with the problems of the dynamics of institutions, of politics, the taking of positions from which what is acceptable or not acceptable is defined. The very psychoanalytic situation itself has been defined as an institution by the South American analyst Bleger, who wrote: 'A relationship which lasts for years and in which a set of norms and attitudes is kept up is indeed an institution' (1967, p.511). But what happens when an individual becomes an institution, for this is the history of psychoanalysis where the institution has been formed by the personality and the work of Freud. Emerson (1920) had some interesting things to say about this also; first, 'An individual is always mistaken'. This might lead us to suppose that institutions can correct the mistakes of the individual and, indeed, this is a basic tenet of group analysis, that the group can represent the norm from which each individual is a deviant. Thus the group under suitable conditions has the capacity for correction of individual errors. It is of course important that the group or the institution does not coerce individuals into conformity with the group norms, but that the situation is such that the individuals who make up the group are able to achieve autonomy and yet arrive at shared points of view.

The second thing that Emerson (1920) had to say about institutions is: 'An institution is the length and shadow of one man'. We need, therefore, to understand better the figure of the man Freud in whose shadow we all live and, in this country, to understand the shadow of Melanie Klein as well.

For a better understanding of these two great figures we have to turn to history, to their personal history, to the history of their times; in Freud's case that of late nineteenth century Austria.

The well-known biographers of Freud do not, in my opinion, do justice to Freud's social context and the dynamics of his personal struggle to evolve within this context. Recent historical work which deals with such aspects as Freud's Jewish identity and how this affected his evolution as a citizen and as a scientist do more justice to Freud in this respect, and enable us to obtain some new perspectives on his personal involvement in the evolution of psychoanalytic theory and practice.

Freud, born into the optimistic Jewish generation of the 1860s, when Jewish emancipation was enforced, was part of the great surge of Jewish talent that entered into the professions. For the first time in Central Europe, Jews could now aspire to high political and professional positions. Freud himself wrote how every clever Jewish boy now carried a minister's portfolio in his knapsack, and this indeed was his own early ambition. He intended to study law in order to take up a political career and it was only in his late teens that he changed to a scientific career. Indeed he was jealous of a young man, a few years older than himself, who had managed to combine a career in politics and in psychiatry, Freud's own profession. This man was Victor Adler, who had a distinguished career both in psychiatry and in politics and who eventually became the first Foreign Minister of the post-war Austrian socialist government. Such was Freud's rivalry that he even challenged Adler to a duel after an angry confrontation in a debate when Freud, worsted in an argument, insulted Adler and wanted to fight with him. Though Adler calmly ignored this provocation their paths crossed yet again. Adler worked in the same laboratory as Freud, that of Brucke, came from a prosperous family and had married at a time when Freud's poverty and uncertainties prolonged his lengthy engagement. In one of his letters Freud writes about this jealousy after having visited Adler in his family home in Bergasse 19, the house which Freud himself later bought on impulse without apparently recognising the dynamics behind his choice.

So here we have the ambitious young Jewish physician whose culture heroes, whose ego ideals, were those great men who had fought the power of the Catholic Church, had advanced the cause of secularism, who had also directly helped Jews to obtain some release from religious and political oppression. There is Cromwell, after whom Freud named his second son Oliver. Cromwell, tolerant of Jews, opposed to Catholicism and, like Oedipus, a regicide. Other heroes included Napoleon, Garibaldi, Bismark; left-wing Jewish political leaders appeared in his dreams, Ferdinand Lasalle and Ernest Lasker. They served as inspirations, these persons who showed that work, talent and dedication could bring about great positions for Jews. But by the 1880s the outlook for Jewish progress had darkened. Anti-Semitic forces had gathered strength and Freud felt the currents running against him. As he struggled to make progress within the Christian medical community of Vienna, he turned more and more to the Jewish brotherhood, the B'nai B'rith, to whom he gave many of his important papers, and certainly much of his warmth and fellowship went towards them. The first 17 members of the Psychoanalytic Society were all Jews. We have to take into account in the development of Freud's psychoanalysis his position of feeling embattled with his environment. A striking example of how strongly Freud felt about the hostility of the environment and which shows his hatred of it is seen in what he himself called his 'revolutionary dream'. Shortly after he had embarked upon his momentous self-analysis, brought about by the impact of his father's death, he had this revolutionary dream. It was provoked by the sight of Count Thun, the Prime Minister of Austria, stalking arrogantly to his special train at Vienna Central Station where Freud, the humble possessor of an ordinary train ticket, was leaving for a holiday. Filled with rage and hatred at the sight of the Count, Freud caught himself whistling Figaro's aria, 'If the Count wants to dance then I'll call the tune'. In his dream Freud is in an angry confrontation with the Count at a political meeting, as he had once had a confrontation with his rival, Victor Adler. In the next scene of the dream Freud retreats from the political meeting into the halls of the University of Vienna, and the final scene of the dream is back at the railway station where he now holds a urinal to a helpless old man. In his analysis of the dream Freud uncovers his oedipal struggle with his father and analyses the final scene as an oedipal victory over his once dominant and potent father. Thus in the dream the political figure, the Count who had precipitated the dream, is reduced to a mere father figure whom Freud can now triumph over. The political reality that the Count actually had power over Freud's whole society is ignored; that the dream retreats from politics into the academic world of the university, which follows Freud's own giving up of political ambitions and becoming a scientist, is unremarked. Thus Freud is able to reduce all environmental conflicts; all situations of rage and helplessness are re-presented in terms of a universal infantile oedipal phase; one aspect of current reality can be pushed aside and the past takes the place of the present. Thus politics is replaced by Freud's invention of psychoanalysis where he himself is the triumphant leader. Psychoanalysis replaces politics and parricide replaces regicide. Where it can be shown that we are all driven by the same instincts, we are all democratically equal and the psychoanalyst can even become a master of the politician.

I suggest that this is one of the significant problems in the psychoanalytic framework, the withdrawal from a full grasp of personal reality, and that the work of many of the so-called deviationists represents natural attempts to re-place society in the psychoanalytic dialectic of human development. One of the most notable early deviants, Alfred Adler, who was an active socialist all his life, emphasised social interest, man's involvement in society. Within the psychoanalytic movement he had embarked on the exploration of narcissism, of feelings of painful inferiority and inadequacy, the defences that we erect against them, over-compensation and grandiosity. He was a sensitive observer of the current social scene and opposed Freud's ideas that the problems of feminine development related to notions of psychic castration; he pointed out that women had very real reasons to feel rendered passive and helpless in society. In many ways Adler was a precursor of Kohut and of self-psychology, a significant recent contribution to psychoanalysis.

Indeed, because Freud was an individual, though an individual of genius, as Emerson (1920) has put it, he was bound to be mistaken, and each of Freud's own mistakes was perceived by his early collaborators and became the focus of great controversy as the group itself struggled to regain the norm from which Freud himself had become the outstanding deviant. Ferenczi, Groddeck and Reich stood for the reconsideration of the body as more than the source of the instinctual impulses; Rank for will, courage and creativity in motivating forces; Jung for a less reductionistic biological position.

Psychoanalysis, one of the highest achievements of nineteenth century science, engages us in the great metaphors that emerge from the eighteenth century age of Enlightenment. Hydraulic and steam power gave us models for mental mechanisms; geological strata for the layering of the mind; archaeology for the uncovering of past cultures; anthropology for the mind of the savage. The German philosophies of Kant and Hegel, Schopenhauer and Nietzsche, German romantic psychiatry, gave Freud the foundation for a model of the mind driven by deep unconscious forces.

History helps us to see how the original psychoanalytic model of an intrapsychic unconscious, a one-body psychology based on neurophysiology, came into existence through man's reshaping of his world view through the evolution of modern science. How did this notion of man's inner life, his interiority appear? For this is the basic substrate for the model of an individual mind driven by instinctual forces. As the phenomenologist Romanyshyn (1982) has demonstrated, in modern psychology psychological life appears in a world that is defined by physics and by physiology, that is, in the world view created by Copernicus, Galileo, Newton and Vesalius. Our psychological life is reflected through the physical world and the physical body, and through these mirrors psychological life is interiorised. Let me illustrate this argument by describing to you the phenomenologist's analysis of the portrait of the Mona Lisa. Painted in the early sixteenth century, the Mona Lisa faces us with her enigmatic smile, her back is turned to the neutral landscape. Her smile separates her from the landscape, none of which reflects the meaning of that smile. Walter Pater wrote: 'Her smile seals an *inner* self who is estranged from the landscape. She is older than the rocks among which she sits and like the vampire, she has been dead many times and learned the secrets of the grave'. By seeing her we are drawn through her smile into a state of blindness from the world. Her portrait was painted 100 years before Descartes dreamt his dream of reason and the Cartesian world view was born. With Descartes we move from a world of subjects into the new world of objects through which we have gained so great a mastery of the forces of nature but, consequently, we have lost much of the vision of man's wholeness in body, mind and spirit. Freud gave to those psychic inscapes of the modern mind their depth and their history. Through a historical perspective we are enabled to recognise that Freud's vision was of an interiorised world, a world in which we are all fundamentally isolated in a democratic world of instinctual forces that act indiscriminately upon us all and where, basically, individual differences disappear. It is through the development of object relations theory, especially in this country through such work as Winnicott's and Bion's, that we have begun to replace this isolated interiority in which we are driven either by lustful, greedy or envious forces. We begin to regain a fuller vision of human interrelatedness. Therefore we are led to reconsider that momentous moment in psychoanalytic history, September 1897 when Freud decided that he could no longer consider his patients' stories of sexual seduction as real. He decided that they must be fantasies that represented unconscious wishes that had not, in most cases, been realised, that had not actually involved other persons' actions. One month later Oedipus appears for the first time in Freud's letter to Fliess. With Oedipus Freud encloses the infantile wish within a universal drama of taboo and of incest. The child's wish, the adult patient's imagination of the wishful child, is not now an index of relatedness with others. It has become a symbol of everyone's internal dilemma. Romanyshyn describes Freud as a Descartes of the depth; in a Cartesian world reality is defined in empirical principles. Either the child is actually seduced by the parent or the child wished to seduce the parent. One or the other is guilty; there is no alternative.

What, then, could be the alternative? It is there if we can change our world view. It is a view of the world in which the relationships between individuals, as well as with the things of that world such as styles of dress, of furniture or of architecture, cover more than they reveal of the living human body and of psychological life in all its complexity. Sexuality becomes the hidden and forbidden wish of the helpless child. The story of what happens between people is replaced by the story of what happens within the isolated child. And indeed how isolated is that child without the nurturance and guidance of caretaking adults whose biology and culture shape their capacities to receive and to respond to their infant's needs. The Kohutian notion of self-objects replaces the primary social unit into its right place as the cradle of sound human relations and development.

In the past two decades we again have become more aware of the reality of adult traumas upon dependent and helpless children. Within psychoanalysis Jeffrey Masson (1984) and Alice Miller (1985) have urged us to reconsider the facts of psychological life and to remove the veil from our eyes that Freud wove in September 1897.

Masson accumulated historical material of Freud's time in Paris when for the first time the reality of parental sexual crimes towards children was properly examined, and shows that undoubtedly this gave a new perspective to Freud's formative experiences. Alice Miller suggests that Freud abandoned his trauma theory for the drive theory because he himself was unable in his great essay in self-analysis fully to relive his early traumas without the help of an empathic non-judgmental person. For without this the pain and the fear of revenge by offended internalised figures are intolerable, and Fliess was unable to play that particular role.

Remember how Freud introduced the figure of Oedipus to explain his own self-uncovering and universalised his lonely experience? Oedipus is the one who is driven by inner forces to kill his father and to sleep with his mother. Just how one-sided a view this is of the Oedipus legend has been strikingly brought to our attention by John Ross (1982). He has enlarged our view of the whole Oedipus myth and shown us Freud's remarkable selectivity in his rendering. In Freud's rendering the figure of the father, Laius, has no real presence other than as the victim of Oedipal rivalry. Yet in the full legend Laius himself is an orphaned child at the age of one, his throne is usurped by his uncle; expelled from his home he becomes a wanderer, a pederast whose homosexual crimes lead to his being cursed by the father of the boy whom he has sodomised. The curse is that he will long remain childless and then be murdered by his son. Thus the prophecy is a revenge that originates from family outrage.

Laius, fearful of the prophecy, abjures sexual intercourse with Jocasta. Finally she intoxicates and seduces him and it is the child of that seduction whom Laius sadistically and fearfully exposes to bring about his death. Laius acts evilly towards his infant son, even pinioning his foot to stigmatise him. As a father Laius is unable to identify with his child, to be a parental self-object. A violent and cowardly man, others have to act for him. He clings greedily and possessively to his wife; understandably the child is orphaned and driven out to become a wanderer.

Oedipus, raised by foster parents whom he leaves to avoid the fulfilment of his oracle, meets this murderous father at the crossroads; he raises his arm against this furious stranger who would strike him down and acts in ignorance and in self-defence.

Nowhere does Freud mention Laius' crimes. He ignores the reality of the family, of the interpersonal reality. His eye is turned inwards towards inner drives and fantasy.

In his old age Oedipus was honoured and shepherded by a daughter, as was Freud by his daughter, and by a good princess. At the end of his life Oedipus is redeemed by Theseus, the slayer of the minotaur, good son of a good loving father who was the civilised opposite of Laius, the fatherless and primitive autocrat.

In today's society we must redream our own vision of childhood, a larger vision than Freud's, and see how we have emerged from an era where the violated child has been focused upon as the source of sexual desire, hatred and envy. What has been ignored is the desire, hatred and envy of the parents. The oedipal theory made it possible to treat the child, now seen as having sexual desires, as an object of adult didactic or therapeutic efforts. One of the founders of Arbours, Morton Schatzman (1973), has contributed signally to this re-vision by his work on Schreber's father, showing the real torments to which he subjected not only his son but a whole generation of German youth.

Alice Miller suggests that we ascribe to children what we are ashamed of in ourselves and would like to be rid of, in keeping with the way in which traditional power structures operate.

This is not to deny that children do indeed have sexual fantasies and desires. This is the great contribution of psychoanalysis. But a taboo in our society, a hidden dimension within our social unconscious, is to recognise and to limit the rights of adults to put children to whatever use they please if it satisfies their needs.

How often do we really appreciate that child murder is much more frequent and cruel a crime than is parricide? In the Latin American world, organisations against filicide have drawn public attention to this danger because of its great prevalence. Once again in Western Europe we are becoming more conscious of this tragic dimension of human existence.

Our historical perspective enables us to recognise the strength and the persistence of the great metaphors of Western science in our late twentieth-century theories and practice. What do we have to add to, and if necessary replace, those great lessons? Surely we must give a prominent place to communication and to linguistics as presented by, say, Rycroft, Sharer and Lacan; the biology of the infant/mother pair, studies initiated by Spitz and continued by such as Emde, Sander and Stern; the child developmental studies of Piaget, which have been integrated with psychoanalytic theories by George Klein and by Kegan, ethology as presented by Bowlby. In 1966 my late friend and colleague James Home issued a bold challenge to us to debate the nature of mind and to ally psychoanalysis with the humanities rather than with the natural sciences. It is my belief that if psychoanalytic training does not reflect these contemporary issues, it isolates itself and becomes a closed system doomed to run down in momentum and in allegiance.

I said earlier that I would return to the question of power and of tradition. I take up this theme again with respect to the nature of institutions. As psychotherapists our working lives and our training are defined by the nature of our training institutions. The American historian, Carrol Quigley (1979), has identified a process that he calls, 'the institutionalisation of instruments' that he considers applies to all institutions.

In the pursuit of progress human beings fashion instruments, entities which aim at progress, discovery, evolution. Imperceptibly, little by little, the entity begins to work for itself, for its own self-preservation. This is like the passage from the poetic to the prosaic, from *mystique* to *politique*. Organisations which are on the way to institutionalisation gradually become less effective in their function, giving rise to discontent, to calls for change and reform. When these are resisted conflict and controversy arise. A tension of development develops between those representing the establishment, as Bion calls them, who enjoy the fruits of the fights acquired by the institution, and the reformers who aim to transform the institution once again into a more efficient instrument.

A culmination of three possible results can develop from this tension development. They are reform, reaction and evasion. Reform re-instrumentalises the institution. In reaction the establishment is the victor. In evasion the institution is honoured and its rights given to a new instrument as, in our country, the monarch retains honour and respect but the task of government is taken over by Parliament and the Prime Minister.

Institutions value and further orderly methods of administration and training. We develop syllabuses that steadily become more comprehensive and rigorous. Within the institution itself there is dynamic tension that can be described as that between organisation and ordination. Organisation, from the word 'organism', represents life, change, development. Ordination, coming from 'order', prevails in hierarchies, libraries and cemeteries. Forests are disorderly but organised. Ordinated systems maintain hierarchy for they are devoted to maintaining privilege and the authority of the establishment. There is a powerful case being made today that Strachey's *Authorised Version* of Freud's writings represents such an ordinated system, that puts forward the privileged viewpoint of E. Jones and his collaborators and represents a significant distortion of Freud's psychoanalysis.

Training (and psychoanalytic training in some respects is a prime example) follows the model of ordination and gives rise to discipleship, to schools of look-alike Freudians, Kleinians and even *mirabile dictu* independents.

One of the most experienced of psychoanalytic educators, Jacob Arlow (1982), has pointed to the conservatism of psychoanalytic education, that it clings to the past, still using as primary textbooks those that are now 75 to 80 years old. 'Like their hysterical patients, analysts suffer too, mainly from reminiscences' (p.18). Psychoanalytic institutes, like many communities, consolidate themselves around mythologies. Ours is that of the mythic hero, the progenitor of the race, Freud (or Klein), who together with a beleaguered band of scholars struggle to promulgate a revolutionary insight into the mind of man. The problem with such myths is that the idealisation and the dogma hide the ambivalence and, by necessity, create opponents who attack the true cause which can then be defended with zeal by the defenders of the faith, the guardians of the sacred flame, the protectors of the remnants of the true cross.

Mythologies are transmitted through initiation rites which to achieve their aims must arouse affect at nodal points of development and education. It is a regrettable fact of psychological life that the most effective affect is that of cruelty. The remoulding of personality then takes place defensively as an identification with the cruel aggressor. The harsher the initiatory experience, in this case the training analyst, the more devoted in the long run is the disciple. Indeed how often seminars and supervisions seem to be conducted in atmospheres of fear and suspicion which therefore block development of dialogue, of free discussion and the development of autonomy in students.

The elders of the tribe, here known as training analysts, enjoy privileges of power and of access to secret information and esoteric knowledge. In the minds of the initiates they are identified with the primal progenitor and thus illusions of grandeur are projected on to them. It follows therefore that it is by the attainment of that idealised status that the members of the community hope to lay to rest forever their nagging fears of inferiority and of incompletion. How, then, are we to bring together the dynamics of the training institutions and the analyst's personal project in his training analysis?

Psychoanalysis demands that the individual discover, recover his unique self and must therefore always be in conflict with his own training institutions, Doestoevsky's conflict of the Grand Inquisitor condemning Christ the Reformer.

The reformers, the dis-established, have to forge their own instruments in order to evolve new ideas and new techniques. For the past 15 years the Arbours Association has formed such a new instrument, putting forward ideas about human development and new ways of working with human breakdown. Now the Arbours has reached the stage of recognition, institutional support and training programmes.

I offer them my congratulations and goodwill and these final thoughts. That, less burdened by allegiance to a past progenitor, they may retain freedom from dogma and cherish a relative ignorance of the workings of the mind for, 'by ignorance we mistake, and by mistakes we learn'. In a recent paper on humanism and the science of psychoanalysis, Lichtenberg compares our present views on the psychoanalytical process with earlier ones. The psychoanalyst used to occupy the position of a scientific observer, objectively monitoring a process equidistant, as Anna Freud put it, from id, ego and super ego. By contrast the contemporary psychoanalyst is deeply involved in a two-person experience in which both parties are under strain. It is at the juncture and interaction of those strains that the dynamic leverage of psychoanalysis takes effect. The shifting strains call for definition and for the discovery of meaningful emotions, discoveries that emerge through inevitable failures, gross or partial, that precede success and understanding. The creativity of the analytic experience emerges when the analyst, staying in a state of 'negative capability', resists premature reaching after knowledge. The work of both parties in the experience is to reach across these failures in communication and comprehension, and this work is the curative dynamic of psychoanalysis.

These are my final thoughts to our hosts, the Arbours Association, to whom by being here we have extended our good wishes for their future: That in psychoanalysis we live with the dynamic tension imposed by these two polarities.

And those who cannot remember the past are condemned to repeat it. And by ignorance we mistake, and mistakes we learn.

References

Arlow, J. (1982) 'Psychoanalytic education: a psychoanalytic perspective.' In *Annual of Psychoanalysis 10*. New York: International Universities Press.

Berke, J.H. (1989) *The Tyranny of Malice*. New York: Simon and Schuster.

Brierley, M. (1951) *Trends in Psychoanalysis*. London: Hogarth Press.

Emerson, R.W. (1920) *The Works of R.W. Emerson. Vol.5*. London: Macmillan.

Erikson, E. (1965) *Childhood and Society*. Harmondsworth: Penguin.

Masson, J. (1984) *Freud: The Assault on the Truth*. London: Faber and Faber.

Miller, A. (1985) *Thou Shall Not Be Aware: Society's Betrayal of the Child*. London: Pluto Press.

Quigley, C. (1979) *The Evolution of Civilizations*. Indianapolis: Liberty Press.

Redl, F. (1966) *When We Deal with Children*. New York: Free Press.

Rickman, J. (1957) *Selected Contributions to Psychoanalysis.* London: Hogarth Press.

Romanyshyn, R. (1982) *Psychological Life, from Science to Metaphor.* Milton Keynes: Open University Press.

Ross, J.M. (1982) 'Oedipus revisited: Laius and the "Laius Complex". In A. Solnit and R.S. Eissler, A. Freud and P.B. Neubauer (eds) *Psychoanalytic Study of the Child 37.* New Haven: Yale University Press.

Schalzman, M. (1973) *Soul Murder. Persecution in the Family.* London: Allen Lane.

Further reading

Klein, D.B. (1985) *Jewish Origins of the Psychoanalytic Movement.* London: University of Chicago Press.

McGrath, W. (1986) *Freud's Discovery of Psychoanalysis.* N.Y. Ithaca: Cornell University Press.

Schorske, K. (1980) *Fin-de-Siecle Vienna.* New York: Knopf.

Szaluta, J. (1983) 'Freud's ego-ideals.' *Journal of American Psychoanalytical Association 31,* 157–86.

CHAPTER 8

What Should a Psychotherapist Know?[1]

When the Association for Psychoanalytic Psychotherapy honoured me with the invitation to deliver their annual address, instantly I knew my title. What more enticing a situation can there be than a captive audience and my very own brief? Now I shall share with you the autumnal harvest of four decades of psychotherapeutic experience – or is it mostly a repetition of one year? – which began as a consumer, with my own venture into training analysis with Adrian Stephen, the brother of Virginia Woolf, at a tender age. I was then a medical student at University College Hospital and slipped off for sessions between ward rounds and lectures. Later, as a psychiatrist at the Maudsley Hospital, I resumed analysis with S.H. Foulkes, somewhat unorthodoxly, as it began in his room in the hospital before we transferred to 22 Upper Wimpole Street. Through Foulkes I came to the wider vision he bequeathed of a psychodynamic psychology that illuminates the difficult dilemmas that beset thoughtful therapists – the relationship of individual to society, biology to culture and how to take account of the immense forces of history in our make-up.

I fear to appear before you in the manner, so beautifully captured by George Henry Lewes, the husband of George Eliot, who wrote of a, 'German actor who excited an admiration which one feels for more mature mediocrity – ripe, perfect, untroubled by a hope of future development'.

The subtitles to my text could well be 'Text and context' or 'How to tell your figure from your ground'. The theme I shall be following is of relating psychotherapeutic ideas and 'facts' to the web of different ideas, ideas of human nature, of self and of mind, of relatedness and society.

---

[1] Association for Psychoanalytic Psychotherapy Lecture, 1989. I dedicate this chapter to the memory of a man whose inspiration, illumination and quite often irritation, stimulated me and so many of my generation. How I would have loved to hear the comments of the late Dr Tom Main.

As an audience you have been in my mind and have already shaped what I shall say to you tonight. Were I speaking in another place not far from here (the Institute of Psychoanalysis) my discourse would be different. The potential reaction of the audience is part of the text and I know that here we are open-minded, friendly fellow-workers in the fields of psychotherapy where our daily task is to practise a psychotherapy that satisfies professional aspirations whilst meeting social needs within the National Health Insurance (NHS). Our foundation matrix, to use a term of S.H. Foulkes, is psychoanalytic psychology, but in our organisation, The Association for Psychoanalytic Psychotherapy in the NHS, we represent several voices. We accommodate other ideas; ours is a forum for dialogue between the most powerful of twentieth-century psychological languages, psychoanalysis, and other languages which will, as Freud wrote, speak in their quiet tones until eventually they are heard. When only one language is heard we are listening to dogma; creative growth comes from constructive dialogue, from the presence of diverse languages called by Michael Bakhtin 'heteroglossia': 'Each culturally predominant group strives to legislate *its* dialect as *the* language, whereas it is, in reality, only one dialect amongst many, albeit the one enjoying the greatest social prestige. That turns other dialects into implicit forms of cultural opposition' (Morson 1986, p.5). As a philosopher of language in Soviet Russia where a plurality of languages was not permitted by the ruling dogmatic ideology, Bakhtin regarded consciousness as the dialogue of 'official language' whilst there is 'an unofficial language' which is suppressed and repressed. This latter he regarded as the language of the unconscious and challenged Freud's ideas that the division between consciousness and unconsciousness is between primary and secondary process. Bakhtin saw Freud 'biologising' that most important and characteristic human resource, language. Some of you may well be shocked at the challenge Bakhtin issues to what he called 'Freudism', that psychoanalysis saves bourgeois man by taking him out of history, by explaining him to himself not as a concrete social entity but as an 'abstract biological organism'. This trenchant statement brings figure and ground together, forcefully admonishing psychoanalysis for having omitted the social. Bakhtin's knowledge of psychoanalysis did not include later developments, the exploration of counter-transference, of the setting, of object relations theory, but his is a voice that should be heard, for we ignore history at our peril. Psychoanalysis will be left stranded if it fails to recognise and to negotiate its ever changing environment.

Let me now tell you a story that I have puzzled over and which I have only recently come to understand. There was a man who owned a fish of which he was very fond. He kept it in its little aquarium where it swam happily, but being a scientifically minded observer he wondered what would happen if he gradually replaced the salty water in which it swam, for this was a salt-water fish, with pure water. So day by day he replaced the salt water with pure water until the fish was happily swimming in unsalted water. The next step in this scientific odyssey was gradually to reduce the amount of water in the aquarium. Daily he took some water out, and by the end of his experiment the fish was quite happily frisking about in no water at all! So he added a perch and a swing and his fish occupied itself jumping around and swinging in the air. The sad end of my story is that one day whilst jumping from its trapeze, the fish accidentally fell into its bowl of water and there it drowned. I have puzzled over the meaning of this sad little tale, as did two German colleagues, who after they had heard me tell this story asked, 'would you please explain the joke because we do not find it funny'. I was not able to explain it then but I believe that I can now. The fish is the figure and the water is its ground; no entity can be removed from its ground without being suspended, as it were, in the air. The cost of doing this is that the organism is no longer adapted to its original medium, so thus the fish that has become bird drowns when it is returned to its matrix.

What sort of history brings psychotherapy and society together as figure and ground? As a model I take Theodore Zeldin's (1977) exemplary work in the Oxford History of Modern Europe: 'France 1848–1945'. Volume Two is entitled Intellect, Taste and Anxiety; chapter headings are: 'Education and Hope'; 'Logic and Verbalism'; 'Privilege and Culture'; 'Good and Bad Taste'; 'Fashion and Beauty'; 'Science and Comfort'; 'Happiness and Humour'; 'Eating and Drinking'; 'Private Lives'; 'Individualism and Emotions'; 'Worry, Boredom and Hysteria'; 'Birth and Death', and as a final flourish, 'Hypocrisy'. What rich readings await us when we can bring the personal, the social and the historical together in a history of this country.

Now I sketch the chapter headings for a book that would present issues with which I believe psychotherapists should engage. It would begin with an historical approach, an historical psychology and anthropology that asks questions about human nature and human society and which shows how inextricably they are woven together. 'Self and society' leads on to 'self and other', to dialogue and alterity, the intertwining of self-knowledge and self-recognition with the awareness and recognition of others. This section might be entitled 'I and me: we and us' and would grapple with relationship issues and 'the effects of relationships on relationships', to use the title of the recent John Bowlby conference. Here the affective, cognitive and conative aspects of personality would be brought together with psychoanalytic, neo-Piagetian and other dynamic developmental studies, all of which show the profound effects of early relationships on the growing infant and which are so clearly seen in infant observation by trained observers. What the observer sees, using eyes and sensitivity, is one vantage point; the other comes from video tape evidence, from Stern, Trevarthen and others, through which we can see the effect of disturbed relationships, and can also see how happy natural relationships are needed and sought for, indeed called out for, by the infant from caregivers. As Trevarthen said, we learn about human development best through the study of happy relationships; just as Bakhtin said that 'alterity is a merry science'. I shall explain that in a moment. Within the field of relationships I would like to see chapters on reciprocity, sharing, friendship, on peer relationships throughout life, 'selfobjects' as the Kohutians term them. Emotions would take a large part of this book, emotions as the moving forces that both connect and separate us with and from others; how emotions originate from the universal physiological anlage of our Darwinian heritage and are then constructed by the opportunities and constraints of family and society: love, desire and need; fear, anger and hate; envy and jealousy; guilt, shame and pride; the wide spectrum of our affective life. There would be an important chapter on the face, that most expressive and communicative organ of the body, which would explore the psychological and philosophical implications of the face-to-face relationship, the I–thou of Martin Buber, the face that asks for the justice and understanding of Emmanuel Levinas. Psychoanalysis has not sufficiently deeply engaged with the eye and the gaze, nor indeed with the ear, with man as a sonorous being, matters to which I shall turn later, if I still have your sympathetic ear.

Then on to those mysterious 'co' words, consciousness, community, common-place, co-operation, common sense, cohesion and coherence. These words are signs to our us-ness, that the human mind is communal as well as personal at all levels. Before there is spoken language there is the language, the choreography, of gesture and response, the proto-conversations, the dialogues, through which the emerging self is in-formed. There would be difficult chapters on language, and psychotherapists would have to re-view the ways in which we offer our hearing and our speech, our sole clothes in the therapeutic domain. We would study how psychoanalysis contributes to the life story as a narrative, notions of action language, of the drive for coherency and would elaborate that mysterious incoherence without which Freud said there could not be a neurosis. The fiendish complexity of Lacan and the French school would have to be tackled. And for the development and significance of language we would have to turn to Russia, to Vigotsky and to Bakhtin whose analysis of language has opened new vistas.

I have already spoken about Bakhtin's challenge to psychoanalysis, that at a critical time in Western history psychoanalysis attempts to save bourgeois man by taking him out of history, explaining him to himself as an 'abstract biological organism', not as a concrete entity. The alternative view to this was put forward cogently by Masud Khan (1972) who wrote:

> Towards the tail end of the nineteenth century when Freud arrived on the psy-chiatric scene, he found a psychiatric patient being treated either as a bizarre so-cial fetish or endured as a familial nuisance. When he isolated this potential

patient into a therapeutic frame what emerged was a therapeutic situation unique in the history of human experience.

But I think Bakhtin has a wider historical scope here than Khan, though of course the creation of the therapeutic setting is Freud's great contribution to twentieth-century culture, the aquarium that we and our patients swim in. The ideas of Bakhtin may be new to many of you, as they were to me, so I shall give you a brief outline:

Bakhtin, a great Russian intellectual, lived from 1895 to 1945. He wrote about language, literature, psychology, history and aesthetics. A sick man for most of his life, from osteomyelitis which led to the amputation of a leg, he spent many years in exile under Stalin and only towards the end of his life was he rehabilitated, his work recognised and honoured. In 1927 he wrote a book on 'Freudianism' under an assumed name and continued to develop his ideas on language and psychology throughout his life. He was an anti-Marxist, though he had to speak through the 'official language' of his era, and his experience of language and thought control clearly influenced the structure of his ideas, just as Freud likened the censorship of dreams to the censorship that he had experienced in the Austro-Hungarian Empire.

Bakhtin's approach can be called 'dialogism', that the 'I' can realise itself verbally on the basis of the 'we'. In becoming aware of myself I attempt to look at myself, as it were, through the eyes of another for I cannot actually see myself. I can only see my face in a physical mirror and my self through the mirroring of another person.

Each of us has a unique position in time and space. No other can see what each one of us sees. We all share uniqueness and each of us has a 'surplus of seeing', our own viewpoint. But we need the other to complete ourselves, to give to us what we cannot see, and we can give to the other the vision that he or she needs to complete his or her self. Bakhtin uses the word 'architectonic' for the way in which the self is constructed. I complete the other as he does me. Thus the self is never whole or complete, we are unfinished projects, which for Bakhtin is not a cause for sorrow but an occasion for celebration. The world needs me to give it meaning, just as I need the authority of the other to define myself: 'The other is in the deepest sense my friend. It is only from the other that I can get myself'. Though alterity is what Bakhtin called a merry science, I am reminded of Wilfred Owen's line, 'You are the enemy I killed, my friend'.

The I–other relationship is figure to ground, as are all organism–environmental relationships. The organism must find a good adaptation to the environment, else it perishes. Bakhtin, unlike Kohut and the self psychologists, clothes his concept of the self in a definition: 'Myself is that through which performance I answer other selves and the world from the unique time and place I occupy in existence'. And what he means by performance is: 'A successful performance between me and the other must be shaped into a coherent performance; thus, the architectonic activity of authorship, which is the building of a text, parallels the activity of human existence, which is the building of a self'.

Some final words from Bakhtin: 'What the self is answerable *to* is the social situation: what the self is answerable *for* is the authorship of its responses'.

Figure and ground

What should therapists know about figure and ground, a concept which does not appear much in psychoanalysis, but which is basic to group analysis? You will no doubt remember it as an interesting aspect of perception, nicely illustrated by Rubin's Vasewhich indicates instability and reversibility but which is not recognisably connected with the process of psychotherapy. Yet I shall argue that it is and that our art is shallow in its absence. The figure–ground concept states that no entity exists in isolation. All is embedded and contextual. An individual is figure against the ground of his network of family, work, the micro- and macro-society. To see a 'patient' is to see a person in a particular context of therapy. Choosing individual, or marital, family or group therapies we change the figure–ground constellation. Therapists should know 'by acquaintance' not only 'by description' the therapeutic potentialities of these contexts and give them equal weighting both in diagnosis and decision-making. Sadly, therapists seem mainly to divide into conflicting camps to the patient's disadvantage, for they lose overall perspective which could enable them to make more appropriate decisions.

I want to go further: each theory stands on the ground of another more encompassing idea. The idea of a psychodynamic therapy stands on the ground of a theory of development and psychopathology which itself is embedded in the history of ideas of its epoch. All ideas, all actions are permeated by history more than therapists appreciate. In our education we are schooled in this or that approach, informed of its correctness, and other approaches are disregarded or said to be deviances. A more encompassing history of psychotherapy will show that most of these so-called deviances have only isolated and identified areas that later are reintegrated with the mainstream. Adler recognised the early forces of aggression and narcissism, described neurotic character formation and emphasised social factors; Jung, the unfolding of individuation and integration throughout life; Ferenczi and Alexander the primacy of relationship over interpretation. The 'Controversial Discussions' of the British Psycho-Analytical Society are well known; self psychology, little regarded in this country, represents a new critical paradigm that I shall turn to later. And outside the psychoanalytic domain, there are the essential contributions of neo-Piagetians and the cognitive psychologists.

The theory and process of group analysis are situated on a figure–ground basis of social and individual psychologies, both intrinsic aspects of the human being.

Group analysis accepts the historical matrix of personality and takes into account the social facts that psychoanalysis seems to discount. An example of this is Foulkes' enthusiasm for the work of Norbert Elias (1978). In his seminal work, The Civilising Process, Elias showed that in the West between the twelfth and eighteenth centuries, the state began to monopolise violence so that individuals were obliged to master their impulses, which led to the growth of social peace; another process was the tightening of interpersonal relations which also brought about more severe controls on emotions. Thereby the characteristic modern individual of Western society emerges as self-controlled and interdependent. 'The particular stability of the apparatus of mental self-restraint which emerges as a decisive trait built into the habits of every 'civilized' human being, stands in the closest relationship to the monopolisation of physical force and the growing stability of the central organ of society'. In these societies we become attuned from infancy to a highly regulated and differentiated pattern of self-restraint which becomes second nature, 'a shift from social constraint to self-constraint'. Elias traced this process through the history of Courtly society which set the patterns which were adopted by other areas of society. Elias laid the ground for 'historical psychology' and, for instance, challenged the concept of an id without history; the relationship between id, ego and super ego changes in the course of the civilising process. The drives are not timeless, universal, outside of history. The impulsiveness of the thirteenth-century man and the impulsiveness of twentieth-century man, their attitudes to their impulses, the permissions and restraints that they experience, are laid down through the historical civilising process. An understanding of historical psychology can release us from the tyranny of so-called correct or exact concepts that claim to grasp the nature of the human psyche, but which represent disguised totalitarian approaches.

The story of Oedipus

The Oedipus Complex is the keystone of Freud's architecture of psychic development and structure. The oedipal stage represents the main doorway into the social world through which we pass to emerge gendered.

But psychotherapists should know that there is far more to the story of Oedipus than Freud chose to present; indeed there is a family history for Oedipus that begins with the story of his father Laius, which would have been well known to the Greek spectators of the oedipal plays. (Here is a seminal example of the separation of figure from ground, of how the whole configuration changes once we reinsert what is missing.)

The father of Laius, the grandfather of Oedipus, died when Laius was but a year old, leaving him in the care of his mother when his uncle usurped the throne. Later Laius was forced to leave both Thebes and his mother. We next encounter him as an adult in Pisa, where he kidnaps and sodomises Chrysippus, the beautiful illegitimate son of his host, King Pelops. The infuriated father curses Laius, invoking also the curses of Zeus and Hera, and condemns him 'long to remain childless', then to be murdered by the son he conceives and, furthermore, that his son will replace him in his wife's bed.

Laius, mindful and fearful of this curse, abjures sexual intercourse with Jocasta until finally in her frustration she intoxicates and seduces him into the conception of their fateful son.

Though there are many other episodes to this family story, let us look at what there is for psychotherapists to learn in this fuller account.

First, there is a perverse history to the father of Oedipus. In Freud's version the dynamic is largely within Oedipus himself and Freud withholds the story of the perverse father, his fear of his son and his filicidal rage.

Next, behind the story of the one is the story of many, of the family and of their society. John Ross (1981), whose account I am presenting to you, writes that, 'we cannot overlook the intricacies of the interpersonal element and the tragic unconscious dialogue even though they mar the classic elegance of our admired theory'.

Third, and this applies to all our reading and learning, we must seek out the source material and read it for ourselves. We should listen to those lone voices who question received knowledge and who ask us to look and to think again, as Freud himself did, and as indeed those who we consider deviants from his work did also.

The return to the aquarium: psychotherapy and swimming

Why should a psychotherapist know how to swim? Well, I ask you to remember how each of us has learned to swim. First feet on the ground, then splashing about, pretending to move in the water, admiring and envying those who can move in this strange new element. Maybe armbands and rings have helped us to get off the bottom into the new experience of floating; a good supervisor helps. One day we find that we can actually swim; we trust this new element, water, to support us; we enter into a new and harmonious relationship with it. So it is with psychotherapy; we learn to trust ourselves in this new situation of encounter with the other in the shared time–space dimension of the psychotherapy situation. From my own novice experiences I recall only too well the awkward silences, the anxious clutching for ideas of what to do (for instance at what was then the popular Finesinger technique, which is to repeat the last few words that the patient has said with an interrogative inflection, still by the way a valid manoeuvre), the search for the right thing to say. Gradually we come to be better listeners, to trust ourselves and our responses, to find that we can actually enjoy being with the other, seeing how the patient can begin to find sufficient support in a therapeutic situation where he begins to be able to float, to suspend unnecessary irritable movements, to await and to accept the emergence of new thoughts, feelings and images.

And, as in learning to swim, the patient has to feel safe. Anxiety blocks the free movement of the mind. I find that what helps our patients to feel safe enough to venture from the shore is the feeling that they will be understood and responded to. To understand is indeed to stand under the other, to occupy the same emotional and mental space for that moment of time that we need to be able to cope with the emergence of the threatening new that separates us from our own familiar and accepted notions of ourselves and that disrupts connection with the other.

Psychotherapists have widely differing ideas of what patients need from them. There is a spectrum difficult to define, but which Lawrence Friedman (1978) described as a, 'running battle between the claims of understanding and attachment'. He sees this as an ongoing battle in Freud's work and which has characterised our idea of the nature of psychoanalytic treatment. The concept of 'attachment' includes components of the therapeutic situation such as the therapeutic alliance, the working relationship and the transference relationship itself. Understanding refers to the role of insight conveyed through interpretation. Friedman first looks at the symposium on the therapeutic process in the 1936 Marienbad Congress where, amongst others, James Strachey gave his important paper on mutative interpretation. In 1936 the emphasis was on the recognition of introjection as a basic developmental and therapeutic dynamic and, as Friedman (1978) writes: 'One might have concluded that psychoanalysis had found a way to investigate how attachment brings about structural change and how affective elements transmit understanding' (p.533). However, in 1961, at the Edinburgh Congress, there was a symposium on the same theme which I dimly remember, and there was a very different atmosphere. Theorists seemed to recoil from the emphasis on the affective relationship as if they feared to be embroiled in their patient's affective net. Indeed, whoever amongst you has listened to or read Heinz Hartmann will understand that, swimming as he did in the realm of the higher metapsychology, he was not in danger of being caught up in the patient's affective net!

Why the change? Friedman suggests that this was a period of such increasing complexity in psychoanalytic theory that theorists, like the struggling swimmer, grasped at something that offered security, a part aspect of the complex subject, holding on as to a raft in the sea when we feel out of our depth; Tolstoy's words from *War and Peace* catch the essence:

> The combination of phenomena is beyond the grasp of the human intellect. But the impulse to seek causes is innate in the soul of man. And, the human intellect, with no inkling of the immense variety and complexity of circumstances conditioning a phenomenon, any one of which may be separately conceived as the

cause of it, snatches at the first and most easily understood approximation and says – here is the cause. (p.1168)

Around this time, from the 1960s onwards, the swimmer's ability to keep afloat in deep waters such as those that we encounter in painful and intense interactions with 'difficult patients' (to whom we largely give the name 'borderline') was aided by the systematic exploration and recognition of counter-transference. Counter-transference enables us to use our own affective imaginative responses in the better understanding of our patients. Therapists' anxieties and affects, the sadness, despair, anger, the erotic arousal and fantasies of intimacy; through accepting these as *legitimate* elements of the therapists' experience we are more able to be open to ourselves and, hopefully, to create a fuller, more adequate response to what the patient brings to us. There are also dangers here, of regarding all our own responses as originating from the patient's affective field, thereby disregarding our own subjectivity. The use of counter-transference can quite easily degenerate into a disguised blaming of the patient for affective or uncomfortable experiences such as irritation, boredom, distraction, confusion and sleepiness. I suggest that these subjective states are inevitable in the course of a long, hard day of emotional and intellectual involvement with disturbed persons – especially after lunch!

Gradually therapists develop the endurance and stamina needed for our work. Mental athletes, like physical athletes, should take into account the necessary conditions for training up to peak condition and for maintaining good condition over long periods of time. Younger therapists may like the sprint or the hurdles, the dramatic dash for short-term therapies, and later settle for the pace of the middle- and long-distance runner, knowing that the art is long and life is short, but still long enough for experience to be accumulated. I do believe that psychotherapists have a good claim to working into advancing years, though admittedly there is a race between the accumulation of experience and the degeneration of capacity.

What should a psychotherapist know about interpretation? First, the meaning of the word. My dictionary has three renderings for 'interpret': one, to explain or tell the meaning of: to present in understandable form. Two, to conceive in the light of individual belief, judgement or circumstance. Three, to act as an interpreter between speakers of different languages. For 'interpretation': the act or result of interpreting; as artistic interpretation, in performance or adaptation.

Do we not act in all these ways according to the situation? We *explain*, tell meanings, hopefully in understandable form, bearing in mind what Sheridan said in one of his plays: 'Begad, I think the interpreter is the hardest to be understood of the two'. We listen to our patients' language, to understand, to translate into our inner language which we then speak out, the inner language now an outer one, for the patient to hear. When we work with groups we are indeed interpreter between many persons and many languages.

All these different aspects have one thing in common: the psychotherapist's interpretive act is the insertion of himself *through dialogue* into the mental life of the other, individual or group. By our speech acts we present and reveal ourselves to our patients. By our words shall we be known; what we say and how we say it matters a great deal to us and to our patients.

Perhaps you will be saying to yourselves, yes, but we already know that, this is our daily toil so what is it you are trying to say?

First, that we should not waste our efforts in uttering words that will not be heard or understood. We want our patients to listen, to enter into the essential dialogue of listening and of speaking that is psychotherapy. I believe that in our concern to understand what is being said to us and to find our own thoughts and words, we often leave out of the account the listening potential of the patient. Winnicott said that if the patient lacks the capacity to play we must help to develop that; the same applies to listening. The ability to listen openly and attentively disappears in situations of danger, the danger of reproof, of judgement, rejection, shaming, of painful exposure. Perhaps most of all the fear of being 'objectivised', of not being in relation. I believe we only listen, take in and respond to what a therapist says if we feel a personal relationship with the other, in a situation of dialogue, for our truths are personal, part of ourselves, even if unwanted or painful and can only be shared under conditions of trust and mutuality. I bless Donald Winnicott for telling us that towards the end of his life he realised that his task as an analyst was not to make clever or apt interpretations, but rather to give back to the patient what he had brought to him. This is an attitude of respect and mutuality, to give back to the person what they have brought, not as a rebuttal but as an acknowledgement that what had previously belonged to only one now belongs to both, shared in the 'in-between'. Therapy takes place in the 'in-between', not within the patient, though the inner work of reflection, connection and insight undoubtedly occurs, but in the room, our words and our patients' words, our ways of being together, live in the overlap of boundaries between us and, as the anthropologists have shown, when boundaries overlap there is an area of the mysterious, the magical and the sacred. It is from being together in this way, by creating and sharing this new space, that we have our power.

On listening and speaking

A therapist's capacity to listen and skills in speaking should ripen as he matures. He develops a capacity for the evenly hovering attention which gives him perspective into the patient's presence and over his life story. This becomes a relaxed form of attention-giving, of being with and being for the patient, an immersion into the movement of the unfolding life. This involves a 'decentring' from oneself that contains some elements of an 'out of body experience' which helps the therapist to reach towards images of the patient's experience. At some point he begins to clothe these images with words, words to reach the patient's attention and which will enable the patient to share the therapist's vision, and thereby to feel understood.

The skills for this are part of the everyday knowledge of the human condition as lived by ourselves and those about us, greatly deepened by psychoanalysis and by the humanities, of history, literature and language. The broader the vision the more we can encompass the infinite variety of human dilemmas which are presented to us. A therapist should be able to draw on what Rickman called the one-, two- and three-body psychologies, the intrapersonal, the interpersonal and the social. Ralph Waldo Emerson (1920) expressed this same vision when he said that, 'in my room there are three chairs, one for solitude, two for friendship, three for society'. The Spanish philosopher Ortega y Gasset answers the question 'Who am I?' with the response: 'I am myself plus my circumstances'. We both create and are created by circumstances, and the work of therapy has much to do with understanding the interplay of self and surroundings.

The patient brings not only the past as experienced in the present, but also brings hopes and fears for the future, the future of relationships, career and, with the older patient, a hunger to find more understanding of his passage through life towards old age and death, work which comes more easily to the older therapist who has his own life experience to draw upon.

Here again my plea is that theory should not be a procrustean bed for us to be tied to and to which we should not attempt to bind our patients. Theories, like lamp-posts are often used for relief rather than illumination!

On correct and exact interpretations

I propose to look at our aim in giving 'correct' interpretations; this is the ground of enlightenment and reason; that the viewpoint of the analyst should enable him to see beneath the surface of the patient's consciousness and to grasp hidden aspects of the person's mental life. He believes that what is in there, present but hidden, corresponds to the analyst's vision. I shall argue that this approach, though necessary, is not sufficient to understand the nature of our work and the process of revelation and understanding. By revelation I mean that the patient has to be in a position to offer up that aspect of being that needs our understanding; it must sound forth for our hearing and we should be attuned to this emergence to which we have a response-a-bility. Then we share a moment of correspondence, a recognition that a new truth has emerged and lies between us and the listening space of the session. 'Spoken truth shrivels when it falls on a tin ear' (Hoffman 1981, p.279).

On how to make incorrect interpretations

Every therapist should have the courage and ability to make inexact and incorrect interpretations. Let me explain this heresy. Years ago Marjorie Brierley (1951), a fine theoretician of the British school, writing about Melanie Klein's contribution, suggested that while we should not be bound by the Old Testament according to Freud, neither should we profit by the Gospel of the Good Object. There is also a dogma of interpretation as laid down by Edward Glover, followed by James Strachey.

Glover (1931) asserted that an inexact interpretation is accepted with relief by the patient, because he is spared the pain that would be aroused by the more deep-reaching and truthful interpretation, and Strachey (1934) maintained that to be effective a correct interpretation should be mutative. Mutative interpretations are articulated in clear form and directed at the 'point of urgency' of a session. Primarily they concern transferential aspects of a patient's relationship to the analyst, and only on this basis are they experienced by the patient as emotionally immediate and relevant. Strachey asserted that vagueness in an interpretation bolsters the patient's resistances. Against these two great authorities I have to set my own experience, as therapist and as supervisor.

First, does the concept itself of the exact interpretation belong in the domain of psychoanalysis? To me it smacks too much of the 'exact' sciences, an attempt to approximate psychoanalysis to physical or mathematical models. By striving for exactness the therapist is doing something to his patient as object; in this model they are not sharing the same intersubjective space. I am reminded of Ornston's observations that in German Freud uses the same terms when he speaks of the patient and of the analyst, whereas Strachey uses different terms to speak about the analyst and the patient. Through language Strachey separates the patient and therapist and does not situate them in the same experiential world and intersubjective space. That Strachey does this can be recognised nowadays through the greater appreciation of the aim of the *Standard Edition*, which was to present to the English-speaking world an acceptable and quasi-scientific model of psychoanalysis that would gain wide acceptance.

Next, what of the concept of the 'correct' interpretation? The implications of the very 'to correct' leads to ideas of correcting mistakes, correct behaviour, correctional establishments, the implication of someone who is doing something to someone else. A therapist's words may correct a misunderstanding of the present or in the past, may elucidate a clearer, possibly more truthful, explanation, but truth and correctness belong more to the realm of the cognitive than to the affective and empathic. We know what it is like to make 'empty' interpretations, banal because they do not go further than the surface, or clever interpretations that represent performances in our analytic role, interpretations that lack tact and sensitivity, interpretations that overwhelm through being mistimed, or which do not connect with the warded-off experience that needs to be reached and released. Patients quickly learn that what we offer to them is not direct help, it is an offer of recognition through understanding. It is through the therapist's responses that the patient will know whether he has been heard, seen and understood. In the analytic situation the therapist is known through his demeanour – appearance, voice, the ambience he creates – most of all he is known through what he says. This comes from his reflecting on his experience and then sharing this with the patient, whereby the patient experiences that another person has the capacity to contain and hold what he brings with him, that what he has brought has been taken in and reflected upon. By what we say to the patient, we show him the image that he has evoked. This response is not Freud's exact surgical mirror, it is a complex human response in a shared situation that is imbued with tensions, dilemmas and feelings. We shape our responses and, at our best, we are able to respond creatively and aesthetically as the artist–interpreter who creates from a text or from a score, not literally through exact repetition, but living in the unique unrepeatable moment.

Winnicott showed us how the infant begins to see himself in the expression of his mother's face, and this is how each of us begins the lifelong task of creating a sense of self. 'I am good or bad to see and to hold. I exist in the eyes and the face of the other'. If the response of the other is empty of feeling, if the response is 'correct', and only correct, I am not held in my continuity of being. This is why I cannot see the value in trying to instruct exact or even correct interpretations, for by this the therapist tells the patient who he *is* rather than sharing with him the possibility of *who he might be* and how he might have come to be himself in relationship to another. The value of an interpretation is in the response that brings to consciousness feelings, memories, ideas that put the patient's life before him. Repeatedly I have had to accept that my 'best' interpretations were those that I have never made! I have made tentative offerings of an understanding which the patient has used creatively, putting into words a self-understanding that goes further, sometimes in quite unexpectedly different directions to that which I had in mind. In every group session a therapist has the opportunity to see this happening. Patients who are not in a social therapist–patient role relationship respond to each other in ways that can be original and creative. If one group member makes a 'therapist-like' response to another, this sticks out like a sore thumb, as a gaffe that offends the mutuality and reciprocity of the group situation. Listening together to the therapist's words they are drawn into a shared activity and the responses that they separately make are acts of differentiation within a shared context. The context of the group dynamic matrix, the cognitive–affective field of a shared life space and life experience that comes to acquire coherence over time.

The face, the eye and the mirror

What, then, should the psychotherapist know of the face, the eye and the mirror? Perhaps because psychoanalysis is more an oral than a visual situation this is a realm as yet relatively unexplored. It offers startling riches to those who are ready to look.

'There is no power to see in the eye itself any more than there is in any other jelly. We cannot see anything until we are possessed with the idea of it, take it into our heads – and then we can see hardly anything else' (Thoreau).

> The glance is natural magic. A mysterious communication established across a house between two entire strangers, moves all the springs of wonder. The communication by the glance is in the greatest part not subject to the control of a will. It is the bodily symbol of identity of nature. We look into the eyes to know if this other form is another self, and the eyes will not lie, but make a faithful confession what inhabitant is there...the eyes of men converse as much as their tongues, the ocular dialect needs no dictionary, when the eyes say one thing, and the tongue another, a practised man relies on the language of the first. If the man is off his centre the eyes show it. The reason why men do not obey us, is because they see mud at the bottom of our eye. (Emerson 1920, p.145)

The face is the most expressive and communicative organ of our bodies. Together with our posteriors it is the part of ourselves which we only see on reflection. So we come to know ourselves by the way in which we are seen and responded to by others. The self image, so linked with self-esteem, accrues through myriads of visual interaction which begin with the mutual gaze of infant and mother, captured in Winnicott's felicitous phrase that the infant's first mirror is the mother's face. Her expression informs him, gives form, of who he is, a delight, a trial, even a no-thing. The abstracted or distant mother can be an empty mirror for the infant, who may adopt this non-reflection into an emptiness at the core of the self.

In warm happy mirroring, gaze-exchanging, we see ourselves recognised and loved, the gleam in the eye of the other. Kohut's self-psychology, not yet given much recognition here, leads to a more accepting and understanding outlook on therapy. For self-psychologists, the self concept is central in therapy. They look to see how the person tries to maintain the coherence of the self in the face of inner and outer pressures. This point of view leads to a way of understanding and to a use of language that patients quickly appreciate and which enables the therapist to move closer to the patient. It lessens the shame that people often feel quickly and powerfully when exposing their weaknesses and dependencies in therapy.

In self-psychology there is a recognition that from birth onwards we are intimately connected with others experienced as parts of ourselves, as self-objects, which is different to part-objects. We are made whole by them and we contribute to their wholeness. We need their powers and their understanding for survival and development. We need to idealise them and have them idealise us, to develop a healthy narcissism, good self-esteem, and we go on using and needing, being used and needed throughout life. I find illuminating the functions that self-objects provide for developing self as outlined by Ernest Wolf (1988), for these functions are responses to needs that will reappear in the transference situation of therapy and which call for recognition in their own right, not as distortions of other baser needs and motives.

And what of the self?

> The Self is a complicated mechanism, and to speak it honestly requires not only sincerity but the agility to catch insight on the wing and the artistry to give it accurate words. It also requires a listener who can catch our nuances as they fly by. Spoken truth shrivels when it falls on a tin ear. (Hoffman 1981, p.279)

Natural language, unlike psychoanalytic language, cannot do without the self. Self-love, self-hatred, self-esteem, selfishness, selflessness, all of these reflexive words curl round the central point of conscious life, of self-awareness and of our unconscious depths. Self-confidence, the background sense of safety, enables a person to respond flexibly and appropriately to a wide range of experiences. This capacity is built up during childhood as the child is exposed to an ever increasing range of experiences, building up an unconscious sense of safety through success in meeting challenges. Throughout childhood we are held in a matrix of self-object relationships, using Kohut's felicitous term for the adult in the child's world whose abilities are there to meet the child's needs and who by their very existence form part of the child's response repertoire. The crescendo in the growing child's abilities to handle the world of self and others is met by a decrescendo in the controlling and protective actions of the self-objects. Kohut calls this 'transmuting internalisation', the building up in the inner world of the capacity to do for oneself what was formerly done by others; Winnicott calls this the mother's task of failing her child. All this works best on a sensitive understanding of each child's constitutional endowment. Heinz Kohut liked to quote Eugene O'Neill's phrase, 'Man everywhere is born broken. The grace of God is glue'. We are not born broken for we have a primary organic unity, a body that works, adapted to a responding environment and these together make the basic human unit of asking self and answering other. We internalise this basic unit into the very groundwork of self on which our conscious experience stands as figure. Where the ground is lacking we can provide some sort of a setting where these fundamental life processes can be re-presented, where there is an asking self and an answering other or others. This for me is the baseline of psychotherapy; the setting, the presence, the presenting, the asking and the answering.

The answering from wisdom finds little place in the office language of psychoanalytic psychotherapy, though I do not doubt that it plays a large part in our unofficial language. After all, one of the compensations and joys of ageing is in discovering wisdom in ourselves. The whole question of answers and answerability goes much deeper. Bakhtin declares that addressability and answerability are basic to the human condition. We are born as people into and through dialogue. To 'be' means to communicate, vertically with ourselves, horizontally with others, for we have both vertical and horizontal depths. To 'be' means to be for another and through the other to be for oneself. How do we communicate? We communicate through *utterances*. An utterance differs from a sentence, which is but a unit of language. An utterance is a unit of communication. The utterance always presupposes the potential response of another and the response is both the most difficult and yet in some ways also the simplest task of the psychotherapist, how to understand that incompleteness of the utterance and to find a response that meets that incompleteness in a setting that makes it possible to hear it. Psychoanalysis teaches a response that is primarily interpretation; self psychology teaches an understanding and explanation based on empathy; Rogerian psychology is for an empathic response without the distancing of interpretation. In group analysis I constantly witness a range of answering responses which exemplify Bakhtin's ethical imperative for linguistic and all other social behaviour: one should address others with a presumption that they are capable of responding meaningfully, responsibly and, above all, unexpectedly. Responses from dogma are essentially irresponsible.

Pride, humiliation, shame and guilt: emotions of self-assessment

There is little that I have to tell this audience about guilt; we are well educated in its sources and of the power of guilt, the burden of the super ego. For Freud this burden is the price of culture: 'Every culture must be built up on coercion and instinctual vicissitudes' – perhaps you hear the sound of Hegel's master–slave relationship here? Freud's opinion of human beings was not high: 'Most of them are in my experience riff-raff' (Pfister). 'Our intellect is a feeble and dependent thing, a plaything and tool of our impulses and emotions'.

The death of the father slain by the sons is the basis of social institutions, for the father's vanished authority has to be replaced by a moral imperative, that brother shall not kill brother in the fight for the woman. Civilisation is founded on the incest barrier but beneath it lurk ancient guilts and desires: 'That which began in relation to the father ends in relation to the community' (Hughes 1979, p.148). Without the restraining power of guilt a neighbour is one who is exploited in work, in sexuality, his possessions are to be seized, humiliation, pain, torture and death his lot. Who amongst us shall gain, says Freud in his pessimism?

However, there are also his words in which he acknowledges that in the weakness of the human intellect, in comparison with the instincts, there is a precious peculiarity: 'The voice of the intellect is a soft one, but it does not rest until it has gained a hearing. Ultimately, after endlessly repeated rebuffs, it succeeds'. But other voices than Freud's ask to be heard, voices that give a different message about mankind's needs and his capacities for facing and hearing others in society, and which draw more than he did on sound and vision, on communication.

Here I turn to shame. A sense of shame restrains us from violating others and upholds our codes of solidarity. Without a sense of shame we have nothing to prevent us from falling to the base and primitive behaviour that Freud described without having seen that forces other than guilt can restrain and motivate us.

For the Greeks, shame and respect were the gifts of the gods that enabled them to live in society, for without them men behave like brutes and destroy each other. A psychology that is based on communication instead of instincts establishes affinity and dialogue as its foundations. The utterance and the gaze require the other, the self requires its self-objects. Without the other there would be no self. Instead of the master and the slave there is the master and the child, the teacher and the pupil. According to Levinas, the face that appears to us says, 'Do not kill me', it is the face of the master who teaches justice and who calls for peace. And here I return to consciousness and communication. These very words express togetherness, that knowledge is found and expressed through thought and language, which exist primarily as social facts.

References

Brierley, M. (1951) 'Trends in psychoanalysis.' *International Psycho-Analytical Library* 39. London: Hogarth Press.

Elias, N. (1978) *The Civilising Process.* Oxford: Basil Blackwell.

Emerson, R.W. (1920) *The Works of R.W. Emerson. Vol.5.* London: Macmillan.

Friedman, L. (1978) 'Trends in the psychoanalytic theory of treatment.' *Psychoanalytic Quarterly,* 544–67.

Glover, E. (1931) 'The therapeutic effect of inexact interpretation: a contribution to the theory of suggestion.' *International Journal of Psycho-Analysis 12,* 397–411.

Hoffman, E. (1981) *Lost in Translation.* London: Mandarin.

Holmes, O.W. (1975) *Human Reality and the Social World. Ortega's Philosophy of History.* Amherst: University of Massachusetts Press.

Holquist, M. (1990) *Dialogism: Bakhtin and His World.* London: Routledge.

Hughes, H.S. (1979) *Consciousness and Society. The Reorentation of European Social Thought 1890–1930.* Brighton: Harvester Press.

Khan, M. (1972) 'On Freud's provision of the therapeutic frame.' In W. Munsterberger and A. Esman (eds) *Psychoanalytic Study of Society.* Vol.5. New York: International Universities Press.

Marson, G.S. (1986) *Bakhtin: Essays and Dialogues on His Work.* Chicago: University of Chicago Press.

Ornston, D. 'How standard is the "Standard Edition"?' In E. Tumms and N. Segal (eds) *Freud in Exile.* New Haven: Yale University Press.

Ortega y Gasset, J. *Man and People.* New York: W.W. Norton.

Rickman, J. (1957) 'Number and the Human Sciences'. In *Selected Contributions to Psychoanalysis*. London: Hogarth Press.

Ross, J.M. (1981) 'Oedipus revisited: Laius and the "Laius Complex".' *Psychoanalytic Study of the Child*. Vol.37. New Haven: Yale University Press.

Strachey, J. (1934) 'The nature of the therapeutic action of psychoanalysis.' *International Journal of Psycho-Analysis 15*, 127–159.

Wolf, E. (1988) *Treating the Self.* New York: Guilford.

Zeldin, T. (1977) *France 1848–1945. Oxford History of Modern Europe Vol.2: Intellect, Taste and Anxiety*. Oxford: Oxford University Press.

Further reading

Holquist, M. (1990) *Authoring as Dialogue: The Architechtonics of Answerability*. London: Routledge.

King, P. and Steiner, R. (1991) *The Freud–Klein Controversies 1941–45*. New Library of Psychoanalysis. London: Tavistock/Routledge.

Levin, D.M. (1989) *The Listening Self.* London: Routledge.

MacGibbon, J. (1997) *There's the Lighthouse. A Biography of Adrian Stephen*. London: James and James.

Pines, M. (1987) 'Shame – what psychoanalysis does and does not say.' *Group Analysis 20*, 1, 16–31.

Pines, M. (1995) 'The universality of shame.' *British Journal of Psychotherapy 11*, 3, 346–357.

Pines, M. (1991) 'Once more the question of revising the Standard Edition.' *International Revue of Psycho-Analysis 18*, 235.

Pollock, G.H. and Ross, J.M. (1988) *The Oedipus Papers*. Madison, CT: International Universities Press.

Tolstoy, L. *War and Peace*. London: Penguin.

Voloshinov, V.N. (probably by Bakhtin) (1976) *Freudianism: A Marxist Critique* (trans. I.R. Titunik). New York: Academic Press.

Zeldin, T. (1988) *The French*. London: Collins Harvist.

PART 3

Historical Perspectives

CHAPTER 9

Psychoanalysis and Group Analysis
The Jews and the Germans[1]

The task that I have been set is a considerable one. The theme of German/Jewish relations and the figure–ground relation of psychoanalysis and group analysis to this long and tormented history is complex. I shall have to draw on studies of history, sociology, philosophy and religion, and in doing so I am bound to make generalisations which may seem unjustified or incorrect. I can only hope that my paper may stimulate thought and discussion.

First I shall deal with some aspects of the relationship between Jews and Germans over the centuries and then, in dealing with the development of psychoanalysis and group analysis, I shall speak about Sigmund Freud and Sigfried Heinrich Fuchs as figures in the landscape of German/Jewish relations. Freud was an Ostjud in the Austra/Hungarian Empire of the mid nineteenth century, Fuchs a Germanised Jew of the early twentieth century. Between the careers of these two seminal figures are the cultural politics of two empires, two different Jewish heritages and different eras in psychiatry.

I want to put German/Jewish history into the context of a wider European history. Spain expelled its Jews in 1492, trying to free itself from the dread that Spanish purity was being defiled by the large numbers of Jews who had been forcibly converted yet secretly continued to practise Judaism. Some of these were very highly placed both at Court and in the Catholic Church itself. This expulsion occurred at the moment of the great Spanish expansion into the New World, fuelled by its conviction that it had a holy mission to carry Christianity to the new continents. Having been in a country that had tolerated conversion and intermarriage, a Jew now became demonified, leading to fears of impurity and defilement. When cohesion was most needed at the time of this great expansion,

1   Opening paper of the 9th European Symposium on Group Analysis in Heidelberg, 1993, proceedings of symposium published by Mattes Verlag, Heidelberg. Published in: *Mind and Human Interaction* (1996) 7, 1, February, 20–30; Center for the Study of Mind and Human Interaction, Charlottesville, University of Virginia.

the Jew represented a fear at the heart of Spain, endangering, it seemed, the very integrity of the nation. This led to the basic assumption solution to expel the Jews and root out the Morranos, the converts who still secretly practised Judaism.

This solution had already been tried in England when the Jews were expelled in the thirteenth century but under Cromwell they were invited back. To the minds of many influential Protestants the British and the Jews were partners, the British themselves were the new Israelites. Though Jews were expected eventually to convert to Christianity there was a respect for, indeed a love for, the teaching of the Old Testament, a conviction that in its final and true articulation Christianity would be informed by Jewish wisdom and piety.

To compare the Spanish and British attitudes to Judaism, the Hispanic world feared a Jewish presence and the Anglophone world came to fear its absence. If Spaniards were anguished at the thought that they might be Jewish, Englishmen became increasingly concerned that they might not be!

Britain and Spain are distinct geographical entities bounded by seas or mountains and at the times of these events both countries had entered into nationhood. By contrast Germany; the Germanic territories, lacking clear protective territorial boundaries, was repeatedly invaded, threatened from both East and West, not yet united into a nation state. The cockpit of the great struggle between Catholicism and Protestantism, the supreme culture of the Germanic lands for one thousand years, was that of Rome. A German Emperor ruled over 'The Holy Roman Empire of the German Nation'. The German lands remained disunited and relatively undeveloped politically, socially and culturally compared with the other major European nations. In these German lands a comparatively large Jewish nation lived in their segregated communities, their ancient culture distinguishing them from the Germans by language, garb and custom, a culture that seemed to retain its own form of consciousness, living within, yet not part of, the surrounding German culture.

As an example of the way in which the Jewish presence disturbed German minds, I shall outline what the philosophers Kant and Hegel had to say about Jews and Judaism (Rotenstreich 1984). Kant proclaimed Judaism and Christianity irreconcilable as the Jewish religion is based upon a fear of the Creator who controls every aspect of Jewish life through the Talmud. Thus the Jew cannot be truly religious as religion can only exist in the heart and soul of autonomous persons who can therefore truly live in morality and in the spirit. The Jew lives by external divine authority in superstition, and the only solution for the Jew, in Kant's opinion, is his own euthanasia, his self-annulment and disappearance from history. Hegel states that Judaism is a stage in the development of religion and that through the Jew the spiritual principle had been made separate from nature, which had opened a new relationship between man and God. But though Judaism had placed God at the centre of spiritual life, Judaism remained ethnic and

Christianity had gone beyond this ethnicity to become a universal religion. Group analysts will find interesting the lively response that Jewish philosophers made to these dicta. Moses Mendelsohn (Sorkin 1987), the first significant Jewish philosopher in modern Germany, responded to Kant defending Judaism. He stated that Judaism stands for human activity which is bound to human society. What makes social life bearable are acts of mutual help and kindness. Mendelsohn stated that sociability is the basic human trait and that we have innate generous impulses and a capacity for beneficence. Human life, essentially social, is grounded in mutual assistance. This emphasis on social life contrasts with Kant's dictum that we live lives of 'unsocial sociability', that our basic nature is made of crooked timber, that radical evil exists within us all. This debate over basic human nature is still with us and is perhaps polarised in the theories of Freud and of Fuchs.

Following the Enlightenment, German philosophers began to explain that the faults in the Jew's character derived from his living conditions, his ghettoisation, his restriction to certain trades predominantly to do with money, and they became concerned that he was withheld from fuller participation in civil and political life. Pressure for Jewish emancipation grew on the grounds that the state, the new modern state, should give constitutional rights to all its subjects and therefore the Jews should also be given political and civil rights. The Jews themselves also began to claim these rights as equal members of modern politically based society. Boundaries and barriers that separated Jews geographically and socially from their Christian neighbours began to be dismantled, and both Jews and Christians had to deal with the consequences of these changes.

The majority of Jews had lived for hundreds of years in small, tightly knit communities, *shtetles*, sharing a common language and customs, organically knit together into a *Gemeinschaft*. Now they had to enter into new forms of social relationship with their Christian fellows, and new forms of civility had to be fashioned for social intercourse with these feared and powerful strangers (Caddihy 1987). They had to enter into civil society before they could enter into political society. Previously Jews had had the safety to express themselves openly with members of their own community, but now they had progressively to be concerned as to how to present themselves to the manners and mores of Western Christian society. Norbert Elias has shown how Western manners evolved slowly over centuries, descending from courtly society down to the lower strata. Only a few Jews, mainly the Court Jews and some privileged merchants, had been exposed to these forms of etiquette. The great majority of Jews had retained their own forms sufficient unto themselves. An argument has been made that the Jewish community had progressively to censor its own behaviour affects and impulses in order to gain acceptance and status in civil society.

Having embarked on the road to social integration and political rights, Jews found they had first to enter into civil society and in order to do that they had to alter some of their own personal characteristics. They encountered the great eighteenth and nineteenth century German demand for *Bildung*, for the education and cultural development which made great demands for social and psychic changes for the Jews. Within the Jewish population great tensions were set up between the generations, for younger generations can adapt quickly to these expected social norms and thereby become alienated from, and ashamed of, their ancestors. In looking at them they no longer see what they aspire to be, they see what they are ashamed to be. The case can be made that the great Jewish thinkers of the turn of the century – Freud, Marx and, in France, Levi-Strauss – were members of that community of Jews thrown into contact with the non-Jewish environment who had no access to political power and resorted therefore to the creation of great theoretical systems. Through these systems they sought to universalise their own personal experiences and responses to the hostile environment.

In psychoanalysis Jews and Christians alike are threatened with castration by their fathers for incestuous love of their mothers. Marx turns outwards and seems to direct his hatred of being Jewish on to Judaism, with the Jews representing a historical stage of the bourgeoisie that will give way to communism. For Levi-Strauss, Jewish identity dissolves into universal categories of binary opposition.

I move now from the philosophical to the diabolical, to come closer to the psychic forces that have made German/Jewish history so traumatic. The philosophers struggled to find reasons, rationalisations, for the uncanniness that was aroused by Jewish presence in German life. Jews were blamed for causing the Black Death through poisoning wells of drinking water. In the sixteenth century there was an epidemic of accusations of Jewish ritual murder of Christian children whose blood was needed to carry out Jewish rituals (Hsia 1988). This epidemic had spread from England to France in the twelfth to fourteenth centuries and passed on to Poland and Eastern Europe in the seventeenth and eighteenth centuries, having peaked in Germany during the sixteenth century. The socio-cultural psychological background to this epidemic, which led to many trials, tortures and executions, seemed to be based on the following factors. First, the Jews had a reputation for possessing magical powers through the Kabbala. Second was the popular belief in the magic potency of blood. During the sixteenth century Christian beliefs in the Passion and the Crucifixion intensified, and it was believed that these beliefs and rituals were being defiled by Jewish sacrilege as Jews needed Christian blood for their own terrible rituals. This belief in Jewish ritual sacrifice of Christian children had power over the population as long as it had coherence, narrative power and persuasive power. Opposition to this belief system came from the Emperor, who exercised imperial power to put Jews under his personal protection. A struggle to protect the Jews, whom the Emperor needed as merchants and financiers, was part of the struggle between imperial power and municipal power. Slowly the power of the Emperor and a proper legal process gained ascendance; trials of the Jews for ritual sacrifice became more searching and it became clear that in many cases Christian infanticide had been covered over by accusations of Jewish ritual murder.

It was a process of secularisation that brought about the substitution of evidence for superstitious belief, and this was part of the great change of mentality brought about by the Protestant reformation under Luther. Though Luther himself was antagonistic to Jews, he attacked a superstition of magic of a corrupt Catholic Church. Gradually the social background no longer supported the belief in Jewish ritual murder, and no Jews were executed on these grounds after the end of the sixteenth century in Germany. However, the demonology of the Jew was replaced by an increasing belief in witches and witchcraft. Following Luther the Hebrew language was studied as a divine language and no longer as the language of magic (Leschnitzer 1956). Nevertheless the symbolisation of the difference between Christian and Jewish blood remained a powerful theme in German consciousness (Bergmann 1992).

In the nineteenth century many Jews, mostly middle class, believed that intermarriage was the only solution for the German/Jewish relationship, that they would be regarded as true Germans, that they would gradually merge with the Christians. But what the Jews hoped for evoked horror in the majority of Germans, for whom Jewish traits of avarice, miserliness, lovelessness and hatred of mankind were thought to be carried in Jewish blood. Thus even if the Jew were to be given political rights in the modern state, he was not to be treated as a fully accepted human being. He was always the loathsome 'other', a container for the dark side of the German nation. We find in German writings right through into the nineteenth century that the Jew is labelled as representing Mammon, Moloch and, above all, Ahasuerus, the undying, eternally wandering Jew. Only in German territories did the myth of the wandering Jew take such a grip on the mass imagination. Ahasuerus is condemned never to die because of his mockery of Jesus on the cross. The Jewish community in its entirety was seen in this light, as a living corpse outside of time, a deposit of the uncanny. Writings about Ahasuerus appear at the beginning of the seventeenth century and begin to replace the Christian religious attitude that Judaism represents a living community gone astray but eventually to be reunited as the keystone in the edifice of the Church. This notion is replaced by a more primitive mentality and the concepts of reparation and redemption succumb to a paranoid superstitious mentality. Is it coincidental that the Faustian myth appears at the same time as that of Ahasuerus?

There is a German longing for redemption that is polarised with the condemnation of the Jew who will never be redeemed (Timms and Segal 1992).

The concept of sinister otherness is deeply rooted in German history in attitudes towards the Jew's body, his very material essence (Gilman 1991). The Jewish nose, the Jewish foot, the Jewish voice, Jewish sexuality are all aspects of his loathsome otherness. It is the Jew himself who is responsible for his loathsome character and not his environment. It is the Jew himself who must change, who must emancipate himself from within, if he can. Schopenhauer and Richard Wagner were amongst the most prominent of those who declared that it is not possible for the Jew to change, that he will always remain loathsome.

By the middle of the nineteenth century the Jew stood in the way of the redemption and triumph of a newly established German spirit and soul. A new German nation was arising, a German revolution that owed nothing to French or to Jewish ideas. The Jew could not take part in this new German identity, however much he identified with its ideas and ideals. This German revolution did not aim at revolutionary transformation. Its aims were the restoration and practice of virtues such as honesty, loyalty, generosity, bravery, piety – proclaimed as the essence of the German spirit. The new German state was a vessel for the embodiment of a social order superior to that of other nations. Pseudo-evolutionary science was used to establish the concept of racial purity, and through the new tool of economic science Marx, a Jew, declared that Jews are responsible for capitalism, for egoism, for the money economy, for all that is the antithesis of the human, the noble and the ideal. Now the word anti-Semitism is coined and anti-Jewish attitude changes from being religious to being racial and national (Rose 1990). Within the Church prejudice against Jews had been contained and restrained, for the redemption of mankind had to await Jewish recognition of Christianity as the true religion. The new German nation did not need Jews and refuted the notion that Aryan and Jew shared a common humanity; the Jew was identified as the agent of the social disease of modernism, of industrialisation.

I shall summarise what it was that the Jew stood for in German mentality and why he was such a threat, such a depository for fear, for evil, for pollution, for magic. Apart from the many socio-economic factors some characteristics stand out:

1. The Jew was always obviously 'other', in his language, garb and custom.

2. The Jew led a life outside of history. His ways of life seemed to go on unchanged over centuries when all about were subject to the forces of society and of change. Because of this the Jew seemed uncanny, petrified and did not act as a benign confirming mirror to the reality, presence and essence of the German. The German could not find a safe

reflection of himself in the Jew, a reflection of the familiar and therefore he reflected the uncanny, the discarded, the dreaded, a malignant mirroring. For examples we can take titles of anti-Semitic tracts such as *Der Judenspiegel* (*Mirror of the Jews*) by Hundt-Radowsky (1819) and the Danzig 'Antisemiten Spiegel' (*Anti-Semitic Mirror*), a journal. Magical beliefs of the pre-oedipal phase of development could all find a place in the Jew's image (Pines 1985). The Jew was seen as one who hates mankind, incapable of proper human love, forever condemned to be the wandering Jew.

We also have to take into account the belief in Jewish hostility to the rest of mankind, of Jewish pride in being a persecuted minority that still retains the concept of being the chosen people who are ethically and morally superior to the Christians.

Malignant mirroring can change when there is dialogue (Pines 1984). Group analysis tries to create opportunities for dialogue over 'impossible' issues.

The power of anti-Semitism in German history is much greater than that found in any other Western European country (Gay 1992). Some of the explanations that I find compelling are as follows. When Jews were segregated socially and geographically, they and the Germans found ways of co-existing but when this co-existence moved up to a much greater mingling because of the lowering of boundaries and barriers, a phase of what has been called 'symbiosis' set in. Symbiosis occurs when a minority whose foreign origin is not forgotten takes over the culture and way of life of its surroundings and becomes more and more like the world in which it lives. However, the environment, the surrounding majority, sees them as foreigners and clinging to older distorted patterns of perception based on history and mythology. They go on seeing the Jew as usurer, uncanny, scheming and dangerous, and whilst the Jew blindly believes himself to be invisible, in the eyes of the environment he is always marked, even his body is different. For not more than 50 to 80 years, in the nineteenth century, Jews and Germans lived in a great period of cultural expansion, a middle-class movement of humanism and neo-classicism, but as middle-class solidarity broke up the alliance between Jews and Germans crumbled. Through the crises and opportunities of industrial capitalism, a new wealthy middle class arose which included many Jews, but at the same time an embittered and impoverished petty bourgeoisie also developed. The Jew became the displaced visible target for this class tension, for through emancipation they had entered higher education and the previously closed professions as well as commerce. This again contributed to a sense of injustice and envy in the immobile and unadaptive lower middle classes. These classes who had despised Jews had to cope with their new higher social status, which added shame of themselves to their already existing envy. Thus enormous pressures built up, as the pressures that lead to volcanoes can build up invisibly until they erupt with frightening force and destructiveness. These pressures built up beneath the facades of obedience and conformism that characterised the lower classes (Graml 1992). It has been said that until very recently Germany, unlike other European nations, did not have a record of successfully seizing political power from those who possessed it, and this is especially marked by the failed 1848 revolution. Jews became a convenient scapegoat for hostility to the real holders of political power, who in their turn would exploit the Jews as scapegoats. Austria set the example with the growth of anti-Semitic political parties that exploited working-class fears and thereby gave politicians the power to manipulate the new mass votes. German Austrians, threatened by numerically superior Slav elements, longed for union with the greater German Reich, the more so as the Hapsburg Empire decayed. In Austria Jews were visibly and realistically rich, more so than in Germany, as they had contributed greatly to the industrialisation of nineteenth century Austria. Also, Austrian society contained so many socially immobile functionaries that tensions were all the greater there.

I am now going to consider Freud and Foulkes, psychoanalysis and group analysis, starting from a position of Foulkes that psychoanalysis and group analysis are complementary. Psychoanalysis explores the vertical intrapsychic dimension, the depth of the individual's unconscious and explores his inner society. Freud's domain of group analysis takes in horizontal depth, the inter- and the transpersonal as well as the intrapsychic. The group analytic situation is the social space of free floating discussion, whereas psychoanalysis began, and for a long time remained, a social space for a restricted dialogue between persons whose social positions were structured by the psychoanalytic situation. I shall try to argue that psychoanalysis became a social space for the return of the repressed whereas group analysis gives an opportunity for the return of the suppressed and the oppressed.

Let us look at Freud's response to Austrian and German anti-Semitism (McGrath 1986). He qualifies in medicine but remains a research worker in biology and neurology until forced to give up research and practise medicine. He enters psychiatry, a branch of medicine of relatively low status and therefore open to Jews, and teams up with Wilhelm Fliess, a Berlin Jew who has also entered a low status branch of medicine, that of ear, nose and throat surgery. But Fliess is attempting to raise the status of his lowly specialty by showing that there is a functional link between the genitalia and the nose, connected by the central nervous system. Freud, enormously influenced for many years by Fliess, supported his theories about the connection between the nose and the genitalia and his numerological calculations about periodicity. Fliess seemed to be trying to demonstrate the universal occurrence of male menstruation and we need to understand why he was doing so. There is an ancient belief in Jewish male menstruation, the stigma of the Jew punished for his rejection of Christ. Jewish male menstruation was a sign of the curse upon him and of his intrinsic deafness that continued to prevent him from hearing the truth of Christianity. The Jew tried to rid himself of the curse of menstruation by taking in Christian blood, another version of the Jewish ritual murder myth. Thus Freud and Fliess together were trying to move signs of Jewish difference to universality that released the Jew from a degrading particularity. The same can be said of the attempt to show that there is a universal connection between the nose and the genitalia and that it is not the Jewish nose or the circumcised penis which can be used as a projection and a depository for sexuality (Gilman 1991). The Jewish body was stigmatised as weak, feminine, evil, dirty, the binary opposite to the blond and virile Aryan. The Jew's nose betokens avarice, his feet are weak and flat and therefore the Jew cannot be a soldier or an athlete. He is the mirror in which the Aryan can relieve himself of his own fear of oral greed, unruly anality and feared, yet wished for, femininity. Psychoanalysis, Marxism, modern anthropology, Zionism, the call for the new muscular Jew at the turn of the century were all aspects of the great unconscious emphasis to re-balance the social forces that discriminated and stigmatised the Jew (Maidenbaum and Martin 1991).

In Freud, Jewish creativeness met with the new attitudes from the Enlightenment and from Positivism (Meghnagi 1993). Freud could look beyond Jewish despair to understand the conditions of all people, Christians and Jews alike. Rejected by culture and chased back into the realm of the demoniacal, Jews had become theorists of the unconscious. It has been said that Judaism came back into culture as a theory of transference. It is also arguable that the process of free association is linked with the Jewish heritage of the constant search for hidden meanings in the scriptures. Through the psychoanalytic dialogue all that seems irremediably suffocated and blocked in society is brought up, and Freud created a privileged situation for the dialogue between Jew and non-Jew. Entering into the medical profession gave Freud the opportunity to meet with patients of the middle and upper classes, often non-Jewish, on mutual territory or, indeed, territory that was privileged by the doctor's status. Psychoanalysis became a place where it was no longer the Jew who represented all that was crude and repressed, and what had been a stigma for the Jew could now be used to liberate both Jew and non-Jew from the forces of repression. I want to argue that in psychoanalysis we have a return of the repressed, of those powerful and censored parts of the psyche which are in conflict with societal norms. This had been the role of the Jew in society and it does not seem strange to me that it was Freud and his Jewish followers who were the first to explore these realms. I shall argue that in group analysis what we find is the return of the suppressed, even of the oppressed. There is a liberation of the social unconscious, of the socially invisible and unthinkable.

By 1930, Foulkes, a Viennese-trained psychoanalyst, believed that patients could hear and understand each other, they did not need a psychoanalyst to translate the meaning of their problems and symptoms. They all had privileged access to the language of the unconscious. This is because by now psychoanalysis had penetrated into culture and was a cultural possession, a reservoir of understanding that could be drawn upon by many persons, not only by the expert. Was Foulkes able to see this and to do this because his position in German society was very different to that of Freud? Foulkes was part of a well-to-do and socially accepted German/Jewish middle-class family, born in Karlsuhe. In that part of Germany Jews were part of the rural community, as wine growers, horse and stock raisers who had lived peaceably with their neighbours for many centuries. He seems to have experienced little anti-Semitic discrimination, took an active part in sports, was a member of the German army in World War I and suffered relatively few problems of anti-Semitism until he was forced to leave in 1933. Through his contact with Goldstein he was introduced to Gestalt psychology and to the concept of the central nervous system as a network. He took this concept of the network from the organic to the psychological and this way, whether he knew it or not, he had connected with a powerful stream in German philosophy and psychology.

The Volk psychology of Wundt, the historical philosophy of Dilthey, the Volk psychology of Lazarus and Steinfeld (Kalmar 1987), all stressed the supra-individual, that the individual can only be understood if he is seen as a nodal point in a historical and social network. To understand the individual you have to understand the forces of language, religion, economics, social forces in general. In Frankfurt, after his psychoanalytic training in Vienna, Foulkes was in contact with the discussions of the Frankfurt school, where economic forces and social forces were given equal status with intrapsychic forces. Here his contact with Norbert Elias led to his understanding of the enormous historical forces at work in the development of the personality. It seems to me that through group analysis we are able to take a more conscious account of the forces of society, such as those of anti-Semitism, than has been the case in psychoanalysis where these forces have left their mark on the psychoanalytic enterprise itself, forces which unconsciously have moulded the shape and form and nature of enterprise (Timms and Segal 1988). Psychoanalysis has developed its own language and to some extent has sought to impose its own language upon the general field of psychotherapy. This is an example of what the Russian writer Bakhtin calls a monoglossia, that is, the situation where only one language is legitimated as the official and valid language; whereas the natural state is that many languages can compete with each other and occupy the same domain. The natural state is not that of monoglossia but of heteroglossia. The language which tries to legislate its own primacy is trying to impose a dialect upon language itself. In group analysis we have our own theoretical language but we value the different tongues that people bring to the group analytic situation and in our interpretive responses we try to weave these languages together but more in an attempt to present a Gestalt, a pattern, than to insist that this is the true meaning of what is being said. This differentiates from the use of Bion's basic assumption language and some aspects of the Tavistock school.

The question has to be asked whether there are any particular psychic factors that can be identified as belonging to the German people that may play a part in this long, painful history of German/Jewish relationships. I shall quote from a book written in the 1920s by the Professor of Aesthetics at Stettin, Richard Muller-Freienfels, entitled *The Germans* (Muller-Freinfels 1936). The author is very expert in psychology, as evidenced by an earlier book, *The Evolution of Modern Psychology* translated in 1935. From his study of aesthetics, of German intellectual life and history, he identifies these characteristics. First, tendencies to abstraction, to the fantastic and to a certain lack of clarity. Germans can lose themselves, 'easily in the fantastic with little contact with the immediate world about them'. Dissatisfied with the present they dream of a better future or revel in considerations of a cherished part. Deep intense emotions can lead to characteristic moods, *'Stimmung'*. In art Germans can tolerate more dissonance, ugliness and greyness than other European nations. The German language, rich, diversified and versatile, can also be obscure, ambiguous and amorphic, which enables concepts to be juggled with. The most interesting point that the author makes is that there is a constant struggle in the German to compensate for these underlying traits and therefore there is an everlasting war, a dissatisfaction with his own nature. Thus there is the combination of a natural disposition, a reaction against this and an over-compensation which leads to a willingness to subordinate himself to laws, norms, and systems and imperatives. This tends to make the German very subject to strong-minded individuals, a willing acquiescence to accept dictates, to make it one's own duty to accept the will of the other but also to remain active and strong willed even when bowing down before the higher authority. Germans are willing to accept the power of such a leader but with the loss of that leader, or in the absence of such, there can be a rapid disintegration. Public opinion is less important in its effect than the leadership of a commanding person.

As regards philosophy, Muller-Freinfels points out that nineteenth century German philosophy is predominately anti-rationalistic and that the rationalistic philosophers are Jewish. The German philosophers are trying to identify those obscure forces, yearnings and impulses which are super-ordinate to anything rational. Of Wagner he speaks of the harmonic structure which envelopes the melodic line, of the mystical many voicedness, the melancholy and indeterminateness that streams forth.

Muller-Freinfels describes what he sees as typical German over-compensations because the latter sense danger in their underlying structure; they accept coercion and voluntary binding of the self which is felt not to be a restriction of freedom but to be a true manifestation of the highest power of the self. In overcoming the individualistic, indeterminate volitional life by means of willing subordination to self-selected authorities, we see the power of logical systems taken to their extremes and the power of bureaucracy.

There is quite an uncanny prescience from this book written in the 1920s with its anticipation of the submission of the German people to the will of Hitler.

I have attempted to bring together a network of ideas about the German/Jewish relationship and how this forms a background to the development of psychoanalysis and of group analysis. In the course of doing this I have had to read a great deal about the history of Germany, of German/Jewish relationships and of the history of ideas, and I hope that I have managed to weave this into some sort of coherent narrative. Born in Britain of Russian Jewish parents, I have had little contact with German life, though none of us has been unaffected by the tragic developments in German history during my lifetime, which includes, of course, the recent reunification of Germany and the enormous impact of this on European history. In the course of reading I have come across this phrase from Goethe that Freud used many times: 'What you have inherited from your ancestor, acquire it yourself in order to possess it'. This has happened to me in the course of this work. I have had to try to acquire for myself more consciously what I have unconsciously inherited from my Jewish ancestry. In some ways I have come into possession of some of this, and I hope that I have managed to convey some of this to you for you yourselves to possess.

References

Bergmann, M.S. (1992) *In the Shadow of Moloch: The Sacrifice of Children and its Impact on Western Religions.* New York: Columbia University Press.

Caddihy, J.M. (1987) *The Ordeal of Civility: Freud, Marx, Levi-Strauss and the Jewish Struggle with Modernity.* Boston: Beacon Press.

Gay, R. (1992) *The Jews of Germany: A Historical Portrait.* New Haven: Yale University Press.

Gilman, S. (1991) *The Jew's Body.* London: Routledge.

Graml, H. (1992) *Antisemitism in the Third Reich.* Oxford: Basil Blackwell.

Hsia, R.P. (1988) *The Myth of Ritual Murder.* New Haven: Yale University Press.

Kalmar, I. (1987) 'The Volkerpsychologie of Lazarus and Steinthal and modern concept of culture.' *Journal of the History of Ideas 48*, 671–690.

Leschnitzer, A. (1956) *The Magic Background of Anti-Semitism: An Analysis of the German–Jewish Relationship.* New York: International Universities Press.

Maidenbaum, A. and Martin, S.A. (eds) (1991) *Lingering Shadows: Jungians, Freudians and Anti-Semitism.* London: Shambhala.

McGrath, W.J. (1986) *Freud's Discovery of the Unconscious: The Politics of Hysteria.* New York: Cornell University Press.

Meghnagi, D. (ed) (1993) *Freud and Judaism.* London: Karnac Books.

Muller-Freinfels, R. (1935) *The Evolution of Modern Psychology*. New Haven: Yale University Press.

Muller-Freinfels, R. (1936) *The German: His Psychology and Culture*. Los Angeles: New Symposium Press.

Pines, M. (1985) 'Mirroring and child development. The mirror: psychoanalytic perspectives.' *Psychoanalytic Inquiry 5*, 2. (See Chapter 2)

Pines, M. (1984) 'Reflections on mirroring.' *International Review of Psychoanalysis 11*, 27. (See Chapter 1)

Rose, P.L. (1990) *Revolutionary Antisemitism in Germany: From Kant to Wagner*. Princeton: Princeton University Press.

Rotenstreich, N. (1984) *Jews and German Philosophy: The Polemics of Emancipation*. New York: Schoken Books.

Sorkin, D. (1987) *The Transformation of German Jewry 1780–1840*. Oxford: Oxford University Press.

Timms, E. and Segal, N. (eds) (1988) *Freud in Exile: Psychoanalysis and its Vicissitudes*. New Haven: Yale University Press.

Further reading

Timms, E. and Robertson, R. (1992) *Psychoanalysis in its Cultural Context. Austrian Studies 3*. Edinburgh: Edinburgh University Press.

CHAPTER IO

On History and Psychoanalysis[1]

Freud claimed that psychoanalysis represented a major assault on human narcissism. This view is only partially correct, for it is largely ahistorical. Freud's view must now be balanced against the historians' perspective on psychoanalysis, which in its turn represents a potential narcissistic blow to psychoanalysis, so long as psychoanalysts isolate themselves from fuller recognition of the socio-cultural matrix of Freud's work.

This article, by a psychoanalyst, presents some of the newer perspectives of historians on the development of Freud's work against the background of late nineteenth century Austrian and German political, cultural and social history. Through understanding this past, we are better able to understand the present dilemmas of psychoanalysis, in particular the relevance of social forces in the development of emotional disorder.

An institution, wrote Ralph Waldo Emerson, is the lengthened shadow of one man. And, he also wrote, an individual is always mistaken. In this article, I outline some aspects of the personal history of Sigismund Freud, for that is the name he was given at birth. He changed it during his adolescence to the more Teutonic form, Sigmund, because by then a character called Sigismund had become the butt of anti-Semitic jokes. It is in his shadow that the institution of psychoanalysis has grown. And, in order to go beyond that individualistic vision which, as Emerson rightly stated, must always be mistaken, I invoke a vision of those historians who take Freud and psychoanalysis as the object of their studies. I draw principally on the work of Decker (1977) on the history of the reception of Freud's ideas in Germany; Levin (1978) on Freud's early psychology; Johnston (1972) on the Austrian mind; Klein (1985) on the Jewish origins of psychoanalysis; and the works of Karl Schorske (1980) and William McGrath (1974, 1986). The latter's recent book, *Freud's Discovery of Psychoanalysis: The Politics of Hysteria* (1986), is a very important contribution to this area of study.

1   This article was presented as a Freud Memorial Lecture at University College, London, England, June 1986. Published in: *Psychoanalytic Psychology* (1989) 6, 2, Spring, 121–135.

Psychoanalytic theory has been used as a tool for the understanding of an individual's history, his-story and, more ambitiously, towards an understanding of historical eras and the sweep of historical change. That is not the subject I address. Rather, I sketch out Freud's own personal history in the context of his family, setting his family in the context of their own cultural and historical era. I then illustrate some enduring personal patterns in Freud's relationship to the socio-political environment of the late nineteenth century in Austro-Germany, suggesting ways in which his ideas may have been shaped by this environment and by the nature of nineteenth-century medicine and science. I also describe how these very subjects themselves were influenced by historical processes.

In Gestalt psychology and in group analysis, we use the concept of figure–ground; that the perception of an object is only meaningful when set against its background and, further, that we can reverse the perceptual field and make background into foreground and foreground into background. This concept helps us to see the relationship of a person to his context. The individual's uniqueness is not reduced by seeing that we are all children of our times. As Freud himself in 1897 acknowledged in a letter: 'One always remains a child of his age, even in what one deems is his very own' (Freud 1985, p.277).

Sigismund Freud was the fortunate eldest son of a young and beautiful mother. Amalia Freud was the third wife of Jacob Freud and was half his age when they married. Martin Freud described his grandmother as being descended from those Galician Jews who fought the Nazis in the ruined ghettos of Warsaw with legendary courage and stubbornness (M. Freud 1983). Sigismund Freud had two much older half-brothers from his father's first marriage: Emmanuel, the elder, and Philippe, the younger. Emmanuel had two children, John and Pauline. John, Sigismund's nephew, occupied an important and unforgettable place in his unconscious (McGrath 1974, 1986). John, a year older than Freud, was his superior in strength and skill. In their relationship, Freud inevitably occupied the position of underdog. Freud (1900) wrote: 'At the age of three, I was in a close relation, sometimes friendly but sometimes warlike, with a boy a year older than myself' (p.198). He went on:

> We had loved each other and fought with each other, and this childhood rela-
> tionship ... had a determining influence on all my subsequent relations with
> contemporaries. Since that time my nephew John has had many reincarnations
> which revived now one side and now another of his personality, unalterably
> fixed as it was in my unconscious memory. (p.424)

Freud and John, his 'companion in crime', began to explore the world of sexuality, together treating Pauline, his niece, in some way 'shockingly' (Freud 1954, p.219). Thus libidinal ties were formed between him and John, which were played out in common rebellion against paternal authority.

McGrath (1974, 1986) elaborated on the reverberations of this relationship with his nephew, John, in Freud's relationships with such brother figures as Breuer, Fliess and the lesser known figures of his schooldays, Heinrich Braun and Victor Adler.

Let us turn to Freud's relationship with Heinrich Braun, a greatly admired 'young lion' (Freud, 1960, p.379) from his early adolescence and later a leading socialist politician. Braun, though two years older than Freud, was his classmate for several years. He introduced Freud to politics, to radicalism and to political action. Until his later adolescence, Freud, like Braun, aspired to a political career, for which the study of law would have qualified him. In his early adolescence, Freud apparently was fearful of his father and greatly admired Braun's ability to speak to his father as an equal. Together with Braun, Freud took part in a rebellion against an unpopular schoolteacher, which led to his being marked down from the highest possible grade of conduct to two grades lower, from which he only recovered in the final years of his school career, after Braun had left. Freud (1960) described his hero worship of Braun:

> I admired him, his energetic behaviour, his independent judgement, compared him secretly with a young lion and was deeply convinced that one day he would fill a leading position in the world ... he encouraged me in my aversion to school and what was taught there, aroused a number of revolutionary feelings within me ... it was understood that I would work with him and never let down his side. (p.379)

Later, Freud did leave Braun's side, becoming his own man in the field of psychology, rather than that of politics, in which Braun went on to become a leading figure. However, some deeper personal feelings came into this break in the relationship with Braun. This was through Braun's relationship with Victor Adler, later to be the founder of the Austrian Socialist Party, the first Foreign Minister in the first Austrian Democratic Republic's government, and the originator of May Day as a celebration of international socialism.

Victor Adler, a Jewish psychiatrist who also worked with Freud's revered mentor, Brucke, aroused Freud's jealousy in many ways. He was a leader in the reading circle of young Viennese intellectuals, to which Freud belonged for five years, which studied the writings of Schopenhauer, Nietzsche and Richard Wagner. It was Adler who Freud challenged in a debate during his student days, and by whom he was defeated. His self-esteem was injured and in an angry outburst Freud even challenged Adler to settle their differences in a duel. Adler coolly rejected the challenge, but this incident reappeared in one of Freud's revolutionary dreams, to which I refer later. Rivalry with Adler seems to have intensified when Adler married Braun's sister and thereupon replaced Freud in his close relationship with Braun. This seems to have activated the antagonistic, competitive side of Freud's memories of his nephew John, and McGrath (1974) relates an interesting sequel to their relationship.

In 1883, Braun had arranged a lunch at Adler's apartment when Freud was still a medical student. Despite the pleasant nature of this lunch, Freud left it in a melancholy mood. At that time Freud, engaged to Martha Bernays, had no prospect of marrying her because of his poverty. He compared himself with Adler, who was married, prosperous, already a father and a respected member of this community. Nine years later, Freud, looking for a larger apartment to accommodate his growing family, chose one that met none of the requirements that he and his wife had carefully drawn up: 19 Berggasse. This was Adler's old apartment and Freud rented it on the spot, not even consulting his wife. According to the analyst Suzanne Bernfeld, from whom this story comes, 'with characteristic intuition, Mrs. Freud realised that Freud had to have this house, and that no other house would do. They did manage to live in this gloomy and impractical house for 47 years' (cited in McGrath 1974, p.40).

McGrath (1974, 1986) has drawn our attention to Freud's identification with Hannibal, Semitic opponent of Rome, with whom Freud deeply identified in his adolescent rebellion against his father, Jacob. You will no doubt recall that famous incident in Freud's adolescence when, contemptuous of his father's response to the anti-Semite who forced him, as a Jew, to step off the pavement into the muddy street, he swore to himself that he would not follow the model of his father. In his place rose up the image of Hannibal, who made an oath to his father to take revenge upon the Romans. Hannibal became the first of Freud's ego-ideals-historical figures, who would include Oliver Cromwell, Napoleon Bonaparte, Garibaldi, Bismarck and, much later, the American President, Woodrow Wilson. What united all these great figures in Freud's mind was that they advanced secularism, contested the power of the Catholic Church and released Jews from oppression.

The only contemporary of Freud's among these ego-ideals was, of course, the German Chancellor, Bismarck. When the latter visited Vienna in 1892, Freud (then 36) waited in the street and made several attempts to get a close look at him. From adolescence, Freud had closely followed Bismarck's career, apparently fired by his exploits. During the Franco-Prussian war when Freud was 14, he took such an interest in this conflict that he acquired a large map which he dotted with small flags to pursue the campaign and enthusiastically gave lectures to his sisters on the strategies of the respective forces. Bismarck's political and military intrigues directly affected the fortunes of Freud and his family. Freud's father admired Bismarck because he brought about German unification. Indeed, when Jacob Freud had to adapt his birthday from the Jewish to the Christian calendar, he showed his esteem for Bismarck by selecting the latter's birthday as his own. Bismarck's unification of Germany fired the pan-Germanic ideals of the generation of Freud's adolescence and early adulthood. Traces of this militant nationalism and of his unconscious conflicts with it have provided Schorske and McGrath with much material for their research. This we come to later.

I have given these vignettes from Freud's youth to illustrate his passionate nature, his radicalism and his strongly vested relationships with brother figures. I hope that they have breathed some youthful life into the image of Freud, whom we usually regard as a stern, ageing patriarch, a Moses. Freud, indeed, strongly identified himself with the biblical figures of Joseph and of Moses. Shengold (1979) pointed out that Freud makes many references to Joseph in the interpretation of his dreams, and himself explained (Freud 1900) that it was easy for him to identify himself with Joseph: 'It will be noticed that the name Josef plays a great part in my dreams. My own ego finds it very easy to hide itself behind people of that name, since Joseph was the name of a man famous in the Bible as an interpreter of dreams' (p.484).

The identification with Joseph goes far beyond this similarity, however. Joseph was the eldest son of Jacob's wife Rachel, and his father's favourite. Note the similarity of the name of the patriarch to that of Freud's own father, Jacob. Joseph is envied by his brothers, who band against him, selling him into slavery in Egypt, but he has his revenge upon them when he rises to great power and eminence there. He triumphs over them, brings his father and the whole of his tribe to live in the land of Egypt, and has his own children adopted by Jacob. He exemplifies in his life the triumph of a man who is assimilated into a foreign culture, acquires power and eminence within that culture, and lives the life of a man of peace. Shengold (1979) has drawn the parallel to the aspect of Freud's character in which he wishes to become the assimilated Jew in the Austro-Hungarian Empire, and rise to high office: 'Every industrious Jewish school boy carried a Cabinet Minister's portfolio in his satchel' wrote Freud (1900, p.193), remembering his childhood in the optimistic liberal era of the late 1860s, the time of the Burgerministerium. The Joseph identification represents the peaceful achievement of power and strength in a hostile world. Joseph the powerful Jew remains in Egypt, the land of the foreign oppressor, and to the end of his life remains a loving son, respecting paternal authority.

Later in his life, Freud's identification moved from Joseph to Moses. He was fascinated by the figure of Moses throughout his middle and later years, and in a reverse of his assimilationist identification with Joseph, tried to prove that Moses was not a Jew but an Egyptian. In his study of Michelangelo's Moses (Freud 1914), he portrayed Moses as a powerful, proud man with a passion over which he had to exert immense self-control in order not to erupt into violence against his people. Moses never entered the Promised Land – this was the punishment for his impulsive nature and for his defiance of his God – but he was the leader who took people out of the land of the oppressors. Likewise, Freud suggested to Jung that the latter was the Joshua who would take the chosen people into the Promised Land that he would never reach.

But for two years Freud lived almost across the street from the man who, in political reality, did become the Moses of his people, the founder of Zionism, Theodore Herzl. Freud's ambivalence to Herzl and to Zionism is starkly illuminated by his words to Herzl's son, Hans, in 1913, nine years after Herzl's death. These words illuminate Freud's own views on the interrelationships of fantasy, reality and politics:

> Your father is one of those people who have turned dreams into reality. This is a very rare and dangerous breed. It includes the Garibaldis ... the Herzls, I would simply call them the sharpest opponents of my scientific work. It is my modest profession to simplify dreams, to make them clear and ordinary. They, on the contrary, confuse the issue, turn it upside down, command the world while they themselves remain on the other side of the psychic mirror. It is a group specialising in the realisation of dreams; I deal in psychoanalysis; they deal in psycho-synthesis. (Falk 1977, p.19)

He went on to say: 'They are robbers in the underground of the unconscious world, stay away from them, young man. Stay away even though one of them was your father. Perhaps because of that' (p.19).

Clearly, Freud here is also speaking of his relationship with his own father, a man who had failed to realise Freud's adolescent, rebellious ideals, who had apparently given in without struggle to anti-Semitism. Freud himself had become the leader of a great movement but, unlike Herzl's political movement, psychoanalysis can be termed a counterpolitical movement in that it moves the heart of the matter from politics to the psyche. Thus not only was Herzl the rival who had succeeded in fulfilling Freud's adolescent wishes, but he was of that breed of politician who knew how to summon from the depths of fantasy the forces which men blindly follow: forces which in Freud's own lifetime had led to mass anti-Semitic movements and which would eventually lead to the ascent of Hitler and Nazism. Hugo von Hofmannsthal, Freud's contemporary, wrote: 'Politics is magic. He who knows how to summon forces from the deep, him will they follow' (cited in Schorske 1980, p.134). Freud had explored the depths of his own intrapsychic journey, but still he feared the forces of the deep when they escaped from the control of the individual's own ego and became subject to the will of a charismatic leader.

When we put together this assemblage of Freud's ideals, his models for identification, we see again some indications of the passionate, proud and warlike nature of this man, who had the intellectual power and emotional courage to enter alone into the dark ravines of the mind.

I now turn from Freud's personality as such to view him in relation to his social context, as figure against social ground.

The conventional history of how Freud began his explorations, his lonely forays into the unconscious, is that they were stimulated by the death of his father in 1896, an event which Freud himself characterised as that great and poignant event in a man's life. Certainly in those years Freud developed symptoms of hysteria which must have driven him to attempt a self-cure both through his own investigations and through his passionate relationship with Fliess. Modern historians, however, tell a somewhat different story. McGrath (1974) wrote:

> An examination of Freud's own political and personal history in conjunction with his political dreams, recorded in *The Interpretation of Dreams*, reveals that much of the very psychoanalytic theory to which Freud reduced man's individual and social actions can itself be seen to reflect historical, sociopolitical conditions of Freud's time. The assurance with which Freud was able to apply psychoanalytic theory to sociopolitical problems may thus be as much a reflection of the sociopolitical origins of psychoanalysis as of the general truth of these theories. In order to trace the ways in which psychoanalytic theory may have been shaped by the historical events of Freud's time, it is necessary to examine the various links tying together in his mind the problems of society and politics with those of the individual human psyche. It is necessary to read Freud backwards, to reintegrate the autobiographical and political fragments he reveals into the personal and social context from which they were taken. Once this is done it becomes possible to see how closely politics and history interacted with Freud's own creative genius in the genesis of psychoanalysis. (pp. 32–33)

Let us consider first the political context of nineteenth century medicine and neurology as outlined by Decker (1977). There was acute political rivalry between France and Germany, a rivalry into which science was drawn. France's brilliant eighteenth century age of enlightenment and rationality contrasted with divided Germany's romanticism and idealism. Whereas French medicine had advanced brilliantly in the early nineteenth century, German medicine was far behind. The universities and centres of scientific research were only just developing in Germany, in contrast to the splendidly organised French system. By the mid nineteenth century, German universities had become much better organised and great advances in scientific medicine were being made, and in these academic centres there was a strong reaction against the older system of romantic medicine. Materialistic attitudes triumphed. In psychiatry, this was manifested through the search for the anatomical basis of mental disorders.

We should never forget that at least 30 per cent of all mental disorders proved eventually to be due to the ravages of syphilis, of general paresis of the insane. This finding greatly strengthened the case of the brain anatomists. Eventually, German physicians began to feel much superior to their French rivals and to regard the French as an inferior people – more degenerate, more prone to hysteria, less industrious and less efficient. This seemed to be confirmed by the triumph of

Prussia in the war of 1870 against the French, when the Prussian medical forces were far better organised than their opponents – Prussian casualties were much lower, the wounded were better cared for and deaths from smallpox were ten times less than among the French. However, French and German psychiatrists were largely united in the belief that knowledge of the anatomy and pathology of the nervous system was the royal path to progress in psychiatry. Freud's teacher, Meynert, was the leading proponent of German anatomical psychiatry and his pupil, Freud, was a leading neurologist in his earlier years.

Once Freud had dedicated himself to a career in psychiatry, he obtained a grant to study with Charcot in Paris for five months. He did not go there to study hysteria and hypnosis. He wrote:

> I was bound to reflect that I could not expect to learn anything essentially new in a German University after having enjoyed direct and indirect instruction in Vienna… The French school of neuropathology, on the other hand, seemed to me to promise something unfamiliar and characteristic in its mode of working, and moreover to have embarked on new fields of neuropathology, which have not been similarly approached by scientific workers in Germany and Austria. (1886, p.5)

Charcot, indeed, was recognised as the leading European anatomist of the nervous system and had occupied a Chair of Anatomy and Pathology at Paris University before a special Chair of Neuropathology was created for him. It was only when Freud was in Paris, in direct contact with Charcot, that Freud discovered the difference between French and German neurologists, which was that for Charcot, 'the work of anatomy was finished and that the theory of the organic diseases of the nervous system might be said to be complete: what had next to be dealt with was the neuroses' (Freud 1886, p.10). Charcot was using hypnosis as his tool to study the working of the nervous system and had clearly established hysteria as a clinical entity that was not based upon anatomical changes in the nervous system. The personal effect Charcot had on Freud was expressed in a letter to his fiancee: 'Charcot, who is one of the greatest of physicians … is simply wrecking all my aims and opinions … when I come away from him I no longer have any desire to work at my own silly things' (Freud 1960, p.185).

But Charcot himself has to be seen in his sociopolitical context. He was a great figure in French intellectual and political life and his school at the Salpetriere has been regarded as part of a tight network of republican politicians and scientist-politicians. His very Chair of Neuropathology at the university was created for him by his close political friend, Gambetta, as part of the anticlerical policy of the republican French government. The whole movement to establish hysteria as a recognised medical condition was part of an anticlerical campaign. Medieval Catholic Church culture had included hysteria in the phenomena of witchcraft; now, scientific thinking was taking over what had once been the Church's domain. Charcot's disciple, Bourneville, laicised the public hospital in 1883.

The conquest of religion by science in France contrasted with the rise of anti-Semitic Catholic forces in Austria at that same time. When Freud returned to Austria as a spokesman for Charcot, whose book he had translated and after whom he named his second son, Jean-Martin, he was pitched into the rivalry between French and German psychiatry and was, therefore, seen as a deviant from the school to which he had formerly belonged. This, in part, accounts for the hostile reception of his ideas on hypnosis and on male hysteria. However, Freud was ready to throw down the gauntlet to Catholic Vienna. He announced in the newspapers that he would open his professional office on 25 April 1886, Easter Sunday — the day on which every other office and business would have been closed.

Freud the psychiatrist in 1886 was not yet Freud the analyst of 1895 onward. I now sketch in the sociopolitical background of this next decade and trace its effect on Freud's psychoanalytic researches. Freud grew up in the liberal, optimistic 1860s. All restrictions on Jews were lifted in 1867. This happy era was short-lived, however, for under the Liberal government's free market policy there was great economic expansion, a stock exchange boom culminating in a great financial crash in 1873. The Liberal government was involved in scandals of corruption, immorality and cynicism (the Ofenheim case) which severely undermined the fragile political prestige of Austrian liberalism. Freud's own letters of that time illustrate his disillusionment with political radicalism and his turning to scientific radicalism. From that point on, his interest in political life, until now strong, was manifested primarily as an undercurrent in his intellectual life, appearing usually in jokes, allusions, asides and unconscious connections. It is this undercurrent that McGrath (1986) brought to our attention.

From 1875 onwards, reactionary anti-Semitic forces began to strengthen in Austrian politics. In the 1880s, Georg von Schonerer had forced the pan-Germanic movement for the unification of Austria and Germany on to an anti-Semitic path. Richard Wagner, a great force in Austrian intellectual life, also espoused racial anti-Semitism. Thus anti-Semitic pressures intensified in Freud's environment. Historians have suggested that these factors played an important role in Freud's turning his attention away from the frustrating external world which blocked his professional advancement, and reinforced his underlying sense that it would be through the exploration of his inner world that he would become master of his environment instead of being a helpless pawn in the world of politics.

Freud's self-analysis dates from 1896, which was the year of the death of his father. But this, and subsequent years, were also times of great political unrest in

Austria, as was reflected in his self-analysis. In 1897, elections were called by the government of Count Badeni, the result of which was an increase in the strength of the anti-Semitic Christian Social Party. Badeni had hoped to create a coalition of Czechs and liberal Germans to avoid an alliance with the clerical conservatives, but the conservatives outbid Badeni in an alliance with the Czechs and established a tenuous Slavic–clerical conservative majority. This tipped the balance of power towards Prague and the Bohemian region of the Austro-Hungarian Empire. The tensions concerning whether Czech or German should be the official language of the Empire aroused those passions with which we are now familiar in other language disturbances (e.g. in Belgium and Sri Lanka). The streets of Vienna were filled with rioting crowds, the university was closed and, as part of the political deal with the Christian Social Party, the anti-Semitic mayor of Vienna, Karl Lueger, was finally confirmed in his post. The Emperor, Franz Josef, had twice refused to confirm him as a sign of his disapproval of his anti-Semitic politics, but in the end he had to give way to politics and to public opinion.

What this political struggle lit up in Freud can only be guessed at and sketched out. In his dreams, Freud touched upon the fact that until the age of two he had a Czech nursemaid, Monica Zajic, and that through her he knew something of the Czech language. She – Catholic, ugly, fascinating – had in some way been his first teacher in the realm of sexuality and had brought him into contact with the mysteries of the Roman Catholic Church. She disappeared from his life at about the time his sister Anna was born, when she was imprisoned for theft. Thus the issue of Czech versus German had a powerful emotional resonance for him. The whole climate of increasing anti-Semitism and political unrest stirred up in him anxieties about the fate of his family and reminded him of the wanderings of the Jews in search of their own land; metaphors of journeys appeared in his dreams and interpretations, whilst his travel neurosis increased in intensity. In his journeys to Italy and to Greece, Freud was going back to the childhood of Western culture at the same time as he was re-exploring his own childhood in his self-analysis. In this period of great emotional turbulence, reflected in his neurotic symptoms, he established a powerful relationship with Wilhelm Fliess. In a very unrealistic way, he saw Fliess as a man who balanced harmony with spirit, who represented the harmony and proportions of classical culture which he contrasted with his own erratic moods. It was on one of his Italian journeys that he made a crucial breakthrough, forming his concept of the oedipal relationship and conflicts which gave him access to a universal and timeless struggle between instincts and repression, and for which he was able to find evidence in Greek mythology. For the first time, he felt that he had attained both intellectual and emotional coherence in his life. It was through his recognition of the oedipal struggle that he felt reconciled to his relationship with his father, and was released from the ambivalence of his mourning; immediately after his return from his Italian visit he joined the Jewish brotherhood, two days before the end of the 11-month ritual mourning period. Now he was able to ignore political uncertainties and dramatic events for he had found safe harbour within the domain of the psyche.

Let us look, however, at some of the details of these turbulent times as McGrath (1986) showed they were alluded to in his dreams. In October 1897, he had a dream which referred to a Dr Lecher: 'I saw in the window of a bookshop a new volume in one of the series of monographs on great artists, on world history, on famous cities, etc. The new series was called 'famous Speakers' or 'Speeches' and its first volume bore the name of Dr Lecher' (Freud 1900, pp.268–269). Of this dream, Freud wrote that:

> It seemed to me improbable that I should be concerned in my dreams with the fame of Dr Lecher, the non-stop speaker of the German obstructionists in Parliament. The position was that a few days earlier I had taken on some new patients for psychological treatment and was now obliged to talk for ten or eleven hours every day. So it was I myself that was a non-stop speaker. (pp.268–269)

It is surprising that Freud should speak of himself as a non-stop speaker in his role as an analyst, where surely he was in a position of being a non-stop listener. Let us see what the occasion was of the non-stop speech by Dr Lecher.

The situation was that the Austrian Parliament had to pass legislation by a certain date in order to renew commercial and economic relations between Austria and Hungary, the two halves of the Empire. Because of the fight between the Czechs and the Germans, the German language faction set out to block the passage of this legislation. McGrath (1986) presents a splendid account of Dr Lecher's speech and the surrounding political events written by Mark Twain (1929), who was in Austria at the time. In the turmoil of an outraged and noisy Parliament, Dr Lecher spoke non-stop for 12 hours, without deviance or repetition, for the rules of the Austrian Parliament were strict in demanding that speeches be relevant to the subject under debate. In Mark Twain's words, Dr Lecher's speech was, 'the longest flow of unbroken talk that ever came out of one mouth since the world began' (p.206), and it was all strictly to the point. 'For twelve hours he stood there, undisturbed by the clamour around him, and with grace and ease and confidence poured out the riches of his mind, in closely reasoned arguments, clothed in eloquent and faultless phrasing' (pp.217–218). At the end of his 12 hours, Dr Lecher had achieved a personal triumph recognised by all, even his enemies. As McGrath (1986) pointed out, there are many factors which would have led Freud to a close identification with Lecher. He:

> had gained the widespread fame and admiration for which Freud longed, and he had won it in a heroic manner reminiscent of Freud's adolescent phantasies of military glory. He was serene and untroubled in the face of the violent emotional storm raging around him; he was a man of masterful intellect who displayed a

comprehensive understanding of the difficult subject under discussion; he responded like a gentleman to insults; he was a polished and eloquent orator. (p.244)

Nevertheless, 'Freud's interpretation of the dream brushed aside any possibility that political sympathies could have brought about his identification with Lecher and pointed rather to professional activities as the real subject of the underlying dream thoughts' (p.225).

McGrath (1986) suggested that the dream of Dr Lecher represented fulfilment of a wish that Freud himself could, like the subject of his dream, overcome all those frustrating obstacles that stood in the way of success and fame. Freud, too, had been held down by his contemporaries when he presented unpopular subjects for public discussion and approval. He had not yet succeeded, like Lecher, in getting his opponents to listen to him and in subduing their passions through the skill and power of his language and of his arguments. In the dream, Lecher's oration was transformed into a book. Having identified himself as the speaker, might that book not have been the one that he was working on, *The Interpretation of Dreams*, which was indeed to become one of the most famous books of our time? And does not that book also contain the results of Freud's self-analysis, his own non-stop speaking?

The crucial point about this dream is that it was the first dream in which Freud gave an 'openly counterpolitical interpretation' (McGrath 1986, p.227) to a political event. The dream interpretation represents a wish to be freed from the power of politics. As McGrath concluded, 'in giving a political dimension to his scientific work on dreams, he provided a therapeutic outlet for his frustrated political drives' (pp.230–231). He began to recognise the power of dream censorship and he quite openly recognised that censorship in dreams recapitulates in microcosm the basic structures and dynamics of the political order. The dream wish is equivalent to popular opinion and the censor is equivalent to the repressive political authority which has to be evaded so that the opinion can reach some disguised form of expression.

I wish to mention just one of three political dreams which McGrath (1986) used to illustrate this counterpolitical stance of psychoanalysis. This is what Freud (1900) called his 'revolutionary dream' of July 1898. It was provoked by the sight of Count Thun, the Prime Minister of Austria, stalking arrogantly to his special train at Vienna Central station, where Freud, the humble possessor of an ordinary train ticket, was leaving for a holiday. Filled with rage and hatred at the sight of the Count, who represented political, Catholic and aristocratic domination, Freud caught himself whistling Figaro's aria, 'If the Count wants to dance, then I'll call the tune'. In his dream, Freud had an angry confrontation with the Count at a political meeting – as he had once confronted his rival, Victor Adler. He felt that he had been carried back to the revolutionary year, 1848, and associated with the unsuccessful attempts of the students to bring about political liberalism. Thus in the first part of this dream he attempted to satisfy the rebellious feelings excited by the Count.

The second scene of the dream replaced revolt by flight. He found himself in the Aula, the great ceremonial hall of the University of Vienna. 'The entrances were cordoned off and we had to escape' (p.210). Eventually, after passing through a series of beautiful government rooms, he reached, 'a corridor, in which a housekeeper was sitting, an elderly stout woman. I avoided speaking to her, but she evidently thought I had a right to pass' (p.210). Here, Freud was referring to the dream mechanism of censorship, perhaps of his dream or perhaps of his book, which might be censored on account of its rebellious dream thoughts. In his association to the second scene, Freud wrote that in a boastful way he was proud of having discovered these mechanisms of dream life, thus bypassing the censorship.

In the third scene of the revolutionary dream there was a tangle of absurdities, and Freud was especially proud of his understanding that absurdity in dreams represents unconscious thoughts involving criticism or ridicule, in this case directed at the Count and also at Freud's brother, who had been included in the associations. Freud reconstructed from this dream the thought, 'It is absurd to be proud of one's ancestry; it is better to be an ancestor oneself' (p.434). Thus he triumphed over the aristocracy by becoming a great and famous scientist, whose descendants should be proud of him.

In the fourth and final scene of this revolutionary dream, Freud found himself alone at the train station with a partially blind old man, whom he understood as being both his father and the Count. He was now in a position of authority over the feeble old man, for whom he had to hold a urinal. That is, he reversed the situation of childhood, when his father had tyrannised him for his own urinary incontinence and, through psychoanalysis, placed himself in a position of authority. Thus in his analysis, 'Freud collapsed the entire range of allusions to social and political rebellion ... into the basic psychological relationship with his father' (McGrath 1986, p.274):

> The whole rebellious content of the dream went back to rebellion against my fa-
> ther. A Prince is known as the father of his country; a father is the oldest, first,
> and for children, the only authority, and from his autocratic power the other so-
> cial authorities have developed. (Freud 1900, p.217)

Through psychoanalysis, Freud was able to reduce all environmental conflicts, all situations of helplessness and rage, to the terms of a universal, infantile, oedipal phase. Aspects of current reality could be pushed aside and the past put in the place of the present. Thus politics was replaced by Freud's invention of psychoanalysis, where he himself was the triumphant leader. As Schorske (1980) wrote: 'In this passage Freud adumbrates his mature political theory, the central principle of which is that all politics is reducible to the primal conflict between father and son ... Patricide replaces regicide; psychoanalysis overcomes history. Politics is neutralised by a counterpolitical psychology' (p.197).

I hope that I have been able to give you some impression of the great interest that historians now take in psychoanalysis and the important ways in which the understanding of historical context enters into our appreciation and appraisal of the validity of psychoanalytic theory. That we are currently in a period of reappraisal is evident. Freud's triumphant discovery that stories of infantile seduction represent fantasy rather than reality is undergoing close scrutiny. Once again we become aware of the frightening power of the environment upon the child. Parental seduction and violence are not situations of fantasy; they are irredeemable reality. We know that Freud was enormously impressed by the incidence of violence towards children that was demonstrated to him during his time in Paris. He never gave up the idea that there were serious emotional traumas inflicted upon children, but we, particularly in this country, have lived through an era where the politics of the family and the exercise of power over children were almost totally ignored by a considerable number of psychoanalysts, who saw all these painful experiences of childhood in terms of the externalisation of the child's own aggressive drives or of the death instinct.

Freud's interpretation of the Oedipus myth entirely left out the filicidal rage of the father, Laius (Ross 1988), yet the significance of the Oedipus story cannot be fully realised until one takes into account the whole family myth in which the father is a central figure. Tragic events and public opinion are making us look again at the reality of childhood. In today's society, we must redream our own vision of childhood, a larger vision than Freud's, and see how we have emerged from an era where the violated child has been focused upon as the source of sexual desire, hatred and envy. What has been ignored is the desire, hatred and envy of the parents. The oedipal theory made it possible to treat the child, now seen as having sexual desires, as an object of adult didactic or therapeutic efforts. The controversial analyst, Miller (1985), suggested that we ascribe to children what we are ashamed of in ourselves, and would like to be rid of, in keeping with the way in which traditional power structures operate. This is not to deny that children do, indeed, have sexual fantasies and desires. However, now we need to redress the balance, to become aware of the hidden dimensions within our social unconscious, those taboos which limit our ability to see further into our social context.

In this urgent and never-ending work of reappraisal of ourselves and society, psychoanalysts and historians can yoke to each other as oxen before a plough, tilling the soil of the unconscious.

References

Decker, H.S. (1977) *Freud in Germany: Revolution and Reaction in Science.* New York: International Universities Press.

Falk, A. (1977) 'Freud and Herzl.' *Midstream 23,* 3–24.

Freud, M. (1983) *Sigmund Freud: Man and Father.* New York: Aronson.

Freud, S. (1886) *Report on my Studies in Paris and Berlin. Standard Edition I,* 5–15.

Freud, S. (1900) *The Interpretation of Dreams. Standard Edition 4,* 1–338, 5, 339–627.

Freud, S. (1914) *The Moses of Michelangelo. Standard Edition 13,* 211–238.

Freud, S. (1954) *The Origins of Psychoanalysis.* (M. Bonaparte, A. Freud and E. Kris eds). New York: Basic Books.

Freud, S. (1960) *Letters of Sigmund Freud* (E.L. Freud, ed). New York: Basic Books.

Freud, S. (1985) *The Complete Letters of Sigmund Freud to Wilhelm Fliess 1887–1904* (J. Masson, ed. and trans.). Cambridge, MA: Belknap Press of Harvard University Press.

Johnston, W.M. (1972) *The Austrian Mind.* Berkeley: University of California Press.

Klein, D.B. (1985) *Jewish Origins of the Psycho-Analytic Movement.* Chicago: University of Chicago Press.

Levin, K. (1978) *Freud's Early Psychology of the Neuroses: A Historical Perspective.* Pittsburgh: University of Pittsburgh Press.

Miller, A. (1985) *Thou Shall Not Be Aware: Society's Betrayal of the Child.* London: Pluto Press.

McGrath, W.J. (1974) 'Freud as Hannibal: the politics of the brother band.' *Central European History 7,* 31–57.

McGrath, W.J. (1986) *Freud's Discovery of Psychoanalysis: The Politics of Hysteria.* Ithaca, NY: Cornell University Press.

Ross, J.M. (1988) 'The darker side of fatherhood: clinical and developmental manifestations of the "Laius motif".' In G.H. Pollock and J.M. Ross (eds) *The Oedipus Papers.* Madison, CT: International Universities Press.

Schorske, C. (1980) *Fin-de-siecle Vienna.* New York: Knopf.

Shengold, L. (1979) 'Freud and Joseph.' In M. Kanzer and J. Glenn (eds) *Freud and his Self-Analysis.* New York: Aronson.

Twain, M. (1929) 'Stirring times in Austria.' In *The Writings of Mark Twain.* Vol.22. New York: Harper.

CHAPTER II

A History of Psychodynamic Psychiatry in Britain[1]

In this chapter, the history of psychodynamic psychiatry in Britain will be traced. Not identical to, though closely linked with, the psychoanalytic school, psychodynamic psychiatry has the characteristically British features of eclecticism, empiricism and individualism.

Some outstanding pioneers

The Morrison Lectures of 1915, given at the Royal College of Physicians in Edinburgh and entitled 'The New Psychiatry' (Stoddart 1915) will be taken as a starting point. They caused a furore, as described by Isabel Hutton (1960), a young Scottish psychiatrist working with Professor George Robertson, the first Professor of Psychiatry at the University of Edinburgh. She described how senior Scottish psychiatrists left the hall in fury and disbelief, shaking their heads at the outrageous ideas put forward by the lecturer. However, George Robertson himself became a convert to psychoanalysis, and stoutly declared himself to be a Freudian from then onwards. Who was this lecturer and what was he laying before his distinguished audience? The man responsible was William Henry Butler Stoddart, Professor of Psychological Medicine to the Royal Army College, former Superintendent of Bethlem, pupil and colleague of Hughlings Jackson and author of one of the most important contemporary textbooks in British psychiatry, *Mind and Its Disorders.* (1921).

Described as placid, apparently lazy, fat, affable and always well dressed, a man who enjoyed good food, good wine and idle days on the river (Rickman 1950), Stoddart laid down the first major challenge to British psychiatry arising from the slow arrival of psychodynamic thought to this country. In his lectures, later published as a book (Stoddart 1915), Stoddart outlined the psychoanalytic theory

---

1   Chapter in *Textbook of Psychotherapy in Psychiatric Practice*, edited by Jeremy Holmes, MRCP, FRCPsych. Published by Churchill Livingstone, 1991.

of mind and the psychopathology of the neuroses and psychoses. It was couched in the libidinal terms and topographic theory of those days, and one can understand how this was strong beer for an audience almost totally unaccustomed to psychoanalytic thinking. Yet Stoddart, who later became Physician in Psychological Medicine to St Thomas Hospital, London, was not a person to be ignored, for he was a significant Establishment figure of the early psychoanalysts; he was the most well established, far more so than Ernest Jones, who had failed to gain entry to the higher realms of British neurology and psychiatry. In 1920, the third edition of *Mind and Its Disorders* was reviewed in the *Edinburgh Medical Journal*. The reviewer attacked, 'the extreme Freudian view presented in a manner which suggests that no-one has any scruples or doubts about its full acceptance' (*Edinburgh Medical Journal* 1920). The book was described as confused, and the author as having a father complex towards Freud. The review ends: 'With regret it must be said that this book is one which will do much to retard the use of psychological methods in the treatment of disease'. However, it was said that attacks bounced off Stoddart; he assumed that they would come, and he assumed that they would cease in time – he could wait. Meanwhile, life was pleasant, and his attackers were, after all, good fellows but mistaken.

The first paper on psychoanalysis given publicly was in 1911, by David Eder at the British Medical Association Neurological Section, and described a case of hysteria and obsessionality treated by Freud's psychoanalytic method. 'When Dr Eder had finished speaking the chairman and the entire audience, numbering about nine, rose and strode out without a word' (Hobman 1949, p.89). But Eder, like Stoddart, was a stout character and not to be put off by such a rebuff. Indeed, he was a powerful and colourful personality whom Freud valued highly, as shown by the letter he wrote at the time of Eder's death in 1936 to the analyst Barbara Low, Eder's sister-in-law. A member of a middle-class Jewish family, first cousin of the novelist Israel Zangwill, Eder was an early socialist who bore a scar on his head from the Bloody Sunday riot in Trafalgar Square in 1887. After graduating from St Bartholomew's Hospital in 1895, he became a general practitioner in Johannesburg, a medical officer in his family coffee and rubber plantations in Colombia, was caught up in South American revolutions, fell ill amongst cannibals and voyaged three thousand miles up the Amazon.

When back in England, Eder was active in socialist medicine, worked at the Margaret McMillan clinic for children in the East End, and promoted the new movement for school hygiene. He became interested in psychoanalysis just before the 1914–18 war, during which he was a medical officer in Malta and had much to do with what he called 'war shock', on which he wrote a significant book (Eder 1917). In 1913, he visited Freud in Vienna, had a brief analysis with Victor Tausk and then, with Ernest Jones as President, he became Secretary of the London Psycho-Analytical Society. He also had a brief analysis with Jones, with whom he afterwards fell out for some years, being attracted to Jung. However, after eight months' analysis with Ferenczi in Budapest in 1923, he rejoined the British Psycho-Analytical Society and remained a prominent member for many years. He was active in developing the Institute for the Scientific Treatment of Delinquency, which later became the Portman Clinic. Eder was a much admired man who mixed in artistic and left-wing circles, and it was through the esteem in which people held him that psychoanalysis became acceptable to these circles. It is possibly through Eder that D.H. Lawrence became involved in psychoanalysis.

In his own writings, Ernest Jones (1959) plays down the significance of Stoddart and Eder as major figures in early psychoanalysis. Jones likes to portray himself as the father figure of British psychoanalysis and, with his combative nature and intellectual brilliance, he did indeed play the most significant part in the British psychoanalytic movement for many years. However, there were negative aspects to his contribution. He drew tight boundaries around the Psycho-Analytic Society, more or less dictated who would be accepted as a psychoanalyst and excluded from the Society many people who had contributed significantly to the widening knowledge and acceptance of Freud's ideas before, during and after World War I.

Probably the most influential proponent of Freud's view was Bernard Hart, physician in psychological medicine at University College Hospital, London. Hart did become an Associate Member of the Psycho-Analytical Society, but never played an active part in it and always maintained a critical, objective view of Freud's work. However, he was probably its most accomplished expositor, through his book *The Psychology of Insanity* (Hart 1912), which went through many editions and was the most widely read introductory book on psychoanalysis.

Psychiatry at the turn of the century

To understand the beginnings of the psychodynamic movement, it is necessary to glance briefly at the position of psychiatry at the turn of the century, and at those individuals who began to introduce the psychological aspects of mind into an area then dominated by an organic and materialistic approach. This was the position of Henry Maudsley and of the great majority of well-established psychiatrists. The great input of Hughlings Jackson had convinced British psychiatrists that the only relevant approach to the neuroses and psychoses was through a study of the brain and of the dynamic functions of the central nervous system.

Jackson (Stengel 1963) had shown how the higher levels of the central nervous system act to maintain the lower levels in suppression, and that a lesion of a higher level would release the actions of the lower level. Freud, who knew Jackson well, later incorporated this into his view of repression, in which the ego controls the manifestations of the id which, however, re-emerge in the form of symptoms when the higher levels are not able to maintain their control (Dewhurst 1982).

Whilst British neurologists were pioneers in dynamic functional neurology, British Psychiatrists were isolated from, or in opposition to, the far more advanced European psychiatry. The re-emergence of a psychology that opposed Jackson's materialism came from the Victorian 'other world' search for a spiritualism, an alternative system of belief that could replace religion. Dominated by Cambridge academics, the Society for Psychical Research investigated spiritualism, possession, dual personality and hypnosis. F.W.H. Myers declared his opposition to Maudsley, emphasising unconscious mental processes with his concept of the subliminal self, although this did not have the dynamic qualities of the Freudian unconscious. At the same time, Havelock Ellis, who had qualified in medicine though he did not practise as a doctor, was knocking down cultural barriers to the recognition of the power of sexuality.

British psychiatry at this time was custodial and therapeutically somewhat nihilistic. However, signs that this intellectual monopoly was breaking down came in the movement to establish both outpatient clinics and hospitals for the treatment of the neuroses. The slow acceptance of psychodynamic psychiatry was due in part to the resistance of the mechanistic approach to psychiatry, in part also to the isolation of the early psychoanalysts.

Pioneers in practice

One such pioneer was Dr Helen Boyle, who founded a small outpatient dispensary in Brighton in 1905, when the Lady Chichester Hospital was also founded (Boyle 1922). Psychotherapy was the main basis of treatment, though Helen Boyle herself was not close to psychoanalysis. The dynamic alternative to psychoanalysis in those days was the French school of Janet, Dubois and Dejerine, where persuasion and suggestion were the main methods, together with the hypnotic approach of Bernheim and the school of Nancy. T.A. Ross, the first Medical Director of the Cassel Hospital, declared his support of the French school, though he later became more of a convert to psychoanalysis, writing influential books on the subject (Ross 1923, 1932).

Another major pioneer before World War I was Hugh Crichton-Miller (1877–1959), who in 1911 opened Bowden House in Harrow on the Hill as a nursing home for functional nervous disorders. He had qualified as a doctor in Edinburgh, and had practised in both Italy and Scotland as a fashionable general practitioner; however he became increasingly fascinated by the functional nervous disorders. In his early years, he was assisted by Maurice Nicol, another significant early figure in psychoanalysis, who later moved to Jung and then, finally, to the spiritual movement of Gurdjief. But during World War I, Nicol was one of a significant group of psychiatrists and neurologists led by the psychologist, C.S. Meyers, who persuaded the army Establishment that shell-shock cases should be treated with psychotherapy, and not be subjected to the practice of some eminent neurologists, who used electric shock and other pain-producing methods to force patients to give up their symptoms (Stone 1985).

In 1920, Crichton-Miller founded the Tavistock Clinic, and remained its Director until his resignation in 1934. He was an eclectic psychotherapist and was eventually to be displaced by the more hard-line psychoanalysts of the 1930s; but without Crichton-Miller's enthusiasm, organisational abilities and capacity for clear communication, the Tavistock Clinic would have had a different and less influential development (Stone 1985).

World War I and shell-shock

It was the impact on psychiatry of the so-called 'shell-shock' of World War I that led to the downfall of the dominant neurological approach. Such distinguished neurologists and physicians as Henry Head, Farquahr Buzzard and Langdon Brown, all later Regius Professors of Medicine at Oxford and at Cambridge, supported the new functional approach. Important figures such as William McDougall, William Brown and J.A. Hadfield worked in this area, and Maghull Hospital, Liverpool became for a while the central training ground for psychodynamic psychiatrists under the direction of R.G. Rows. It is regrettable that the history of Maghull Hospital over this period is not yet fully available.

W.H.R. Rivers

One of the most interesting psychotherapists of this period was the experimental psychologist and anthropologist, W.H.R. Rivers (Slobodin 1978). Rivers was an Establishment figure of even more prominence than Hart and Stoddart. He was the director of the first experimental psychology laboratories in the Universities of London and Cambridge, and became a Fellow of the Royal Society. Rivers qualified from St Bartholomew's in 1882, in 1888 became MD and FRCP, and in the 1890s worked at Queen Square with Hughlings Jackson and Victor Horsley before going to study in Germany. In 1898, he was a member of the famous Torres Straits Expedition, the pioneering expedition that established modern British anthropology, in which he was accompanied by C.S. Myers, William McDougal and Charles Seligman. This turned him towards anthropology for several years, although during this period, in 1903, he co-operated with Henry Head in the famous Head–Rivers experiment on peripheral sensory mechanisms, that led to the subsequently influential theories of protopathic/epicritic sensations.

This division of sensation into the lower, primitive form and the higher, more differentiated, form, can now be seen as analogous to Freud's division of the mind into the higher and lower forms of organisation, and both are related to Jackson's doctrine of levels of the central nervous system. In 1915, Rivers, who was already familiar with the works of Freud and Jung, was introduced, at Maghull, to psychotherapy of the war neuroses. His work became famous through the autobiography of Siegfried Sassoon, whom he treated at Craiglockhart Hospital, near Edinburgh. Sassoon had mutinied against the slaughter in France and would have been court-martialled had not his friend, the poet Robert Graves, succeeded in persuading him that he was suffering from a nervous breakdown. (Sassoon and Graves called the hospital 'Dottyville'.) Sassoon was forever grateful to Rivers for his help at this crucial period, and ascribed his mental maturity to his contact with the mind of Rivers.

Rivers became the first President of the Medical Section of the British Psychological Society, and wrote a book, *Conflict and Dream* (Rivers 1923), which described many of his own dreams and in which he both agreed and disagreed with Freud on dream mechanisms. Rivers brought his anthropological approach to bear on the study of mental life, unable to accept what he saw as Freud's limited view of the Western family, to which he had given universal significance. Tragically, Rivers died in 1922 from a strangulated hernia, but he had left his stamp on the 'new psychiatry', a psychodynamic view of mind and its disorders. However, Jones, Edward Glover, John Rickman and other pioneer analysts vehemently opposed the work of people such as Rivers, who they saw as purloiners of Freud's ideas, without being true disciples. It was this intransigent view held by Jones and his followers that helped to maintain the longstanding isolation of psychoanalysis from the mainstream of British psychiatry.

The Brunswick Square Clinic

An example of this intransigence is the fate of the first London Clinic for Psychotherapy, a medico-psychological clinic, later known as the Brunswick Square Clinic, founded in 1912 by Dr Jessie Murray and Miss Julia Turner (Boll 1962). Murray had attended Janet's lectures in Paris, and conceived of a clinic to treat functional nervous disorders with new eclectic therapeutic methods influenced by, but ranging much wider than, psychoanalysis. The clinic changed its name on its move to Brunswick Square, and had departments for medicine, psychology, psychotherapy, physical exercises and education. One of the clinic's early physicians was Dr Hector Munro, but the best known of its early staff was James Glover who was Director of the clinic. James Glover was later joined by his brother, Edward, and other students who later became prominent as psychoanalysts, including Sylvia Payne, Ella Sharpe, Susan Isaacs and Marjorie Brierley. However, this clinic was to be short-lived. When James Glover went to Berlin for analysis with Karl Abraham, he returned determined to oppose eclectic psychotherapy and suggested affiliation with the British Psycho-Analytical

Society. This amalgamation took place in 1922, and little acknowledgement has ever been paid to the pioneering eclecticism of the Brunswick Clinic.

War neuroses

After World War I, the Ministry of Pensions opened up outpatient clinics to treat the thousands of ex-combatants with severe functional symptoms. This, indeed, was the route that led to the establishment of outpatient clinics using psychotherapy. Many psychiatrists who had become converted to psychotherapy did not become psychoanalysts but established outpatient clinics at hospitals in London and in the provinces, such as at Littlemore, Oxford (Good 1930).

The Cassel Hospital was founded after World War I in response to demands that had been placed on psychiatry by the war neuroses.

Mapother and the Maudsley

The history of the post-war years must give prominence to the Maudsley Hospital under Edward Mapother (Lewis 1979). In addition to an offer he had made in his lifetime, Henry Maudsley had left money to London County Council in his will for the establishment of a hospital that would end the isolation of psychiatry from general medical knowledge and research, and which would admit only voluntary patients. Building was begun in 1913, but between 1915 and 1919 the hospital was used for the care of neurotic patients in the services, with Maudsley's consent.

Mapother, born in Ireland in 1881, entered psychiatry in 1907 at Long Grove. There, the Superintendent was Hubert Bond, who had gathered around him a group of brilliant young psychiatrists, including Bernard Hart. There was interest in Janet and Freud, and Mapother's contact with psychodynamic ideas was increased during his training at Maghull Hospital in 1917.

In 1919, Mapother went to the Maudsley, and in the early 1920s visited advanced European centres for psychiatry. In his first annual Maudsley report, Mapother wrote that he encouraged unprejudiced trials of every form of treatment, and that he was extremely glad that there was, 'a considerable proportion of definite adherents of psychoanalysis amongst the clinical assistants and that there was no doubt of great advances introduced by these schools in our understanding of cases' (Lewis 1979, p.148). Mapother continued to advocate the provision of psychotherapy at the Maudsley, and to provide facilities for it, but he became increasingly opposed to the Tavistock Clinic, particularly to the Christian approach of Crichton-Miller, Hadfield and others, dubbing it 'the parson's clinic'.

J.R. Rees, who remained a personal friend of Mapother's, thought that he had strong feelings of jealousy towards the psychotherapeutic strength of the Tavistock Clinic. However, at the Royal Society of Medicine's memorial meeting for Freud, Mapother wrote that, 'Freud brought to psychology and psychiatry more of the imagination of the great artist than of the solid objectivity and rigid logic of the scientist' (Lewis 1979). It is noteworthy that Mapother had written a paper with R.D. Gillespie from the York Clinic, in which they demonstrated the process of Freudian mechanisms such as unconscious homosexuality in cases of paranoia. Perhaps this was in anticipation of his later, somewhat paranoid, attitude towards psychoanalysis, as represented by the Tavistock 'parson's clinic'. However, psychoanalytic psychotherapy did continue at the Maudsley under Mapother, represented in particular by W.L. Neustatter, who wrote on the results of 50 cases treated by psychotherapy at the Maudsley in 1935 (Neustatter 1935). Later developments at the Maudsley, particularly after World War II under Aubrey Lewis, will be referred to later.

Opponents of the psychodynamic movement

It is true that psychoanalysis is past its perihelion and is rapidly retreating into the dark and barren depths from which it emerged. (Mercier 1916)

Freudism, notwithstanding the diligent efforts made to acclimatise it, will, I feel sure, never take root in this country. (Crichton-Browne 1920)

I have now completed a task which, in spite of its repugnant nature, I have felt it my duty to perform. That the invidious poison, which is being instilled into the minds of the young by countless psychoanalysts, is doing untold harm is known to many and should be known to all. (Bolton 1926; J. Shaw Bolton was the first Professor of Psychiatry in England, holding the Chair at Leeds.)

These extracts give a flavour of the strongly emotional opposition to psychoanalysis aroused in some prominent psychiatrists. Two Fellows of the Royal College of Physicians, Sir Horatio Bryan Donkin, a criminologist, 'a sociable man and prominent at the Saville Club', and Sir Robert Armstrong-Jones, a former Superintendent of Claybury Hospital and a Visitor in Lunacy, attempted to censure other FRCPs, presumably Stoddart primarily, for practising psychoanalysis, but the move was blocked by other Fellows.

The British Medical Association set up a committee to report on the status of psychoanalysis in 1927, after allegations had been made of patients being harmed. A young lawyer's suicide had been attributed to psychoanalytic treatment, but his therapist, Dr Millais Culpin, a distinguished member of the early psychoanalytic circle, was able to satisfy the coroner that the lawyer had in fact not been in psychoanalytic treatment. After many deliberations, the Association decided to acknowledge psychoanalysis as a recognised form of training and treatment associated primarily with Freud's work (British Medical Association 1929). Although the committee would go no further in its support for psychoanalysis, this acknowledgement was seen by Jones and Glover, who had been active in giving evidence on that committee, as a triumph for the movement, as it gave recognition and respectability to psychoanalytic training. Thereafter, opposition to psychoanalysis became less raucous and extreme, but was still steadily maintained by Mapother and other leading figures.

Psychoanalysis and psychiatry pre-World War II

It was the intransigent attitude of Ernest Jones that blocked the development of a psychoanalytic influence in general psychiatry. Until World War II, Jones actively forbade psychoanalysts to work at the Tavistock Clinic, as he saw this as a dilution of the pure gold of psychoanalysis. Thus developments at the Tavistock Clinic until after the war were spearheaded by eclectic psychotherapists who represented the 'new psychiatry'. J.R. Rees, assisted by H.V. Dicks, succeeded Crichton-Miller as Director, with J.A. Hadfield in charge of training. Hadfield practised what he considered to be psychoanalysis, but one of his analysands, W.R. Bion (1985), many years later referred contemptuously to him as, 'doctor feel it in the past'.

However, Jones' embargo had positive as well as negative results. It allowed for a freshness of thought for psychiatrists such as Ian Suttie and John Bowlby, who were not caught up in the powerful controversies between the 'English school' of psychoanalysis, headed by Ernest Jones and much under the influence of Melanie Klein, and those Freudians who adhered more closely to the teachings of Vienna and Berlin.

Newcombe and Lerner (1982) have written about the historical context of Bowlby's attachment theory, looking at the psychological and social changes that followed World War I. They suggest that as well as the impetus given to psychotherapy by the treatment of shell-shock, there was the post-war atmosphere of bereavement and the change in mourning customs. Freud wrote *Mourning and Melancholia* during World War I and later, in *Beyond the Pleasure Principle*, struggled with the phenomenon of recurrent battle dreams. The impact of bereavement was enormous: roughly three-quarters of a million Britons died in the war, and about one-third of the dead were married, leaving about 248,000 widows and 381,000 fatherless children. The funeral and mourning customs that had signified loss before the war became impractical due to the enormous number of dead and the comforts of religion generally became less significant to the bereaved. When Bowlby was working at the Maudsley in 1933–34, he apparently became aware of bereavement as a fact in psychosis. This sensitised him to the significance of early separation, which he then studied in his analysis (Bowlby 1946) of a series of 44 cases of juvenile thieves seen at the London Child Guidance Clinic in 1936 and 1937.

Bowlby had been alerted to the significance of early attachment and the consequences of its disruption by the work of Ian Suttie. In his book, *The Origins of Love and Hate* (Suttie 1988), Suttie took issue with Freud and contemporary

Freudian instinct theory. He stressed what would now be called object relations, the prime significance of the early attachment of infants to mothers, and the trauma of separation anxiety that antecedes later generators of anxiety. Suttie was widely read in anthropology and sociology, and he brought this knowledge to bear on his outline of a form of psychology broader than Freudian psychoanalysis, a move from individual to social psychology.

It seems likely, as Dorothy Heard (1988) writes in her Introduction to the reissues of *The Origins of Love and Hate*, that Suttie was influenced by Ferenczi. Suttie's wife, Jane, had translated many of Ferenczi's papers, and in the Preface to the translation Ferenczi writes, 'it gives me great pleasure to lay my work once more before Anglo-Saxon readers, particularly because I have found that with their broad-mindedness, they often strive to view such opinions as mine without prejudice, whereas elsewhere these are turned down on account of their novelty or their boldness'. Much more than did Freud, Ferenczi emphasised the clinical aspect of psychoanalysis, the love between therapist and patient and the patient's need to find in the therapist a secure attachment in order to relive and recover from early conflicts and deprivations in the mother–infant relationship.

The Hungarian school of psychoanalysis had emphasised attachment almost from the start, and Ferenczi's pupil, Michael Balint, later brought this development to British psychoanalysis. Suttie described the infant as having from birth an innate need for companionship which is the infant's only way of self-preservation, and showed how the infant and child always tries to restore harmonious relationships with care-givers. He believed that a psycho-biological framework needed to be developed, with a language that would comprehend the individual and social phenomena of infancy. This viewpoint, later developed by Bowlby, clearly leads on to the work of Fairbairn, Winnicott and the Independent Group of psychoanalysts in the British Psycho-Analytic Society. Suttie's early death, shortly after the publication of his book, prevents us from knowing how he would have developed his theories and his technique. The book was thoughtfully received within psychoanalysis, and may have influenced the work of W.D. Fairbairn, who was working in relative isolation in Edinburgh and who in his later papers advocated the replacement of the theory of libidinal drives by the theory of object relations.

W. Line, a Canadian psychologist, provides an interesting viewpoint on British psychiatry in the 1930s in his article, 'Some impressions of British psychiatry' (1934–35). He affirms that the story of British psychiatry is essentially one of individuals, rather than of schools and systems, and that each outstanding personality drew more from the setting in which he worked than, for example, from any university tradition, which would have a particular philosophical culture and outlook. Thus he tactfully underlines the fact that British psychiatry had not penetrated into the universities. Of the psychoanalysts, he writes:

they constitute the only group manifesting an easily recognised point of view, concerning which evangelical enthusiasm and energetic defence must be displayed. But, the main influence of psychoanalysis in Britain is not to be sought in the work of such extremists as Ernest Jones, but rather in the attitude toward the analytic system of thought reflected in the psychological trends of the country. (p.1060)

He contrasts the 'near-analysts', such as McDougall, Hart and Yellowlees, all termed 'subjectivists' and who adhered to the European emphasis on the individual, with the 'objectivists', such as R.D. Gillespie and Aubrey Lewis. Of Mapother, he writes, 'the critical genius of Mapother appears to be a pertinent example; for his discussions of the weaknesses – systematic and practical – of analysis, and his penetrating descriptions of disordered mental states, reflect not a little the influence of process psychology' (i.e. the work of the psychologist, Spearman).

Line poses the question of why the psychoanalytic approach of McDougall had had so strong an influence in Britain. He compares the reception of psychoanalysis in the 1930s in Britain and America, and suggests (contrary to the commonly held view), that psychoanalysis had a somewhat more cordial reception in Britain than in American. He attributed this to the greater emphasis on experimentation in American psychology; British psychologists had considerably less confidence in experimental psychology when applied to complicated problems of personality.

It seems that British psychology and psychiatry adapted psychoanalysis in a way that is characteristic of British thought, tending to appreciate the value of systematic thinking but not to formulate systems. As Line saw it, the 'British mind', with its interest in life and events as they are, seeks the aid of whatever systematic formulation seems most pertinent, and does not hesitate to import many systems, conflicting though they may be, when radically different problems demand solution. British thought retains a certain mobility, and British philosophers have always applied their ideas to the nature of society and its problems rather than developing purely abstract philosophical systems, as in France and Germany. The empiricism of Locke is typical. Systems tend to isolate thinkers, forcing them to defend a particular point of view and preventing their participation in matters of social policy, where breadth of purview is essential. (This well describes the position of Ernest Jones and the Psycho-Analytical Society.) Application must be eclectic, and the British use any system as long as it works; they import systems but then proceed to compromise them by adding a great deal of common sense. Line thus convincingly outlines the setting that enabled Suttie and Bowlby to integrate social psychology with psychoanalysis in their ideas.

In the 1930s, a variety of articles appeared on the application of psychodynamic methods to inpatient and outpatient clinics. T.S. Good (1930) of Littlemore Hospital described how, after 1922, using wartime experience, it was possible to run a mental hospital almost entirely on the open door system, using psychology to understand delusions and hallucinations. He emphasised that 'mental analysis' is the most certain of all methods, as it reveals to the patient the causes of breakdown which he can avoid in future. Ian Skottowe, Lindsay Neustatter and, later, James Flynd all wrote on the early treatment of the neuroses by psychotherapy in outpatient clinics.

The only centre for serious inpatient psychotherapy in the 1920s and 1930s was the Cassel Hospital under its Director, T.A. Ross (1923, 1932). Ross was a general practitioner who turned to psychotherapy during World War I, and had the confidence of powerful figures both in the army and in medicine. R.D. Gillespie was on the staff of the Cassel from 1925–26 after working with George Robertson in Edinburgh and, later, Ronald Hargreaves, an important wartime figure in psychiatry and, for a short while, Professor of Psychiatry at Leeds. W.C.M. Scott, a pioneer psychoanalyst in the psychotherapeutic treatment of psychosis, spent some years at the Cassel. The respect in which Ross was held by psychiatrists was important in maintaining a psychotherapeutic influence in psychiatry, but it was not until after World War II that the Cassel reached eminence under the dynamic leadership of T.F. Main (1989).

Another important centre of psychodynamic influence was the Institute for the Scientific Treatment of Delinquency. The Institute was given this name in 1932, but had begun to form in 1931 under the influence of Grace Pailthorpe, a psychoanalyst who had researched on women prisoners at Birmingham prison under the guidance of Dr Hamblyn Smith. Later, Pailthorpe continued her research at Holloway Prison in London, and it was this work that led to the formation of the Institute. In 1933, the Institute opened the 'Psychopathic Clinic', the forerunner of the present day Portman Clinic. The most active workers in the early years were Edward Glover, Emmanuel Miller and Dennis Carroll. Glover is the best known of these today, but Miller, a pioneer in child psychiatry and family therapy, and Carroll, a psychoanalyst who had an international reputation in the field of delinquency, were equally important.

Thus the direct influence of psychodynamics on British psychiatry before World War II was apparently limited to a few small centres, such as the Tavistock Clinic and the Cassel Hospital. However, its influence diffused out into many areas of general psychiatry and, in particular, shaped the development of outpatient clinics, where psychotherapy was able to help in the treatment of war shell-shock and other neuroses for which organic psychiatry had little to offer.

The psychoanalytic scene in Britain between the wars

Despite being isolated from the mainstream of British psychiatry, the British Psycho-Analytical Society became an important contributor to the international world of psychoanalysis. Under the leadership of Ernest Jones, who was joined by Melanie Klein in 1926, British psychoanalysis developed a form distinct from that of Vienna. Melanie Klein, who had been analysed by Ferenczi and later by Abraham, came to England at the suggestion of James and Alix Strachey. Alix Strachey had been living in Berlin, undergoing a second analysis with Karl Abraham, after a not very successful analysis with Freud. She had become friendly with Melanie Klein and was impressed by her ideas. Alix and her husband, James, arranged a lecture tour for Klein, who was eager to find a new platform for her ideas. Jones took to her and invited her to work and teach in London and also to undertake the analysis of his own children.

The leading British psychoanalysts, amongst them Jones, Edward Glover, John Rickman, Joan Riviere, Sylvia Payne and, later, Winnicott and Bowlby, were all significantly influenced by Klein's work. Through her analysis of young children, Klein outlined her ideas on the early development of mind, suggesting that Freud's four libidinal phases of development (oral, anal, phallic and genital) be replaced by what eventually she termed the schizoid-paranoid and depressive positions. She outlined an elaborate system of phantasy structures of the infant in relationship to the mother's body; suggested that oedipal phantasies developed much earlier than Freud had proposed; and emphasised the great strength of infantile sadism and destructiveness, the latter concept deriving from her insistence on the importance of Freud's death instinct, an idea which she espoused from the start and maintained throughout her life (Grosskurth 1986).

Klein, a strong and ambitious character with a great drive for power, in many ways dominated the British psychoanalytic scene until the arrival in Britain of Sigmund and Anna Freud and the Viennese refugee analysts in 1938. It is sad to note that Melanie Klein, in a letter to Ernest Jones, accused him of, 'having done much harm to psychoanalysis' (Grosskurth 1986, p.255) by inviting Freud and his daughter to this country. This revealed how much she feared that her influence would now be diminished and that she had come to equate psychoanalysis in Britain with her own work.

The arrival of the Viennese analysts led to a vigorous struggle for power within psychoanalytic society. The new arrivals were shocked at Klein's influence, and regarded her work as constituting so radical a break as no longer to be recognisable as psychoanalysis. During the war, this struggle led to a series of 'Controversial Discussions', in which a number of important issues were clarified, and which later led to the British compromise of three independent but interdependent groups within the British Psycho-Analytical Society – the

Freudians, the Kleinians and the Independent Group – which agreed to share and to divide training procedures (King and Steiner 1990).

Klein's explorations of the early mechanisms of mind, which she likened to psychotic phenomena as shown in manic depression and schizophrenia, were important because they led to pioneering efforts by Bion, Rosenfeld, Winnicott, Little, Segal and others to treat the psychoses with psychoanalysis in the post-World War II period (see below).

The impact of World War II on British psychiatry

Just as World War I was a turning point for psychotherapy through the treatment of shell-shock, so World War II was a turning point for the application of a psychodynamic social psychology to institutions. Ahrenfeldt has described in some detail the application of such thinking in the British army during the 1939–45 war (Ahrenfeldt 1968). J.R. Rees, Director of the Tavistock Clinic, became Director of British Army Psychiatry, aided by Ronald Hargreaves, and under his leadership psychoanalysts found themselves actively involved with others in the fashioning of new forms of organisation for the treatment of the war neuroses, and for the selection and training of officers and other ranks. W.R. Bion, John Rickman, A.T.M. Wilson, J.D. Sutherland, S.H. Foulkes, Harold Bridger and T.F. Main are amongst the most significant of these workers. Eric Trist (1985), a historian of these times and a close wartime associate of Bion's, has called these Tavistock members 'the invisible college', in that they maintained collegial links with each other throughout the war years.

This group achieved striking success through significant innovations in military psychiatry but also in army policy. How was this achieved? Sir Ronald Adam, who became Adjutant General, the second highest post in the British army, supported these innovations largely through his relationship with Ronald Hargreaves. The psychiatrists took part in social model-building:

1. To identify problems.

2. To look for new solutions when old ones had failed.

3. To collaborate with military personnel in the structure of the models.

4. Finally, to hand back the innovations to the military. These innovations included a method for the selection of officers (W.R. Bion and the War Office Selection Board) and the concept of a 'command' psychiatrist, in which a psychiatrist with a roving commission was attached to each of the five army commanders in the Home Forces and later overseas.

Another innovation (by Bion, Rickman and Foulkes) was the concept of therapeutic community. Psychiatrists were also used to prepare propaganda and analyse the mentality of enemies. Henry Dicks was prominent in this field.

In these and other ways, dynamic psychiatry showed itself useful to the military and became an effective part of modern military administration. Psychiatrists were involved with the intake of soldiers and finding appropriate tasks for them; the promotion and training of officers; the treatment of psychiatrically disturbed soldiers; the rehabilitation of such soldiers when possible; and helping on the return from active duty. Later they became concerned with the rehabilitation of prisoners of war returning from the Far East, who had to be helped to overcome the enormous physical and mental traumata to which they had been subjected, to enable them to return to civilian life. Psychiatrists were involved in the study of the creation, maintenance and breakdown of morale; for example T.F. Main was asked to investigate the background of the Salerno mutiny.

Therapeutic community

British psychiatrists generally were not well equipped to organise rapid rehabilitation for the psychiatric casualties of war. The first steps towards this new methodology came from Wilfred Bion and John Rickman. Rickman was a senior psychoanalyst who was deeply interested in, and well informed about, sociological and anthropological matters; he and Bion, his former analysand, were responsible for the setting up of the 'First Northfield Experiment' (de Mare 1983; Main 1989). Northfield, a large military psychiatric hospital near Birmingham, was not meeting the wartime needs of the army for the identification and treatment of recoverable cases of mental breakdown, and the discharge of the unrecoverable. Bion and Rickman were put in charge of a wing of the hospital, where they introduced a radical and psychodynamic treatment regime; discipline was restored and the patients treated as soldiers on active service. The main technique adopted was group discussion. Neurosis was treated as the enemy; soldiers had to be taught to turn and to face this enemy and to develop the courage to do so successfully. Bion's experience as a young tank officer in World War I stood him in good stead, both through his practical experience and because it meant he was accepted by the military as a fully fledged fighting man himself (Bion and Rickman 1943).

The experiment lasted only six weeks, possibly because Bion and Rickman did not fully understand the effects of change on a whole social system, but during that short time they managed to revolutionise the structure of a ward and laid the foundations upon which others were to build. The next, more lasting, phase, the Second Northfield Experiment (Foulkes 1948), was based on the work of Foulkes, Bridger, Main and others, and laid the foundations of the study of a hospital as a therapeutic institution, as described by Main (1989) in his pioneering papers.

Whilst these innovations were taking place in military psychiatry, Maxwell Jones, who originally set out to study psychosomatic conditions leading to fatigue and exhaustion in soldiers, was working under the auspices of the Maudsley. His work was important in the development of the social psychiatry movement, exemplified by his work at Henderson Hospital and, later, at Dingleton in Scotland. Jones did not come from a psychoanalytic background; his work relied more upon the concept of a 'living–learning environment' and concentrated on the examination of roles in relationship to work tasks.

Another important development during World War II was Anna Freud's residential nursery. Together with a devoted band of psychoanalytic co-workers, she cared for homeless and separated children and began the systematic observations of children for which the post-war Hampstead Child Psychotherapy Clinic became justly famous.

Anna Freud carried on her father's work and added to it her own contribution to child analysis which, in contrast to Melanie Klein's work, was based upon the systematic observation of children in different circumstances such as nursery schools, the care of wartime children in residential settings, and the observation of children with physical deficits such as blindness. The systematic analysis of these data was greatly aided by the construction and development of the Hampstead Index, a method for the systematic classification and analysis of the clinical data of the many children in treatment. This was systematised under the direction of Joseph Sandler. Anna Freud herself contributed the concept of the *developmental line*, the observation of the way in which the child progresses within certain defined areas of behaviour. Thus one such developmental line is from emotional dependency to independence, from dependency on others for bodily care and gratification to self-sufficiency in this respect. This concept of developmental lines has proved very helpful in the study of children, adolescents and, eventually, adults. Anna Freud's considerable contribution to the systematic development of psychoanalysis and its impact on child psychiatry is well brought out in the recent biography by Young-Bruhl (1988).

The post-war Tavistock Clinic

The 'invisible college' gathered together in the post-war years under the leadership of W.R. Bion. This group took control of the Tavistock and eventually ousted the pre-war members, in particular those who did not accept the psychoanalytic approach. Most undertook psychoanalytic training, as hardly any of them had begun or attempted training in the pre-war years. The isolation of the Institute of Psycho-Analysis and the Tavistock Clinic began in this way to break down, but some problems arose directly from this. The Tavistock psychiatrists, despite their psychoanalytic training, were imbued with enthusiasm for a social psychiatric model. The training analysts, particularly Melanie Klein, saw these moves as resistance to a true psychoanalysis and therefore discouraged group therapy and associated explorations in social psychiatry. However, the enthusiasm of the staff maintained a great impetus in the field of group therapy for many years. They adopted the model of W.R. Bion and, later, that of Henry Ezriel. The latter in particular applied a strictly psychoanalytic object relations model to the group phenomena, attempting to establish the nature of the group's transferences to the therapist, and to examine both the anxieties that these evoked and the defences against them. Though this produced a number of significant papers, Ezriel (1950) was unable to complete his research, and a follow-up study of group therapy at the Tavistock Clinic by David Malan (1963) did not appear to support the clinical relevance of this approach.

Research into social psychiatry at the Tavistock became split off into the Institute of Human Relations, partly as a result of the changes that had to be made when the Tavistock Clinic entered the National Health Service. The Rockefeller Foundation gave a large grant to the Institute to enable it to continue the work begun in wartime conditions on the application of psychodynamic models to organisation and to social issues.

The Tavistock Clinic itself began to be well known through the work of John Bowlby in the Department of Children and Parents, and it was largely through Bowlby's work and the films made by his collaborator, James Robertson, that the world of medicine and psychology, and later the wider community, began to understand the importance of the early mother–infant bond and the dangers of its disruption through hospitalisation (Robertson 1958).

R.D. Laing

Probably the best-known Tavistock figure of the post-war years was Ronald Laing. He wrote *The Divided Self* (1960) whilst still in training both at the Tavistock and at the Institute of Psychoanalysis, and he became the central figure of a significant movement. Laing brought the European existential and phenomenological approach to bear on psychoanalysis and this had an immediate appeal both to psychiatrists and to the lay public. Propelled into instant fame, he abandoned formal psychoanalysis and became involved in the Kingsley Hall Experiment, in which psychotic and borderline patients and a whole variety of disturbed personalities lived together with the therapists in a new form of community. Many claims were made for their clinical successes, inspired by their early enthusiasms.

Laing's writings, together with those of collaborators such as Esterson, Cooper and others, became linked with the 'anti-psychiatry' movement, which challenged the authority of psychiatrists to diagnose and treat patients, especially with drugs, although psychotherapy and psychoanalysis were also targets for a while. It was at this time that the humanistic psychology movement was challenging psychoanalysis as the most significant model in psychotherapy.

Laing's writings have remained popular. Although he never repeated the impact made by his first book, *The Divided Self*, his lasting contribution may be that psychology, psychiatry and psychoanalysis are now much more in the public domain, and the boundaries of psychiatric influence more open to community pressures.

The Balints

Another important innovation which spread the reputation of the Tavistock very widely was the introduction by Michael and Enid Balint of discussion groups for general practitioners, in which all aspects of the doctor–patient relationship could be examined. This had a profound effect on general practice, and the model of the 'Balint group' has now been widely applied to many groups other than general practitioners, for example psychiatrists, paediatricians, health visitors and occupational therapists (Balint and Balint 1961).

Group analysis

The work of Foulkes and of his collaborators at Northfield Hospital – de Mare, James Anthony and others – led to the formation of the Group-Analytic Society and, later, of the Institute of Group Analysis. Foulkes carried on his research and clinical activities first at St Bartholomew's Hospital and later at the outpatient department of the Maudsley, where he trained generations of psychiatrists in the elements of group analytic psychotherapy. Foulkes' model differed significantly from the strictly psychoanalytic, and in some ways more limited, viewpoint of Bion and Ezriel. He devised a new framework based not only on his psychoanalytic training but also on his understanding of social psychology and Gestalt psychology, the latter through his work with Kurt Goldstein in the treatment and rehabilitation of brain-injured German soldiers of World War I. Foulkes' holistic, organismic model, which gave a comprehensive theoretical framework to the practise of group analytic therapy, has proved fruitful and enduring.

Brief therapy

In the post-war era, some analysts began to see the need for effective forms of short-term psychotherapy that could be based upon psychoanalytic principles. The work of Michael Balint's short-term psychotherapy workshop, its staff drawn from the Cassel and the Tavistock, was described by David Malan (1963), and this led to a brief psychotherapy research programme at the Tavistock Clinic. This further enhanced the international reputation of the Tavistock.

The staff at the Tavistock taught the principles of psychoanalysis and dynamic psychotherapy to a very wide range of disciplines, especially to doctors, psychologists and social workers. Much of this programme was coloured by the predominantly object relations and Kleinian orientation that characterised the post-war Tavistock. This again, rather like the state of the British Psycho-Analytical Society before the war, led to a certain separation and isolation of the Tavistock from mainstream psychiatry. Many psychiatrists regarded the Tavistock as an elite group who were not prepared to modify their attitude or their techniques to bring them more into line with their psychiatric colleagues – an unfair accusation, especially if the work of Balint, Bowlby and Malan is considered. In recent years, the Tavistock has made attempts to become much more in touch with developments in psychiatry and other forms of psychotherapy, to extend its work into the community, and to learn from others as well as trying to teach.

The National Health Service (NHS) and psychotherapy

Since the war, psychoanalytic psychotherapists have helped to develop training in psychotherapy throughout the country. Through their work on the committees of the Royal College of Psychiatrists and on the Committee of the Joint Higher Committee for Psychiatric Training, they have helped to fashion and to implement a network of psychotherapy services and training in most parts of the British Isles. Senior Registrar posts are now available in many regions, and the psychoanalytic monopoly on training for future psychiatrists specialising in psychotherapy no longer holds. Senior Registrars, who are often alone or in very small numbers in regions distant from London, can yet obtain a fairly comprehensive training. Psychotherapists within the NHS have come together to form the Association for Psychoanalytic Psychotherapists, which now publishes its own journal and has created a platform for psychotherapists within the NHS.

Changes in mental hospital practice

The work of Maxwell Jones and Tom Main was influential in bringing about many changes in hospital practice. The move away from custodial practices was accelerated by the creation of ward discussion groups, and the attempt to create therapeutic communities in parts of psychiatric hospitals or in small specialist units characterised the first two decades after the war. Though these experiments were not uniformly successful, they did help to change the climate of mental hospital psychiatry. Some units attempted the difficult task of a psychotherapeutic approach to psychoses, notably at Shenley Hospital near London and at the Maudsley. The programme at Shenley was controversial and was eventually much toned down, and the programme at the Maudsley, carefully fostered by Henri Rey and Murray Jackson, seems to have come to an end with their retirement.

Research into, and the practise of, the psychotherapy of psychosis, carried out in America within institutions such as Chestnut Lodge, has not had the same opportunities in this country. NO facilities have been set up for intensive psychoanalytic therapy of schizophrenia, and therefore this work has largely had to be done within the realm of private practice. Pioneers such as Bion, Rosenfeld, Segal and others, largely drawn from the Kleinian group, have greatly enlarged our understanding of psychotic mechanisms, though their clinical results have not been systematically evaluated (see Chapters 13 and 14).

The most careful systematic psychoanalytic work in psychosis is that of Thomas Freeman (1988). Trained in the classical tradition of Anna Freud, Freeman has worked in the relative isolation of Scotland and Northern Ireland and has combined the career of psychoanalyst with that of consultant psychiatrist. His work with chronic schizophrenia, with delusions and hallucinations and with borderline patients, is an important contribution. Together with his colleagues, Yorke and Wiseberg, Freeman has recently co-authored a book which links the developmental aspects of psychoanalysis with the phenomena of clinical psychiatry (Yorke, Wiseberg and Freeman 1989).

British psychoanalysis

This section will briefly review some of the outstanding contributions made by British psychoanalysts to international psychoanalysis. These come from the Kleinian school, the Independent Group and, as outlined above, from Anna Freud's group. The achievements of the Independent Group are well set out in Kohon's *The British School of Psychoanalysis: The Independent Tradition* (1986). An interesting synthesis of British contributions to psychoanalysis, unfortunately excluding that of Anna Freud, is that of Hughes (1989), *Reshaping the Psychoanalytic Domain. The Work of Melanie Klein, W.R.D Fairbairn and D.W. Winnicott.*

The English school of psychoanalysis had already started to develop along its own lines in the 1920s, before Melanie Klein arrived in 1926. This can be related to the geographical distance of London from Vienna, to some of the cultural features that have been alluded to above in discussing the work of Suttie and Bowlby, and also to the particular character of the early generations of British psychoanalysts. Those with a medical background were mostly well-established neurologists and psychiatrists who were attracted to psychoanalysis because they saw it as a sound development within psychiatry, and a liberation from dogmatic neurological materialism. There was also a significant number of lay analysts and they, like most of the psychiatrists, came from the British upper-middle class. Some came from, or had close links with, the group of Cambridge intellectuals who formed an important part of the Bloomsbury Group, and who were well connected socially and were part of a progressive intellectual elite. James Strachey, the translator of Freud, was the brother of Lytton Strachey; Adrian Stephen was the younger brother of Virginia Woolf, and his wife, Karen, a philosopher, had studied under Bertrand Russell – both qualified in medicine to become psychoanalysts; Joan Riviere was a member of the distinguished Verrall family of Cambridge intellectuals; John Rickman came from an upper-middle-class Quaker family, and the Glovers from Scottish Presbyterian families. The British group – solid, progressive and professional – thus contrasted greatly with the rather polyglot collection of early Viennese analysts, many of whom came from rather Bohemian and artistic circles, were highly neurotic though talented and, as a group, were often rent with conflicts and rivalries.

The very fact that Melanie Klein was invited to Britain and received the attention and support that she did, shows that the British group was ready to explore her radical approach to the child's mind. Reflecting the influence of Ferenczi and Abraham, Melanie Klein's work emphasises the importance of very early object relations; the importance of projection and subsequent re-introjection under the influence of the child's instinctual drives, in particular of destructive aggression; and the very early establishment of oedipal relationships. The significance of the real relationship with the mother seems at times almost to have disappeared under the power of projection, although Klein does maintain that good mothering experiences are important in enabling the child to survive the very painful and dangerous early experiences of infancy, when the infant has begun to conceive of, and to perceive, the mother as dangerous and bad.

W.R.D. Fairbairn, much influenced by Klein's work but working in isolation in Edinburgh, moved further from Freud than had Klein, in that he discarded the concept of the libidinal drive altogether. For Fairbairn, the libidinal aim is the establishment of satisfactory object relations, and the prime need is not the release and relief of libidinal tension but a gradual consciousness of emotional dependency. Fairbairn's developmental line is from immature dependency to mature dependency, that is, he regards the person as always engaged in dependent relationships, by which he primarily means the dependency upon internal objects. For Fairbairn, the concept of the impulse, the instinctual drive, is replaced by a dynamic structure, and thus he is able to dispense with Freud's theories of mental energy which, for Fairbairn, represent an outmoded and irrelevant scientific model (Hughes 1989).

Although Fairbairn sees the mother as being the essential object of the child's needs, he devotes relatively little attention to the actual behaviour of the mother and the way in which she significantly affects the child's development. It was Donald Winnicott, a paediatrician who had moved to psychoanalysis, who placed the mother in a central position in the developmental situation. How the mother handles her child, how she responds to the child's needs and how she adapts herself actively to the child's development is at the centre of Winnicott's contribution (Hughes 1989). The mother is both environment and object. She is that which surrounds the child from birth, replacing the intra-uterine environment with an extra-uterine one in which all the child's biological and physiological needs have to be met by her. She is also the object mother, the person who has to be found and subjectively created by the infant, the 'subjective-object' who gradually becomes an 'objective object' as the child's capacities to deal with reality develop. She is also the object who has sensitively to begin to 'fail' her child, that is, gradually withdraw her ministrations so the child can begin to take over from her and meet his own needs. Naturally, Winnicott links his ideas about the significance of the mother's holding of the child in the maternal setting to the analytic situation. For him, the setting of analysis, the constancy and reliability of the analyst, his presence and his way of being with his patient, are of the greatest significance in the analysis, particularly in the analysis of patients who have regressed to very early developmental stages. Winnicott's work is full of stimulating paradoxes, such as his statements that when he interprets to a patient, it is basically to show him that he does not understand him! By this, Winnicott means that the analyst has to show his patient that he is not omnipotent and omniscient.

This developmental line of Klein, Fairbairn and Winnicott characterises the British school of object relations. Much of this work has been accepted by the followers of Anna Freud, although considerable differences still exist, such as the Freudian rejection of the Kleinian concept of the death instinct, and of seeing the transference situation as being based almost entirely upon the patient's projections, and in the nature and timing of interpretations.

Analytic psychology (Fordham 1979)

There was little in the way of an organised school of analytical psychology in the 1920s and 1930s, although Jung had a considerable influence in Britain and made several visits. In 1914, he was invited to address the annual general meeting of the British Medical Association in Aberdeen. In 1919, with William McDougall in the Chair, Jung addressed the Section of Psychiatry of the Royal Society of Medicine, to whom he spoke again 20 years later in 1939. He held two seminars, one in 1923 and one in 1925, and in 1935 gave five seminars at the Tavistock Clinic. In 1938, Jung chaired a conference of the International General Medical Society for Psychotherapy, in Oxford.

Jung's principal disciple and exponent was H. Godwin Baynes. An Oxford rowing blue and an important member of Rupert Brookes' circle of friends, the 'neo-Pagans', Baynes both translated Jung's work and represented it stoutly. Before the war, the Analytical Psychology Club and the Society of Analytical Psychology were formed; the latter was the training organisation and consisted originally of medical analysts. The predominance of medical analysts is built into the structure of the Society, of which Michael Fordham has been the leading member for many years. Fordham, who worked in child analysis as well as adult analysis, has made many important contributions to both theory and technique. Jungian ideas were represented at the Maudsley by E.A. Bennet and by Robert Hobson, but Jungian thought is conspicuous by its absence at the present day Tavistock Clinic.

There are interesting similarities between many aspects of analytic psychology and the object relations school of British psychoanalysis, particularly the work of Klein, Winnicott and Fairbairn. Samuel, in *Jung and the Post-Jungians* (1985) has sought to demonstrate a steadily increasing approximation of Jungian and psychoanalytic ideas.

Psychoanalysis and psychiatry

Psychoanalysis in Britain has a good international reputation and is probably more recognised abroad than it is within this country. Academic psychology and psychiatry has maintained a distance and a resistance to psychoanalysis, though it has absorbed and integrated many psychoanalytic concepts without fully acknowledging them. Whereas before World War II psychoanalysis was isolated from mainstream psychotherapy and psychiatry, there has since then been a useful diffusion across the boundaries of the discipline.

Psychoanalysts are now much more engaged in the practise and teaching of psychiatry and of psychoanalytic psychotherapy, although this work does remain concentrated in London. Psychoanalysts have contributed to the development of a psychotherapeutic service within the NHS in the areas of individual, group and family therapy. Psychoanalytic theory has been greatly revised under the impact of the British school of psychoanalysis, and this work has led to interesting prospects for the understanding and treatment of the more severe personality disorders and the borderline and psychotic states. Child analysis has flourished in this country under the rival influences of Melanie Klein and Anna Freud. General practice has been greatly influenced by the work of Michael Balint and his followers, and the Balint-type discussion group has been adopted in many other areas of medicine and psychiatry. The British Psycho-Analytical Society has become much more open in recent years, and its influence should grow as a result.

Conclusion

Seventy years ago the psychodynamic approach began strongly to influence psychiatric practice in Britain through the experience of World War I, when large numbers of patients had to be treated and quickly rehabilitated. The British psychodynamic approach was largely based on Freud's ideas, but the influence of the small number of psychoanalysts was limited by their need to maintain a separate identity and only to practise psychoanalysis, which of necessity took place entirely in the private sphere.

The outpatient clinics, such as those at the Tavistock and the Maudsley and the York Clinic at Guy's Hospital, and the inpatient units, such as at the Cassel and some of the progressive mental hospitals, were staffed by psychiatrists who utilised some psychoanalytic and psychodynamic principles and practices, and combined these with an empirical approach, using counselling, suggestion and persuasion.

Changing social attitudes to the mentally ill in the 1920s and 1930s allowed more optimistic and liberal forms of treatment to take place in the mental hospitals, and the staff of these hospitals began to establish outpatient clinics for the diagnosis and early treatment of psychoses and neuroses. However, psychoanalysts and psychiatrists remained relatively isolated from one another until World War II, when they came together as teams for the first time. Psychodynamic and sociodynamic concepts, inspired mainly by the former staff of the Tavistock Clinic, were then accepted, tried and made their impact in military psychiatry. These psychiatrists and their pupils became a significant force over the next two decades, accelerating the pace of change in the mental hospitals and pressing for the acceptance of, and training in, psychotherapy for general psychiatrists. In this respect, there have been significant changes, and psychiatric training now has a definite psychodynamic component.

The post-war years have also seen the emergence of the new profession of clinical psychology, which now seeks autonomy and parity with psychiatry. Many clinical psychologists are analytically trained, and treat and teach in geographical areas where psychoanalysts, who still largely cluster in and around London, do not practise. Psychologists who have subscribed to behavioural methods are often in practice combining psychodynamic and behavioural principles.

Group psychotherapy has emerged as a strong force, and clearly has an important and growing place in the NHS and Community Psychiatry and in the sphere of the Social Services.

Psychoanalysts and analytical psychologists have contributed significantly to NHS psychiatry, and the pre-war isolation of psychoanalysts from psychiatry no longer pertains. However, few academic positions within psychiatry are filled by psychoanalysts, and at the time of writing there is only one Chair in psychotherapy in Britain, in sad contrast to the situation that exists both in other European countries and in North America. It is to be hoped that this will not be the case for long.

In retrospect, psychodynamic psychiatry has a good record in Britain. There is much yet to be done, but progress cannot occur faster than society will accept and foster. The great social changes of the past two decades – much greater awareness of mental health issues, the closing of the large mental hospitals and consequent need for improved community health resources, and the changes in social consciousness which have both allowed for, and been stimulated by, the rise of feminism – bode well for the psychodynamic approach in contemporary psychiatry. Public recognition that psychiatric needs cannot be met solely and simply by pharmacotherapy should exert considerable pressure on the psychiatric profession and its masters to improve the provision of psychodynamic services, despite the real difficulties that exist in practising psychotherapy or using psychodynamic approaches within the setting of the NHS.

References

Ahrenfeldt, R.H. (1968) *Military Psychiatry in Medical Services in War*. London: HMSO.

Balint, M. and Balint, E. (1961) *Psychotherapeutic Techniques in Medicine*. London: Tavistock.

Bion, W.R. (1985) *The Other Side of Genius*. Abingdon: Fleetwood Press.

Bion, W.R. and Rickman, J. (1943) 'Intra-group tensions in therapy.' *Lancet 27*, 678–681.

Boll, T.E.M. (1962) 'May Sinclair and the Medico-Psychological Clinic of London.' Proc. *American Philosophical Soc. 106*, 310–326.

Bolton, J.S. (1926) 'The myth of the unconscious mind.' *Journal of Mental Science 72*, 25–38.

Bowlby, J.(1946) *Forty-four Juvenile Thieves*. London: Baillère, Tindall and Cox.

Boyle, H.A. (1922) 'The ideal clinic for the treatment of nervous and borderline cases.' *Proceedings of the Royal Society of Medicine (Section of Psychiatry)*, 39–48.

British Medical Journal (Suppl) (1929) 'Report on psychoanalysis.' *British Medical Journal 29*, 6.

Crichton-Browne, J. (1920) 'Notes on psychoanalysis and psychotherapy.' *Lancet*, 5 June, 12.

Dewhurst, K. (1982) *Hughlings Jackson on Psychiatry*. Oxford: Sandford.

Eder, M.D. (1917) *War Shock*. London: Heinemann

Edinburgh Medical Journal (1920) 'Review of Stoddart's "Mind and its disorders".' *Edinburgh Medical Journal 24*, 263–264.

Ezriel, H.A. (1950) 'A psychoanalytic approach to group treatment.' *British Journal of Medical Psychology 23*, 59–74.

Fordham, M. (1979) 'Analytical psychology in England.' *Journal of Analytical Psychology 24*, 279–297.

Foulkes, S.H. (1948) *Introduction to Group-Analytic Psychotherapy: Studies in the Social Integration of Individuals and Groups*. London: Heinemann.

Freeman, T. (1988) *The Psychoanalyst in Psychiatry*. London: Karnac.

Good, T.S. (1930) 'The history and progress of Littlemore Hospital.' *Journal of Mental Science 76*, 606–621.

Grosskurth, P. (1986) *Melanie Klein*. London: Hodder and Stoughton.

Hart, B. (1912) *The Psychology of Insanity*. Cambridge: Cambridge University Press.

Hart, B. (1927) *Psychopathology*. Cambridge: Cambridge University Press.

Heard, D.H. (1988) 'Introduction.' In I.D. Suttie (ed) *The Origins of Love and Hate*. London: Free Association Books.

Hobman, J.B. (1949) *David Eder: Memoirs of a Modern Pioneer*. London: Victor Gollancz.

Hughes, J. (1989) *Reshaping the Psychoanalytic Domain. The Work of Melanie Klein, W.R.D. Fairburn and D.W. Winnicott.* Berkeley: University of California Press.

Hutton, I. (1960) *Memories of a Doctor in War and Peace.* London: Heinemann.

Jones, E. (1959) *Memories of a Psychoanalyst.* London: Hogarth (Reprinted by Free Association Books, London, 1988.)

King, P. and Steiner, R. (1990) *The Freud–Klein Controversy 1941–5.* London: Routledge.

Kohon, G. (1986) *The British School of Psychoanalysis: The Independent Tradition.* London: Free Association Books.

Laing, R.D. (1960) *The Divided Self.* London: Tavistock.

Lewis, A. (1979) 'Edward Mapother and the making of the Maudsley Hospital.' In *Later Papers.* Oxford: Oxford University Press.

Line, W. (1934–35) 'Some impressions of British psychiatry.' *American Journal of Psychiatry 91*, 1059–1077.

Main, T.F. (1989) *The Ailment and Other Psychoanalytic Essays.* London: Free Association Books.

Malan, D.H. (1963) *A Study of Brief Psychotherapy.* London: Tavistock.

de Maré, P.B. (1983) 'Michael Foulkes and the Northfield Experiment.' In M. Pines (ed) *The Evolution of Group Analysis.* London: Routledge and Kegan Paul.

Mercier, C.A. (1916) 'Psycho-analysis.' *British Medical Journal,* December, 897–900.

Neustatter, W.L. (1935) 'The result of fifty cases treated by psychotherapy.' *Lancet* April, 796–799.

Newcombe, N. and Lerner, J.C. (1982) 'Britain between the wars: the historical content of Bowlby's theory of attachment.' *Psychiatry 45*, 1–12.

Rickman, R. (1950) 'Obituary.' *International Journal of Psycho-Analysis 31*, 286–8.

Rivers, W.H.R. (1923) *Conflict and Dream* London: Kegan, Paul.

Robertson, J. (1958) *Young Children in Hospital.* London: Tavistock.

Ross, T.A. (1923) *The Common Neuroses.* London: Edward Arnold.

Ross, T.A. (1932) *Introduction to Analytic Psychotherapy.* London: Edward Arnold.

Samuel, A. (1985) *Jung and the Post-Jungians.* London: Routledge.

Slobodin, R. (1978) *W.H.R. Rivers.* New York: Columbia University Press.

Stengel, E. (1963) 'Hughlings Jackson's influence in psychiatry'. *British Journal of Psychiatry 109*, 348.

Stoddart, W.H.B. (1915) 'The new psychiatry.' *Lancet,* March 20 and 27.

Stoddart, W.H.B. (1921) *Mind and Its Disorders.* London: H.K. Lewis.

Stone, M. (1985) 'Shellshock and the psychologists.' In W.F. Bynum, R. Porter and M. Shepherd (eds) *The Anatomy of Madness, Vol 2.* London: Tavistock Press.

Suttie, I.D. (1988) *The Origins of Love and Hate.* London: Free Association Books.

Trist, E. (1985) 'Working with Bion in the '40's; the group decade.' London: Routledge and Kegan Paul.

Yorke, G., Wiseberg, S. and Freeman, T. (1989) *Development and Psychopathology: Studies in Psychoanalytic Psychiatry.* London: Yale.

Young-Bruhl, E. (1988) *Anna Freud.* London: Macmillan.

PART 4

Other

CHAPTER 12

Coherency and Disruption in the Sense of the Self[1]

'Man is born broken. He lives by mending. The grace of God is glue' (Eugene O'Neill). Heinz Kohut's (1978, p.781) use of this powerful tragic statement demonstrates the importance he gave to cohesion in building up the self-concept and developmental line of what he came to call Tragic Man.

Cohesion is a key concept in Kohut's model of the stages of growth of the self (1971), for example:

> The developmental step from auto-erotism to narcissism is a move towards increased synthesis of the personality due to a shift from libidinal cathexis of individual body parts, or of isolated physical or mental functions, to a cathexis of an (albeit at first grandiose, exhibitionistic and unrealistic) cohesive self. In other words the narcissism of the body self and of the mental self coalesce and form a superordinated unit.

Thus 'Growth of the self experience as a physical and mental unit that has cohesiveness in space and continuity in time' (Kohut 1971, p.215), it is implied, is supported by the maternal response to the whole child, for, 'a relationship to an empathically approving and accepting parent is one of the preconditions of the original establishment of a firm cathexis of the self' (Kohut 1971, p.118).

Kohut seems to me to use the term 'cohesion' to describe the achievement of a structured, integrated, stage of mind, for example, 'the cohesive structured total mind self' (p.120).

Mother's responses play a crucial role through a 'cohesion-establishment' involvement with her…total child (Kohut 1977, p.76) and this message is repeated many times. Mother aids the child to achieve self-cohesion through her

1   'Coherencia y ruptura en el sentido del self.' Published in: *Clinica y Analisis Grupal* (1986), Jul.–Sep., *10*, 41, 425–43.

acceptance and empathic responses to the needs of the emerging creative self for empathy, mirroring, for joyous pleasure in his achievements.

Kohut's original belief was that, 'the self...was formed through the coalescence of its parts – that the child's experience of himself as a body–mind unit ... established itself gradually through the coalescence of the experiences of single, unconnected body parts and of isolated bodily and mental functions' (Kohut 1978, p.746).

He revised this theory later when he became doubtful about the correctness of a theory that the formation of the self comes about by such a 'coalescence' of the experiences of fragments, parts, self-nuclei. He moved to a theory in which, 'the progressively toned experience of a single part and function has become related to the total experience of a cohesive part – the parts, in other words, do not build up the self, they become built into it' (Kohut 1978, p.749).

He now develops his concept of the 'double nature of man', that is, Guilty Man and Tragic Man. One developmental line is that of the establishment of the mental representation of separate parts, single drives and functions. This is the developmental line of Guilty Man, with the concomitant and inevitable oedipal complex and accompanying castration anxiety.

The other developmental line is his beginning experience of himself as a larger *coherent* and enduring organisation, as a self. Here suddenly, without explanation, the term 'coherency' is introduced as crucial to the description of the total self experience: 'From early on, the child's empathic environment reacts to him with two sets of responses: one is attuned to his beginning experience of himself as a larger, coherent and enduring organisation, i.e. to him as a self' (Kohut 1978, p.755).

Ornstein (1978) points out this crucial 'small' change in Kohut's theory, that the development of parts and of the whole self is viewed along two separate lines. However, Ornstein omits the concepts of organisation and coherency in his exposition of this theoretical development and refers only to cohesion and continuity.

Indeed, Kohut does make much more use of the concept of cohesion than that of coherency, and the latter term is only adopted when he later describes the developmental line of 'Tragic Man', the experience of the wholeness of self that does not arise from the coalescence of parts.

I propose now to compare and contrast these terms – cohesion and coherence – and to see how they have been used in psychoanalysis.

Some dictionary definitions of cohesion and coherence make little distinction between these terms, both being descriptions of the attachment of parts to each other. Other definitions do clearly, however, distinguish them on the basis of an organisational principle, which applies to coherency but not to cohesion.

Thus in Webster's *New Dictionary of Synonyms* we find the following definitions. Cohesion presents, 'the unity of material things held together by a physical substance such as cement, mortar, glue or by a physical force such as attraction or affinity'. Coherence represents:

> Unity of immaterial, of intangible things, such as the points of an argument, the details of a picture, the incidents, characters and setting of a story; or of material and of objective things that are bound into a unity by a spiritual, intellectual or aesthetic relationship, as through their clear sequence of their harmony with one another; it therefore commonly connotes an integrity which makes the whole and the relationship of its parts clear and manifest. (p.157)

Among psychoanalysts it is Hans Loewald (1980) who has paid most attention to this principle of coherence. He points out some important passages in Freud that relate to coherence.

In *Beyond the Pleasure Principle* (Freud 1920), and dealing here with the repetition compulsion, Freud points out that is it not the repressed that demonstrates resistance in the course of therapy, it is a repressing source that arises from the higher stratum and systems of the mind which originally carried out the repression. The resistances and the motives for them are unconscious, and, therefore, Freud points out, we should not make a contrast between the conscious and the unconscious but between the *coherent* ego and the *repressed*. Much of the ego is itself unconscious, notably what we may describe as its nucleus; only a small part of it is covered by the term 'preconscious'. The patient's resistance therefore can be seen to arise from the ego; the repetition compulsion must be ascribed to the repressed and organised unconscious.

In *Beyond the Pleasure Principle*, dealing with the repetition compulsion, Freud again points out that it is not the repressed that demonstrates resistance in the course of therapy, it is a repressing source that arises from the same higher stratum and system and, 'we know that the stability of this new acquisition is exposed to constant shocks' (p.19). Here Freud seems to be equating the coherent ego with a conscious ego, and the unconscious ego is equivalent to the repressed ego.

However, in *The Ego and the Id*, Freud (1923) writes that through working with resistance:

> We have come upon something in the ego itself which is also unconscious, which behaves exactly like the repressed. Therefore we cannot derive neurosis from a conflict between the conscious and the unconscious and have to substitute for this antithesis another – the antithesis between a *coherent* ego and the *repressed which is split off from it*. (p.17, author's italics)

The consequences are that the unconscious does not coincide with the repressed; all that is repressed is unconscious, but not all that is unconscious is repressed. A part of the ego undoubtedly is unconscious and not latent like the preconscious.

Here Freud is moving away from a topographical model and is beginning to talk about the characteristic of being unconscious as a quality which can have many meanings.

Freud (1923) writes: 'In each individual there is a coherent organisation of mental processes which we call the ego. It is to this ego that consciousness is attached' (p.17). Again Freud does not distinguish between the conscious and the unconscious ego, and attach the quality of consciousness to the coherent ego and the repressed which is split off from it' (p.17).

In *The Ego and the Id* Freud points out that even subtle and difficult intellectual operations can be carried out preconsciously, such as finding the solutions to difficult mathematical or other problems during the state of sleep which are then available to the person on awakening. The faculties of self-criticism and conscience, mental activities that rank extremely highly, are unconscious and produce effects of the greatest importance. Therefore we speak of an unconscious sense of guilt, and therefore aspects of ourselves that are of the highest value in the ego can be unconscious. This again shows that the coherent, organised ego extends into the unconscious.

Freud, as we see, makes the interesting and important distinction between the *coherent* unconscious and the *repressed* unconscious. Thus the unconscious ego represents an unconscious, organised, coherent stratum of the mind and can be contrasted with the incoherent and repressed unconscious. The unconscious does not coincide with the repressed; all that is repressed is unconscious but not all that is unconscious is repressed and in an incoherent state; coherency is a principle established in unconscious areas of the mind and informs some unconscious mental processes.

Loewald (1980, p.78) makes use of this principle of organisation represented by coherency in his arguments about the nature and process of internalisation:

1. What is internalised becomes an inherent part of the coherent ego.

2. What is repressed is split off from the coherent ego.

3. The super ego is a further differentiation of the coherent ego.

Loewald (1980) writes that:

> it is of the utmost importance both theoretically and clinically, to distinguish more clearly and consistently than Freud ever did between processes of repression and processes of internalisation. The latter are involved in creating and increasing the coherent integration and organisation of the psyche as a whole, whereas repression works against such coherent psychic organisation by maintaining a share of psychic processes in a less organised, more primitive state. (p.76)

Loewald emphasises that psychic development takes place in the *setting* of an interactional psychic force field, a polarity in which the mother represents the more organised pole and the child the lesser organised. In the course of development the child comes to acquire and to resemble the characteristics of the more organised person, the mother. Another way of describing this is that where 'other' was, now stands 'self', or ego.

How does this process take place? Through internalisation, as already described, through the mother's recognition and satisfaction of the infant's needs. Basically mother organises the infant's relatively unco-ordinated urges (Loewald 1980, p.237) and through their mutual responsiveness, what the infant introjects is the response pattern of the caring person, the internalisation of an interaction process (p.231). This is not simply the internalisation of an object but the internalisation of the *interaction process* as an essential element in ego development.

Loewald does not assume the existence of a separate psychic apparatus or organisation, however primitive, from the beginning. He posits an original psychic field or matrix within which individuation processes begin. Here he differs from Kohut's later formulation of a developmental line of 'Tragic Man', of the wholeness of the psyche from the very start. Unlike Kohut he finds a place for the concept of drives but does not need to differentiate the instinctual drive organisation from the evolving self, for the drives themselves at the stage of the mother–infant matrix (Loewald 1980, p.270) consist in differentiating and integrating processes within the psychic matrix and not in unilateral experiences emanating from the infant. Instinctual drives, as motivational psychic forces, are formed by interaction within the original psychic matrix. Instinctual drives, 'never relinquish their character as *relational* phenomena' (1980, p.292; author's italics).

The child's central identity develops through his being centred upon by his caretakers. The parents offer to the child is in tune with the 'core of being' that the child presents to the parents. Empathic parents present the child with a, 'more articulate and more integrated version' of this core of being (Loewald 1980, p.229). Another way of putting this is that the parent inserts meaning and coherency at a higher level of organisation into the less organised psyche of the infant through the interaction processes and patterns which are laid down between them, and this, 'move in organisation and significance is what external reality, here the analyst, has to offer to the individual' (1980, p.239).

Where else in psychoanalysis can we look for examples of this principle of coherency?

The concept of coherency, based as it is on the principle of organisation, of parts fitting together, is closely related to the principle of adaptation, which is another term for 'fitting together'. Heinz Hartmann, who introduced the concept of adaptation into the realm of ego psychology, addressed this issue in *Ego Psychology and the Problem of Adaptation* (Hartmann 1958).

'Adaptation and fitting together'

According to Hartmann there are two areas for study: the equilibrium of the organism in relationship to the environment and mental states of equilibrium and their stability. The relationship of the organism to the environment is considered under the principle of adaptation, and the maintenance of mental states in equilibrium can be considered under the principle of 'fitting together'. Adaptation and fitting together are interdependent. Fitting together is a biological principle, 'the lawful correlation of the organism's individual parts' (Hartmann 1958, p.40) and correlates with adaptation, the maintenance of equilibrium between organism and environment. In the psychological realm, fitting together is represented by the synthetic function of the ego, a function which becomes increasingly important in the ascent of the evolutionary scale:

> In phylogenesis, evolution leads to an increased independence of the organism from its environment, so that reactions which originally occurred in relation to the external world were increasingly displaced into the interior of the organism ... thus fitting together (in the psychological realm, the synthetic function) gains in significance in the course of evolution. If we encounter – as we do in man – the function which simultaneously regulates both the environmental relationships and the interrelations of the mental institutions, we will have to place it above adaptation in the biological hierarchy. (Hartmann 1958, p.41)

Hartmann used a wealth of observations to demonstrate the importance of adaptation and fitting together in the development of the child, and referred to Spitz's work based on infant development. He would, I do not doubt, have used the information which has become available to us in more recent years through intensive observation of infant–mother behaviour, which I shall refer to later.

Let us turn, however, to Spitz and see what he has to say about coherency. In *A Genetic Field Theory of Ego Formation*, he says that:

> the emergence of the smiling response marks a turning point in the psychology development of the infant. A polarity has been established in terms of the pleasure–unpleasure principle. It is as if a number of functions have been brought into relation with each other and linked into a coherent unit. A structural pattern emerges which did not exist before in the psyche. After the establishment of this integration, the response to experience will no longer be in terms of unrelated, discrete components, but in terms of the integrated operation of the unit as a whole. (Spitz 1959, p.27)

With this, a new and better adapted mode of functioning is introduced. The response and behaviour take on a different, a more goal-adapted pattern. The new mode of functioning makes rewards available which ensure its continued working. The channelisation of the drive forces creates a force field which influences the further steps in development (Spitz 1959, p.61).

Later, in discussing the principles of organisation and the concept of field theory and how this can be applied to principles of psychic organisation, Spitz quotes the embryologist Waddington:

> When elements of a certain degree of complexity become organised into an entity belonging to a higher level or organisation, we must suppose that the coherence of the higher level depends on properties which the isolated elements entered into certain relations with one another. That is to say, a new level of organisation cannot be accounted for in terms of the properties of its elementary units as they behave in isolation, but is accounted for if we add to these certain other properties which the units only exhibit when in combination with one another. (Spitz 1959, p.62)

If we take it here that the elementary units are the mother and the child, then together they represent a new level of organisation. 'However, the road which leads to this integration of isolated functions is built by the infant's object relations, by experiences of an affective nature' (Spitz 1959, p.84).

Spitz states that, 'from the very beginning the ego shows a strong tendency to form a cohesive structure which regulates a dynamic symmetry' (1959, p.85). This principle of equilibrium he links up with the integrative function of the ego, and in discussing abnormalities of ego development, developmental imbalance or the concept of the fragmented ego, he states: 'Normal integration between development and maturation can be disturbed through the absence or through the abnormality of object relations' (1959, p.86). As a result of such disturbances, abnormal ego nuclei may then become the constituents of a 'fragmented ego' and constitute one of the origins of fixation points. Through the integrative tendency of the ego these abnormal ego nuclei will, 'in due time be integrated into a more or less coherent structure, the normally developing one on the one hand, the maturational factors on the other, however apparent and out of balance the resulting ego may be' (Spitz 1959, p.88).

I find it interesting that, so far as I can see, there is only this one mention of cohesion in this monograph. Cohesion is linked with the Nirvana principle and with homeostasis and therefore represents the activity of the organism considered in isolation. Where Spitz uses the term 'coherency' it is in connection with the organisation of isolated units into a higher level of development, and this seems to presuppose the interrelationship of infant and caretaker.

Spitz was the first psychoanalytic researcher to describe and discuss the mother–infant relationship in terms of 'dialogue' (Spitz 1963). The creative interplay of gestures, sounds, of interactive rhythms, builds up the matrix of their relationship which gradually becomes transmuted into the child's own psychic structure. Dialogue is another concept that intrinsically includes coherency, the meaningful organisation of the response actions of the partners in dialogue. (You will recall that one of the commonest usages of the term 'coherency' refers to speech, whether a person's utterances are coherent or not.)

The psychoanalytic views on the child's development of language have recently been reviewed by Litowitz and Litowitz (1983), though the notion of 'dialogue' has been researched more intensively by non-psychoanalytic authors such as Schaffer, who has been associated with the work of John Bowlby.

Schaffer (1979) characterises all social interactions as dialogue, for they all involve highly intricate and closely synchronised sets of behaviour patterns contributed to by two or more individuals. Dialogues are generally characterised by an impressive 'smoothness', though the rules according to which these dialogues are conducted are often obscure.

Schaffer declares that it is *dialogue*, not monologue, which is the basic speech unit, for the primary function of speech is to communicate. It is against a background of already well-established ways of shared meanings that language arises, against a background of 'turn-taking'. A great deal of mother–infant reactions involve turn-taking, 'now me, now you', the precursors of dialogue, 'pseudo' or 'proto' conversations. Mothers attribute meaning and intentions to their infant's gestures and vocalisations, and thereby insert meaning and coherency into the developing interactions. It is the mother's response to her child, her seeing, embracing its action 'as-if' they had intentionality and purpose that is a vital element in the creation of a genuine dialogue. She talks to her child, she assumes that her child responds by wishing to talk back to her and connects random sounds and gestures by what becomes meaningful to her. By being meaningful to her they become so for her child and hence to them as a couple, establishing the sense of 'us', of 'we-ness'.

I shall not pursue the development of dialogue further, other than to say that it is at the end of the first year that the child begins to be aware of the process through acquisition of the capacities of reciprocity and intentionality (Bornstein and Kessen 1979). Reciprocity is the realisation that a dialogue needs to be sustained by both partners; intentionality that the child has the capacity to direct both its own activities and those of others. On the basis of reciprocity and intentionality the child enters more fully into the social world, gathering ideas about its own competence and begins to find its place.

The Neo-Piagetian approach

Coherency is an important principle in the synthesis that Robert Kegan has made of psychoanalytic and Piagetian approaches to personality development (Kegan 1982).

Kegan describes the evolution of personality as the evolution of meaning-constitutive activity. In the realm of object relations, an object is that which some motion has made separate or distinct from ourselves and then has to be related to. In the course of psychic development we both 'create' objects (differentiation) and relate to them (integration). Object relations are therefore always subject–object relations and the distinction between subject and object is brought about through the very beginning of this development, a process which continues throughout the life cycle. There is a series of qualitative differentiations of the self from the world, each time thereby creating a qualitatively more extensive object to which to be in relation to. The sequence is from 'embeddedness in' to 'relationship to'. Any given person differs from us not only by his distinctness from other persons but by the different ways in which we ourselves make sense of him, of which differences none may be so important as the extent to which we distinguish him from ourselves.

The infant gradually emerges from embeddedness and this is the dawn of an object world. By differentiating itself from the world and the world from it, the organism brings into being that which is independent of its own sensing and moving. As the infant develops, rather than 'being' his reflexes, he now 'has' his reflexes. The 'I' appears as that which co-ordinates or mediates the reflexes in a new form of subjectivity. This creates a world separate from me, a world to relate to rather than to be embedded in.

Through the development of object permanence and the separation–protest phases we can get some idea of the rhythm of psychic development. In separation distress, separation from the object can be seen as separation from the self, from that which was 'me' before 'me' and 'other' were differentiated. Through the process of development the object from which I separate was previously experienced as 'me'; there is a change in the subject–object balance from which I am not yet sufficiently differentiated to be able to integrate the new me and the relationship to the other, therefore I am distressed.

Anxiety and depression are the affects of experiences of the wrenching activity of differentiation in its first phases, but sooner or later the balance as to which self is 'me' shifts and the old equilibrium can be 'reflected upon' from the new position that has emerged. The old equilibrium is now taken as 'object' in the new balance and is often reacted to affectively with anger and repudiation. Emergence from embeddedness involves a kind of repudiation, an evolutionary recognition that what before was me is now not me. *The other is first of all a not-me before he is really an-other.*

Thus object-creating means subject-losing, and subject-losing can lead to object-finding. This is a central rhythm of personality development. In this neo-Piagetian model of development, coherence is given a prime place; it is the greater coherence of its organisation which is the presumed motive of development, a transorganic motive shared by all living things. The organism is moved to make meaning, to resolve discrepancy, it is moved to preserve and to enhance its integrity. From birth onwards the organism is prompted not to return to the homeostatic state of the foetus but to bring its organisation into coherence, to take account of the greater complexity with which it is faced, not to return to an old reality, but to establish a meaning for, or to make sense out of, its present reality.

This is the life history of qualitative reconstructions of self and other, each one emerging out of the process of differentiation and integration.

Kegan proposes a schema of six different levels of subject–object relations throughout the lifespan which are not relevant here, but which constantly reflect the need for coherence within the organism.

When he turns to what he terms 'natural therapy', which is, 'those relations in human context which spontaneously support people through the sometimes difficult process of growth and change' he writes:

> We may hear grief, mourning and loss, but it is the dying of a way to know the world which no longer works, a loss of an old coherence with no coherence im-mediately present to take its place. And yet a new balance again and again does emerge. This is the incredible wonder that makes clinical work worship before great mysteries. (Kegan 1982)

We can comprehend the individual's grief and mourning at the sense of loss of coherency, from which he recovers and establishes a new balance, a new coherence. Through these lines of the poet John Donne, we can also look at the portrait of an age when men feared that a new balance might never emerge, that the world, corrupt, ageing, ailing, was dying. The world Donne knew was, 'all in pieces, all coherence gone'.

This complaint has been explained by the scholar, Victor Harris (1966): 'The idea that the world decays – an idea inherited from the Middle Ages – was part of the Renaissance cosmic order. For two centuries it was particularly important to man's rational and spiritual life' (p.1).

Recurrent in man's intellectual history is a suspicion or a fear, and often a philosophical conviction, that his world is disintegrating. For this belief he finds many reasons. The race of men seems to grow feebler, society more confused, and all nature old and weary. This sense of decay of the universe, the corruption of plants and creatures or of the heavens themselves, is confirmed by the unresolved conflicts within man's mind. He has before him the tragic disparity between the ailing world he lives in and an ideal world which he envisages. Old men remember the happier days of their youth. Legend cherishes the dream of the golden or heroic age, or an era of giants or miracles, of a Garden of Eden untouched by sin or death:

> Through the 16th and 17th centuries there was still no serious challenge to the notion that the world was created for man's use and man, internal, for God's glory. All the universe was included as a closely linked hierarchy of forms. Every

unit held its appointed place in a magnificent harmony extending downward from God to the angels to man; from the heavens to the elements of fire, water and earth; from macrocosm to microcosm; from man to woman; from rational humanity to the brutish beasts; from the sentient to the vegetative; from the subtler spirit at God's right hand to the grossest matter of ashes and dust. (p.1)

But man, by denying his proper obedience to God, had violated the symmetry of the whole pattern. 'Tis all in pieces,' Donne lamented, 'all coherence gone; all just supply, and all relation'.

This world view in which the world must decay, represents the decay of a closed system where all parts must fit together, when man reflects nature. Because man is corrupt and sinful and eventually decays and dies, so also must nature:

> This philosophy is replaced by one wherein our knowledge is understood to be fragmentary and the all-inclusive image of microcosm and macrocosm is regarded as a misleading figure of speech. No argument may be so extended from man to nature, it is asserted, for any defection in the part has its compensation in the continuity of the whole. Because the powers of nature are unchanged and unchangeable, any variation in the forms or the state of nature is temporary and local. (Harris 1966, p.203)

It is striking that in the ontology of consciousness, when this world view of an unchanging equilibrium had to be given up, it was accompanied by grief, loss, mourning and even panic. The feeling of loss of coherency, as exemplified by Donne's poem, was eventually replaced by a newer form of coherency, now at a higher level of organisation and development, through new scientific and philosophical knowledge, just as in the state of personal evolution early stages of equilibrium are given up with grief and mourning before they can be replaced by higher levels.

Conclusion

It seems to me that the psychology of the self should pay considerable attention to this concept of coherency. The fitting together of the parts of the self to make an integrated and individuated super-ordinate self, the relationship of the self to others, the 'fitting in' with its environment, these two processes are intrinsic to psychological development. Goethe wrote that, 'the self could not value itself apart from its world; a self includes the love of its circumstances' (quoted in Weintraub 1978). Individuality is not to be found in isolation from the world in which it moves. The individual is a being forever forming and transforming himself in a never ceasing interaction between himself and his sustaining natural ground and social world, a being individualised only by his mental awareness of continuous experience. Individuality is not to be known without the world with which, in which, by which, it is coming to be and in which it constantly re-enters by its own activity. A man knows himself insofar as he knows his world; he is aware of this world only within himself, and he is aware of himself only in this world. A self is a self only in its fruitful interplay with its world; it is a self by making its world a part of itself, and itself a part of its world. The value of individuality lies less in its separate uniqueness than in its unique way of making itself a part of its world.

I find the concept of coherency useful in understanding certain states of mind of patients in analysis. I find it particularly important in persons who seem to be struggling towards achieving a sense of unity within themselves and sorting out this developing unity from what is represented as a confusing, dangerous or fragmenting relationship with the environment, whether it be to a single individual or to a family group. (I have also applied this concept to the evolution of the 'matrix of analytical group psychotherapy') (Pines 1981, 1983.)

Brief examples

1. In thinking about her father and in trying to understand him and her relationship to him, the patient begins to see him as a man with such different aspects to his personality that to her he now appears a very split and divided man, which he had not done previously. She then begins to think that perhaps when she looks inside herself the fragmentation, confusion and splitting that she finds, is not because she herself is a fragmented, confused and split person or self, but that what she finds inside her is this internal father and family who are so confusing, fragmented and divided that no coherence is possible. Thus the incoherence inside may not represent the incoherence of herself, rather it is the external family which has become internalised.

2. The patient had developed a very intense cathexis of, and dependency upon, the therapeutic space. She had reached the point at which she could now begin to reflect upon this and to wonder why this space meant so much to her. She now saw it in relationship to her mother who could never locate in herself any viciousness, badness and so on, who always saw herself as being sweet, loving and good. Thus for the patient it meant that badness had no location and therefore spread widely into space and into the whole environment, and when she left the session she always took that sense with her. It seemed likely that her intense earlier need to provoke the therapist into rage and to feel relieved when she succeeded in this, was because then badness had become located in the therapist and on the therapeutic space and was a shared experience on common ground.

For badness, helplessness, was actually verbalised and shared; coherency was established.

Since writing this paper I have come across an article by Louis Sander (1983), in which the concept of coherency is given a central place in the psychic development of the infant.

References

Bornstein, M.H. and Kessen, W. (1979) *Psychological Development from Infancy*. Hillsdale, NJ: L. Erlbaum.

Donne, John *An Anatomy of the World*. London: Penguin.

Freud, S. (1920) *Beyond the Pleasure Principle. Standard Edition 18*. London: Hogarth Press.

Freud, S. (1921) *Group Psychology and the Analysis of the Ego. Standard Edition 18*. London: Hogarth Press.

Freud, S. (1923) *The Ego and the Id. Standard Edition 19*. London: Hogarth Press.

Harris, V.I. (1966) *All Coherence Gone*. London: Frank Cass.

Hartmann, H. (1958) *Ego Psychology and the Problem of Adaptation*. New York: International Universities Press.

Kegan, R. (1982) *The Evolving Self*. Cambridge, MA: Harvard University Press.

Kohut, H. (1971) *The Analysis of the Self*. New York: International Universities Press.

Kohut, H. (1977) *The Restoration of the Self*. New York: International Universities Press.

Kohut, H. (1978) *The Search for the Self*. New York: International Universities Press.

Litowitz, B.E. and Litowitz, N.S. (1983) 'Development of verbal self expression.' In A. Goldberg (ed) *The Future of Psychoanalysis*. New York: International Universities Press.

Loewald, H. (1980) *Papers on Psychoanalysis*. New Haven: Yale University Press.

O'Neill, E. *The Great God Brown*.Quoted in Kohut, H. (1977) *The Restoration of the Self*. New York: New York Int. Universities Press.

Ornstein, P.H.(1978) *Introduction to the Search for the Self*. New York: Int. Universities Press.

Pines, M. (1981) 'The frame of reference of group psychotherapy.' *International Journal of Group Psychotherapy 31*, 3.

Pines, M. (1983) Keynote address to the Canadian Association of Group Psychotherapy. Banff, 29 October. (See Chapter 3)

Sander, L. (1983) 'To begin with: reflections on ontogeny.' In J.D. Lichtenberg and S. Kaplan (eds) *Reflections of Self Psychology*. Hilldale, NJ: Lawrence Erlbaum.

Schaffer, R.H. (1979) 'Acquiring the concept of the dialogue.' In M.H. Borstein and W. Kessen (eds) *Psychological Development from Infancy*. Hillsdale, NJ: L. Erlbaum.

Spitz, R.A. (1959) *A Genetic Field Theory of Ego Formation*. New York: International Universities Press.

Spitz, R.A. (1963) 'The evolution of dialogue.' In M. Schur (ed) *Drives, Affects, Behaviour*. Vol 2. New York: International Universities Press.

Webster's New Dictionary of Synonyms. (1973) Springfield, MA: G&C Merriam & Co.

Weintraub, A.J. (1978) *The Value of the Individual: Self and Circumstance in Autobiography*. Chicago: University of Chicago Press.

Notes on the Author

At an early age Malcolm Pines decided to study medicine in order to become a psychiatrist and psychoanalyst. His basic training was at the Maudsley Hospital, where he met one of the three major influences in his life, Dr S.H. Foulkes, founder of group analysis, who became his training analyst. The other two were Dr Tom Main and Dr Noë Pines, his father. From his Russian background, he inherited a sense of history, widespread family connections in Eastern and Western Europe, and an insatiable desire to travel. Tom Main, a man of vision, inspired him to find his own vision and develop a strong sense of humanity in the treatment of the mentally ill.

Had he chosen another career, it might have been as a historian or scholar. With his insatiable appetite for knowledge, it is not difficult to imagine him happily ensconced in a vast library. His explorations of the mind cover an enormous territory, and these have been paralleled by his endless travelling. He is a global intellectual and lecturer, much in demand. What drives him to do so much? Is it the challenge of relating to other language groups and establishing similarities and differences? When he is on a foreign assignment, he is an inveterate foot soldier, quickly exploring local geography, assimilating the culture, storing information in his active mind – ignoring the weather and the normal fatigues of the traveller. He can get off a plane and walk through a city whilst others are recovering from jet lag or disorientation. He could be termed a 'professional rubberneck'. If he could take music with him, he would choose Bach cantatas and fugues, Schubert sonatas, Beethoven quartets and Delius. As for books, he would need a cabin trunk full of diverse reading.

Although he has written and lectured so much and encouraged others to write, this book is a first for him. He finds writing a formidable intellectual task which would mean disturbing his journeying. He wishes he had more time for research and writing but sees himself as a 'creative mirror', gathering the insights of others – more an investigator than a discoverer. Occasional creative moments he finds difficult to encapsulate and synthesise. When I was sitting next to him on the plane once and he was writing a lecture to be delivered the next day, I asked him whether the high altitude stimulated his thought processes or was he just disorganised? He protested it was not the altitude, but a facility he had to reinterpret, to outline a schema, to improvise and fill in. He finds this more fun than struggling to 'complete' a paper and, after all, 'what is complete?'.

It is not difficult to see how Malcolm Pines was attracted to the multiple facets of group analysis and how eventually he became a founder member of the Institute of Group Analysis (IGA) in 1972. After Foulkes' death, he clearly (to my mind) was the Heir Apparent but he has never formally assumed this role. He has devoted a great amount of his career to teaching. He enjoys putting his knowledge to use and especially enjoys the dialogue and interaction with students. He sees the group analytic profession extending its influence in the coming years through our graduates as teachers and practitioners, with more publications and exchanges with other psychotherapies. He says the time for Freud is over. What we need are synthesisers, a Freud who is not so determined to create his own image and school.

At the IGA 24 years on, he is still actively teaching, lecturing, sitting on committees and generally keeping an open and reflective eye on group analytic phenomena. He has held many offices there, but has never wanted to be Institute's Chair. He has, however, been President of the International Association of Group Psychotherapy.

Politically, theoretically and technically he is a successful and esteemed practitioner of individual and group analysis, working privately and collegiately at the Group Analytic Practice and internationally.

It has been a complex task to sort out what should be published, as he has written enough papers for ten books. No sooner was one article selected, then another was being born and added to the collection. However, this volume is a start and will please the many analysts whom he has always encouraged to get into print, myself included.

Meg Sharpe
Group Analytic Practice

Malcolm Pines Bibliography

Journal Articles

'Bion: a group-analytic appreciation.' (1987) *Group Analysis;* September, 20(3), pp.251–262.
Discusses the differences between Freud's and Bion's concept of psychosis. Rather than the eruption of instincts causing breakdown, Bion considers that failures in the mother/infant dyad cause incapacity to receive, process and dream about emotional experience.

The therapeutic style of the group leader working in the style of Bion is compared with that of S.H. Foulkes. Argues that as Bion always dealt with the group as a whole, resisting the needs of the individual, Foulkes' style is a more mature understanding of the individual and the group.

'The borderline personality: concepts and criteria.' (1986) In M. Jackson and M. Pines (ed) *Neurologia et Psychiatria,* pp.34–67.
Historical and current use of the concept of the borderline personality disorder is given, followed by clinical examples of the features of this condition.

'The borderline personality: psychodynamics and treatment.' (1986) In M. Jackson, B. Stevens and M. Pines (eds) *Neurologia et Psychiatria,* pp. 66–88.
Borderline personalities have a history of failure in the mother–baby relationship which then threatens the coherency of the self. A detailed explanation is given of the treatment/management offered by the Unit at the Maudsley Hospital.

'Borderline personality disorder and its treatment.' (1989) *Current Opinion in Psychiatry,* 2, pp.362–367.
Considers the category of borderline personality disorder, and reviews the current literature on the treatment of these patients.

'Change and innovation, decay and renewal in psychotherapy: The Arbours Lecture – 11 February 1986.' (1987) *British Journal of Psychotherapy,* 4(1), pp.76–85. Now published in this volume.
Discusses the psychotherapeutic process in understanding the disorders of mental and emotional life. The styles and development of psychotherapy training institutions are considered.

'Coherencia y ruptura en el sentido del self.' (1986) (Integration and fragmentation of sense of self.) *Clinica y Analisis Grupal;* Jul.–Sep., 10(41), pp.425–438. Now published in this volume.
The concept of self and integration/fragmentation of self, and the normal and psychopathology of the sense of self are discussed.

'Coherency and its disruption in the development of the self.' (1986) *British Journal of Psychotherapy,* 2(3), pp.180–185.
Asserts that the concept of coherency is a basic principle of the psychic development of the human being. Examines the work of significant psychoanalysts such as Freud, Bion and Loewald regarding coherency.

'Discussion.' (1984) *International Journal of Group Psychotherapy,* 34(2), pp.225–228.
S.H. Foulkes' approach to group analysis, particularly his concept of the matrix, is discussed with a consideration of current developments in psychoanalysis, especially that of the dyadic relationship.

'"Elaboration of the negative" and other concepts: A tribute to Eduardo Cortesao. Portuguese Group-Analytic Society Eduardo Cortesao Memorial Meeting, 1991, Lisbon, Portugal.' (1992) *Group Analysis*, June, 25(2), pp.151–167.
Examines the work of the analyst with negative emotions expressed within the group setting, using clinical examples. Considers the elements of dialogue, language, hearing, listening and sonority as parts of the therapeutic process.

'An English Freud?' (1990) *Psychoanalytic Psychotherapy*, 5(1), pp.1–9.
Could Freud have been an Englishman? – so begins the article. Compares the work of early pioneers of psychoanalysis in this country during the late Victorian and Edwardian period, with the culture of Europe that enabled growth over there. Notes the effect of the work of neurologists on psychiatry, which eventually led to the formation of the Psycho-Analytical Society and the foundation of institutions such as the Tavistock Clinic.

'The frame of reference of group psychotherapy.' (1980) *Group Analysis*, April, 13(1), pp.16–21. Paper given at Applied Section of the British Psycho-Analytic Society. (1979)
The basic dynamics of the dyadic situation and that of the group are discussed.
   A number of people are taken into the group to form their own society to observe and work on their difficulties and reactions to fellow group members. Comparison is made between psychoanalysis where 'one-body psychology' and the constant relationship are emphasised and that of the group situation where the patterns of relationships are constantly changing. Group processes are discussed from both the social psychology and the psychoanalytic points of view.

'The frame of reference of group psychotherapy.' (1981) *International Journal of Group Psychotherapy*, 31(3), pp.275–285.
As previous entry.

'Framework patients.' (1978) *Group Analysis*, December, 11(3), pp.245–247.
Provides observations on patients who have sought help after leaving the institution of school, which provided a boundary and thereby a definition of themselves. Ego boundaries and boundary functions are discussed.

'The group-as-a-whole approach in Foulksian group analytic psychotherapy. Special Issue: The group-as-a-whole.' (1989) *Group*, Fall–Winter, 13(3–4), pp.212–216.
Discusses the concept of coherency, linking with the concept of wholeness through to the concept of group-as-a-whole. Argues that coherency is both conscious and unconscious. Also looks at Foulkes' concept of the group matrix.

'Group analysis and healing.' (1989) *Group Analysis*, December, 22(4), pp.417–429. Now published in this volume.
Defines healing so as to bring about wholeness and links this with the group-as-a-whole. The interaction of the individual and the social are examined.

'Group analysis and the corrective emotional experience: Is it relevant?' (1990) *Psychoanalytic Inquiry*, 10(3), pp. 389–408.
Clinical examples of patients in group analysis are given to illustrate the concepts of 'affirmative' and 'appropriate' responses, which Pines prefers, although accepting the phrase 'correctional emotional experience'.

Roberts, J. and Pines, M. 'Group-analytic psychotherapy.' (1992) *International Journal of Group Psychotherapy*, October, 42(4), pp.469–494.
The theories and methods of S.H. Foulkes are outlined and discussed with reference to other forms of analytic group psychotherapy. Particular reference is made to Foulkes' seminal concept of the group matrix.

'Group analytic psychotherapy and the borderline patient.' (1984) *Analytic Psychotherapy and Psychopathology,* 1(1), pp.57–70. **Now published in this volume.**
Four aspects of the borderline syndrome condition are considered: anxiety of fragmentation in self-representation and self-organisation; organisation of the personality structure; the model of the inner world; and narcissistic development and psychopathology. Argues that interpersonal disturbances in early development cause a weak structure to the personality, and that the group analytic setting creates a container for the borderline patient.

'Group analytic psychotherapy of the borderline patient.' (1978) *Group Analysis,* 11(2), pp.115–126.
Gives a clear outline of the characteristics of borderline patients despite the difficulty of defining this condition. Looks at crises of reconciliation, Kernberg's ego weakness, and Winnicott's transitional object.
Pines considers that the demands of borderline patients can be tolerated within the group setting; whereas in psycho analysis, those demands can be experienced so intensely that the treatment becomes too painful for patient and analyst.

'The group-analytic view of culture and civilization: response to Yiannis Gabriel.' (1983) *Group Analysis,* August, 16(2), pp.145–151.
Response to previous paper in the same journal: Y. Gabriel. Discontents and illusions: the inevitable costs of civilisation, pp.130–144.
Argues that Freud was a man of his time, that is, the nineteenth century, who provided a greater understanding of man as an individual. The development of S.H. Foulkes' theories and the individual in the social context are explored.

'Group psychotherapy: frame of reference for training.' (1979) *Group Analysis,* December, 12(3), pp.210–218.
Paper given at International Congress for Medical Psychotherapy, Amsterdam, August 1979.
Looks at the shorter history of training in group analysis compared with that of psychoanalysis, and shows the effect of the development of object relations theory and studies of group processes by social psychologists. Three principal schools of analytic group psychotherapy are presented, followed by a résumé, of the training (including a training group analysis) offered by the Institute of Group Analysis at that time.

'How a group develops over time.' (1979) *Group Analysis,* August, 12(2), pp.109–113.
The phases of development of the group from the viewpoint of the group analyst and that of the patients(s) are considered, along with the various processes of the group and the response of the conductor to these phases.

'"Human sexual response" – a discussion of the work of Masters and Johnson.' (1968) *Journal of Psychosomatic Research,* 12, pp.39–49.
A view of the psychoanalytic theories of sexual instincts, following a clear outline of the work of Masters and Johnson.

'L'influence de John Rickman et de Melanie Klein sur W.R. Bion.' *Revue de Psychotherapie Psychanalytique de Groupe,* 5–6, pp.13–19.

'Malcolm Pines interviewed by Gary Winship.' (1996) *Therapeutic Communities,* 17(2), pp.117–122.
This special issue of *Therapeutic Communities* contains papers by Main, Bridger, Foulkes and Bion (first published in the *Bulletin* of the Menninger Clinic). Pines recollects and responds to his re-reading of the articles.

'The matrix of group analysis: An historical perspective.' (1991) *Group Analysis*; June, 24(2), pp.99–109.
Outline of the development of group analysis in England, with reference to European philosophers and historians of the late nineteenth and early twentieth century. Foulkes' work in the 1930s when he came to Exeter and his writings are discussed.

'Mediation papers: a group-analytic response.' (1988) *Group Analysis*; March, 21(1), pp.57–59.
A concise presentation of the similarities and differences of the roles of mediators and group analysts.

'Mirroring and child development.' (1985) *Psychoanalytic Inquiry*; 5(2), pp.211–231. Now published in this volume.
Looks at the early experience of the infant of the mirroring of the infant by the mother. Compares the view of Lacan that the infant's experience is alienating with that of Winnicott which is the mother and confirmation. Pines also looks at negative mirroring and self psychology.

'On history and psychoanalysis.' (1989) *Psychoanalytic Psychology*; Spring, 6(2), pp.121–135. Now published in this volume.
This was a Freud Memorial Lecture at University College, London in June 1986 and looks at the current reappraisal of Freud and psychoanalysis by using the works of historians with particular reference to Freud. The historical context of Freud's development of psychoanalysis – regarding the social context of Freud's own development – is discussed.

'On mirroring in group psychotherapy.' (1983) *Group*, Summer, 7(2), pp.3–17.
Contends that mirroring in a group provides information to the patient through the social processes within the group, and is considered to be part of the foundation of the group matrix. Observations are made on the use of the term 'mirroring' in psychoanalytic writings and general literature. Two types of mirroring phenomena are considered, one that is primitive and destructive, the other which is dialogical where differences can be tolerated. Clinical vignettes are included to illustrate the concept.

Pines, M. and Wisbey, R. 'Once more the question of revising the *Standard Edition* and Guest Editorial.' (1991) *The International Review of Psycho-Analysis*; 18(3), pp.325–330.
Discussion of the dissatisfaction with, and the defence of, Strachey's translation of Freud.

'A prospect of group analysis.' (1977) *Group Analysis*, April, 10(1), pp.49–55.
The effect of the anthropologist Jean Pouillon upon Pines and his work in the field of group psychotherapy are examined. Pines postulates that the group offers patients chances to rework their early experiences in the family.

'A psychoanalytic view of sleep.' (1976) *Postgraduate Medical Journal*, 52, pp.26–31.
Sleep and dreams are examined. A clinical example of a patient sleeping during the analytic session is presented.

'Psychic development and the group analytic situation.' *Group*, 9(1), pp.24–37. Now published in this volume.
Looks at the concept of coherency and the development of processes in the mother/infant dyad. Within the group analytic situation it is the development of coherency that arises from the development of a group matrix. The work of Freud on group psychology and that of Loewald and Lichtenberg – all looking at the early mother/infant relationship – are discussed.

'Psychoanalysis.' (1981) *British Journal of Psychiatry*, August, 139, pp.164–167.
Psychoanalytic theory and technique are considered within the context of the author's personal preference. Reference is made to psychoanalytic journals and annuals, with a suggestion of a basic text for a more detailed study of psychoanalysis.

'Psychoanalysis and group analysis.' (1978) *Group Analysis*, **April, 11(1), pp.8–20.**
First given to the Danish Psychoanalytic Society, 1977.
   The two systems of psychoanalysis and group analysis are defined and followed by this paper, which looks at the shift from the instinct model to the object relationship in psychoanalysis and its consequent effect on group analysis. The paper concludes that the similarities are more important than the differences.

'Psychoanalysis and group analysis.' (1983) *International Journal of Group Psychotherapy*, **33(2), pp.155–170.**
Compares psychoanalysis and group analysis looking at the basic model of group analysis as defined by S.H. Foulkes.

'Psychoanalysis and group analysis: Jews and Germans. Figureground relationships.' (1993) *Mind and Human Interaction.* **Now published in this volume.**
Originally presented at the 9th European Symposium in Group Analysis 'Boundaries and Barriers', Hiedelberg. 1993.
   The development of psychoanalysis and group analysis is viewed within the context of German/Jewish relations, and the two 'founders', Freud and S.H. Foulkes, both Jewish and born half a century apart as discussed.

'Psychoanalysis, Psychodrama and Group Psychotherapy: Step-Children of Vienna.' (1986) *Group Analysis*, **June, 19(2), pp.101–112.**
The step-children of Vienna are Freud, Moreno and Foulkes. Their work and their links are explored within the European culture of the late 1800s and the early twentieth century.

'Reflections on mirroring.' (1982) *Group Analysis*, **15, Supplement. Now published in this volume.** *6th S.H. Foulkes Annual Lecture of the Group Analytic Society.*
The term 'mirroring' is defined and discussed within the context of group analytic thought and cultural discourse. The terms 'benign' and 'negative' mirroring are explored.

'Reflections on mirroring.' (1984) *International Review of Psycho-Analysis*, **11(1), pp.27–42.**
The concept of 'mirroring' is defined and considered within the context of loving relationships. The role of the group analyst as a mirror is explored.

'Reflets en miroir: facteur therapeutique en groupe-analyse.' (Mirroring: therapeutic factor in group analysis.) (1983) *Connexions*, **No. 41, pp.53–77.**
Mirroring as a therapeutic process within group analysis is discussed and contrasted with that of individual psychoanalysis.

'The self as a group: the group as a self.' (1996) *Group Analysis*, **9(2), pp.183–190.**
The identity of the individual and how this is attained is explored within the social context. Group analysis emphasises this social aspect and enables the group member to discover their 'self' and those of the other members. Kohut's school of self-psychology is discussed.

'Shame – What psychoanalysis does and does not say.' (1987) *Group Analysis*, **March, 20(1), pp.16–31.**
The reasons for Freud neglecting shame are briefly examined before a detailed consideration of more recent work.

'Standard-bearer for group analytic psychotherapy: an interview with Dr Malcolm Pines.' (1981) *Group*, **Winter, 5(4), pp.55–62.**
Describes Dr Pines' family background, training in psychoanalysis and group analytic psychotherapy, and his thoughts on the future of group therapy.

'Therapeutic factors in group analytic psychotherapy.' (1980) *Connexions*, **No. 31, pp.11–24.**
An outline of group-analytic theory.

'The universality of shame: A psychoanalytic approach. Conference on Shame: Theoretical and clinical aspects. (London, England, 1990).' (1995) *British Journal of Psychotherapy*, **11(3), pp.346–357.**
Shame is considered historically, developmentally and culturally. Four particular aspects of shame are presented: 'shame by disgrace', 'privacy and shame', 'shame and the self' and 'shame and the face'. It is asserted that the sensitive recognition of shame by the group analyst enables understanding of the patient.

'What to expect in the psychotherapy of the borderline patient.' (1980) *Group Analysis*, **December, 13(3), pp.168–177.**
Basic cautionary information about the treatment of these patients is followed by a discussion of treatment with reference to the use of group psychotherapy. Hospitalisation of these patients as a treatment is presented.

Chapters Within Books

'The contributions of S.H. Foulkes to group analytic psychotherapy.' (1976) In Wolberg and Aronson (eds) *Group Therapy: An Overview.* **New York: Stratton Intercontinental, pp.9–29.**
Considers the work of S.H. Foulkes within the field of analytic group psychotherapy and the development of his theories.

'The development of the psychodynamic movement.' (1991) In G.E. Berrios and H. Freeman (eds) *150 Years of British Psychiatry, 1841–1991.* **London: Gaskell (Royal College of Psychiatrists), pp.206–231.**
Takes World War I as the starting point following the experience of treating shell-shock victims. Describes the founding of the Tavistock Clinic and the Cassel Hospital; the tension between psychiatry and neurology; the entry of psychotherapists into the psychiatric domain; the post-war formation of the British Psycho-Analytical Society; the criticism as well as support of psychoanalysis; and the links with the Bloomsbury Group and the Hogarth Press. With the creation of the NHS there came a growth in the provision of psychodynamic psychiatry.

'The frame of reference.' (1993) In: T.E. Lear, (ed) *Spheres of Group Analysis.* **Co. Kildare: Leinster Leader Ltd, pp.20–28.**
See entry under journal articles.

Pines, M. and Hutchinson, S. 'Group analysis.' (1993) In A. Alonso and H. Swiller (eds) *Group Therapy in Clinical Practice.* **Washington: American Psychiatric Press, pp.29–47.**
The development of Foulkes' work is outlined and compared with the Tavistock model and other forms of group-as-a-whole therapy. Group analytic therapy is elaborated and the role of the conductor is explored.

Pines, M. and Marrone, M. 'Group analysis.' (1990) In I. Kutash and A. Wolff (eds) *Group Psychotherapist's Handbook.* **New York: Columbia University Press, pp. 61–77.**
Demonstrates the differences between group analytic psychotherapy as fostered by S.H. Foulkes and psychoanalytic group psychotherapy as fostered by W.R. Bion, which is often referred to as the Tavistock approach.

Pines, M., Hearst, L.E. and Behr, L.H. 'Group analysis.' (1982) In G.M. Gazda (ed) (3rd edition) *Basic Approaches to Group Psychotherapy and Group Counseling.* **Springfield: Chas. C. Thomas, pp.132–178.**

Gives autobiographical information on S.H.Foulkes and his work with colleagues at Northfield Hospital. Outlines the theory, the social foundations, the dynamics and the therapeutic factors of the small slow-open group. Basic details of the format of group psychotherapy are discussed, along with the expected functions of the group therapist. N.B. The large group experience, that is, ward group, is described.

'Group analytic psychotherapy and the borderline patient.' (1990) In B.E. Roth, W.N. Stone and H.D. Kibel (eds) *The Difficult Patient in Group: Group Psychotherapy with Borderline and Narcissistic Disorders*. American Group Psychotherapy Association monograph series, Monograph 6. Madison, CT: International Universities Press Inc., pp.31–44.
Four aspects of the borderline state are considered: fear of fragmentation of self-representation and self-organisation; organisation of the personality structure; model of the inner world; and narcissistic development and psychopathology. Argues that interpersonal disturbances in early development can create a weak personality structure, and that the group analytic setting provides a container for the borderline patient.

'Group psychotherapy in the United Kingdom.' (1983) In H.I. Kaplan and B.J. Sadock (eds) (2nd edition) *Comprehensive Group Psychotherapy*. Baltimore: Williams and Wilkins, pp.340–343.
An outline of the development of psychodynamic services within psychiatry and the NHS in the twentieth century is given. Group analytic psychotherapy and the Tavistock model are presented.

Pines, M. and Hearst, L. 'Group analysis.' (1993) In H.I. Kaplan and B.J. Sadock (eds) (3rd edition) *Comprehensive Group Psychotherapy*. Baltimore: Williams and Wilkins Co., pp.146–156.
Short article on the history, theory, technique and clinical issues of group analytic psychotherapy as defined by S.H. Foulkes.

'Group therapy with "difficult" patients.' (1975) In Wolberg and Aronson, (eds) *Group and Family Therapy: An Overview*. New York: Stratton Intercontinental, pp.102–119.
'Difficult' patients do not have the level of socialisation that the majority of patients have and are often described as borderline. Describes the problems faced by the group therapist of an extremely demanding monopolising rage-filled patient with destructive tendencies, who can provoke the counter-aggression of other group members. Refers to the literature of Kohut, Kernberg and Foulkes.

'A history of psychodynamic psychiatry in Britain.' (1991) In J. Holmes (ed) *Textbook of Psychotherapy in Psychiatric Practice*. Edinburgh: Churchill Livingstone, pp.31–55. Now published in this volume.
A detailed résumé is given of the historical development of psychodynamic psychiatry, beginning with psychiatry at the turn of the century, the recognition of shell-shock during World War I and the post-war work of psychoanalysts such as Rivers and Jones. The impact of World War II on British psychiatry through the work of military psychiatrists is discussed. The foundation of the Tavistock Clinic and the growth of group analysis are described.

'Interpretation. Why, for whom and when.' (1993) In D. Kennard *et al.* (eds) *A Work Book of Group-Analytic Interventions*. London and New York: Routledge, pp.98–103.
Defines the term 'interpretation' in four ways and elaborates (with clinical examples) on these definitions from the perspective of a group analyst.

'Mirroring and child development: Psychodynamic and psychological interpretations.' (1987) In T. Honess and K. Yardley (eds) *Self and Identity: Perspectives Across the Lifespan.* Boston, MA: Routledge and Kegan Paul Inc.
An outline of psychological and psychoanalytic knowledge of visual interaction in infancy and early childhood.

'The question of revising the *Standard Edition*.' (1988) In E. Timms and N. Segal (eds) Freud in exile: *Psychoanalysis and its Vicissitudes.* Cambridge, England: Yale University Press, pp.177–180.
See entry under journals.

Books

EDITOR

Bion and Group Psychotherapy (1992). London and New York: Tavistock/Routledge.
Contains contributions showing the influence of Bion both as a person and in his writings on associates in group work, researchers, others who have debated the theoretical concepts and Bion's work during and post war through to his work at the Tavistock Clinic and the Tavistock-style conferences.

The Evolution of Group Analysis (1983). London and New York: Routledge and Kegan Paul.
Contributions include those from Foulkes' military hospital experiences, colleagues from the early days of group analysis in England, and colleagues from America and Europe.

JOINT EDITOR

Roberts, J. and Pines, M. (eds), *The Practice of Group Analysis* (1991). London: Tavistock/Routledge.
An account of the clinical experience of the Group Analytic Practice. Pines has two personal contributions within the chapter, 'Special categories of patients in groups': 1. 'The borderline patient' (pp.97–99) and 6. 'Interminable patients' (pp.112–114).

Pines, M. and Rafaelsen, L. (eds) *The Individual and the Group. Boundaries and Interrelations. Volume 1: Theory. Volume 2: Practice* (1982). New York: Plenum Press.
Proceedings of the VIIth International Congress of Group Psychotherapy, Copenhagen, 1980. Two excellent volumes with a multitude of contributions.

V.L. Schermer and M. Pines (eds) *Ring of Fire: Primitive Affects and Object Relations in Group Psychotherapy* (1994). London and New York: Routledge.
Contributors offer personal insights and techniques for the treatment of patients who are very disturbed. Pines shares a joint editorial introduction with Schermer, as well as providing Chapter 6, 'Borderline phenomena in analytic groups'.

Subject Index

World War I, shell–shock 187
World War II, British psychiatry 196–8

Zurich Institute 111

Author Index